DISPOSSESSED LIVES

EARLY AMERICAN STUDIES

Series editors:
Daniel K. Richter, Kathleen M. Brown,
Max Cavitch, and David Waldstreicher

Exploring neglected aspects of our colonial,
revolutionary, and early national history and culture,
Early American Studies reinterprets familiar themes
and events in fresh ways. Interdisciplinary in character,
and with a special emphasis on the period from about
1600 to 1850, the series is published in partnership with
the McNeil Center for Early American Studies.

A complete list of books in the series
is available from the publisher.

DISPOSSESSED LIVES

Enslaved Women, Violence, and the Archive

Marisa J. Fuentes

UNIVERSITY OF PENNSYLVANIA PRESS

PHILADELPHIA

Published by
University of Pennsylvania Press
Philadelphia, Pennsylvania 19104-4112
www.upenn.edu/pennpress

1 3 5 7 9 10 8 6 4 2

LibraryofCongressCataloging- in-PublicationData
ISBN 978-0-8122-4822-7

For my dad, Jose de Jesus Fuentes and Ula Y. Taylor,
for all that you have given me.

CONTENTS

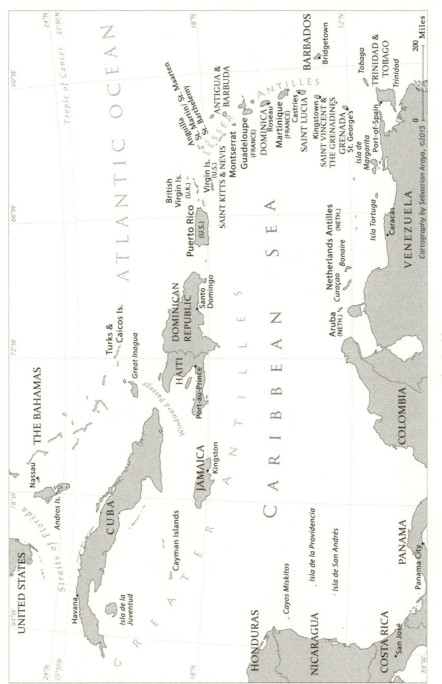

The Caribbean

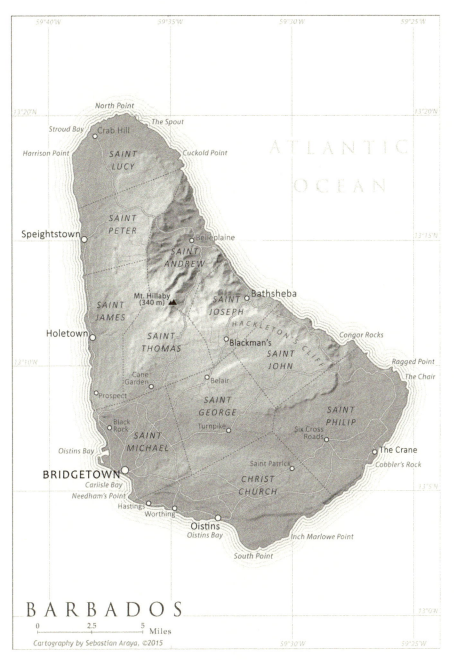

Barbados

Introduction

Dispossessed Lives constructs historical accounts of urban Caribbean slavery from the positions and perspectives of enslaved women within the traditional archive.[1] It does so by engaging archival sources with black feminist epistemologies, critical studies of archival power and form, and historiographical debates in slavery studies on agency and resistance. To trace the distortions of enslaved women's lives inherent in the archive, this book raises questions about the nature of history and the difficulties in narrating ephemeral archival presences by dwelling on the fragmentary, disfigured bodies of enslaved women. How do we narrate the fleeting glimpses of enslaved subjects in the archives and meet the disciplinary demands of history that requires us to construct unbiased accounts from these very documents? How do we construct a coherent historical accounting out of that which defies coherence and representability? How do we critically confront or reproduce these accounts to open up possibilities for historicizing, mourning, remembering, and listening to the condition of enslaved women?

This study probes the constructions of race, gender, and sexuality, the machinations of archival power, and the complexities of "agency" in the lives of enslaved and free(d) women in colonial Bridgetown, Barbados. A microhistory of urban Caribbean slavery, it explores the significance of an urban slave society that was numerically dominated by women, white and black. By the turn of the eighteenth century, Barbados sustained an enslaved female majority whose reproduction rates contributed to a natural increase in the slave population by 1800.[2] Similarly, white women made up a slight majority of the island's white population and owned predominately female slaves who, in turn, allowed white women a measure of economic independence.[3] This unusual demography and the underexplored, intra-gendered relationships between different groups of women mark an important shift from the extant scholarly focus on white men's domination of black and brown women in slave societies.

Despite its small size in relation to other Caribbean islands, an

Figure 1. Prospect of Bridgetown in Barbados, by Samuel Copen
(London, 1695). Courtesy of the Barbados Museum and Historical Society.

examination of Barbados, and in particular Bridgetown, enhances our understanding of how race, gender, and sexuality were formed in British Atlantic slave societies and how these constructions of identity directed and
influenced the life experiences of urban enslaved women. Unlike similar
works on enslaved women of the antebellum U.S. South that draw on the
limited voices of the enslaved, this book does not feature sources written by
enslaved people themselves.[4] On the contrary, the very nature of slavery in
the eighteenth-century Caribbean made enslaved life fleeting and rendered
access to literacy nearly impossible. Yet the women who appear in the archival fragments on which this book draws offer a crucial glimpse into lives
lived under the domination of slavery—lives that were just as important as
those of more visible and literate people in this period, who most consistently
left an abundance of documentary material. Throughout this work I interrogate the quotidian lives of enslaved women in Bridgetown and account for
the conditions in which they emerge from the archives. This is done to bring
attention to the challenges enslaved women faced and the continued effects
of white colonial power that constrain and control what can be known about
these women in the archive. Instead of a social history of enslaved life in
Bridgetown and Barbados, I examine archival fragments in order to understand how these documents shape the meaning produced about them in
their own time and our current historical practices. In other words, this is a
methodological and ethical project that seeks to examine the archive and historical production on multiple levels to destabilize the British colonial discourse invested in enslaved women as property. The impetus to "recover"

knowledge about how enslaved women made meaning from their lives is an important aspect of the historiography of Caribbean slavery. A significant amount of historical scholarship now exists showing how these women enacted their personhood despite their experiences of dehumanization and commodification.[5] This book builds on that scholarship; indeed, it has allowed me to ask a different set of questions concerning the body of the archive, the enslaved body in the archive, and the materiality of the enslaved body. This work seeks to understand the production of "personhood" in the context of Bridgetown and this British Caribbean archive, while troubling the political project of agency.[6] It articulates the forces of power that bore down on enslaved women, who sometimes survived in ways not typically heroic, and who sometimes succumbed to the violence inflicted on them. Each chapter examines one woman in the context of eighteenth-century Bridgetown as she came into archival view. The chapters are titled after the women who are named in the fragments I explore when possible, in order to contest their fragmentation and to challenge the impetus of colonial authorities to objectify enslaved people in the records by generic namings such as "Negro" or "slave."

Dispossessed Lives sets out to answer several questions pertaining to enslaved women in the urban Caribbean. How did these women negotiate physical and sexual violence, colonial power, and the demands of their female owners in the eighteenth century? In what ways did urban enslavement differ from the plantation complex? How was freedom defined in this slave society? How did architectures and symbols of terror—such as the Cage that held runaway slaves, and the execution gallows—shape how enslaved women were confined and controlled in an urban context? And finally, what do the archival fragments describing enslaved women alternately uncover and refuse to reveal about their racial, gendered, and sexual experiences as enslaved subjects?

In answering these questions this book thematically illustrates the connections between gender, urban space, and enslavement. Chapter 1 follows an enslaved runaway named Jane through the streets of Bridgetown revealing the precarity of fugitive bodies in urban areas and within colonial discourses in runaway advertisements. Chapters 2 and 3 concentrate on the production of enslaved female "sexuality" dialectically connected to white female identities and enslaved prostitution. These issues are addressed by revisiting the archives of a free(d) mulatto brothel owner and in chapter 3, closely reading an elite white adulteress's deposition about her sexual affair. In Chapter 4,

Molly, an enslaved woman executed for allegedly attempting to poison a white man, characterizes the construction of enslaved (female) criminality and the empty terms of "guilt" and "innocence" in the Barbados legal system governing slavery, which denied the enslaved the ability to testify in any courts. Executions of the enslaved map the functions of physical urban spaces in rituals of colonial punishments, and the power colonial authorities mobilized to invade enslaved afterlives. Finally, in Chapter 5, I bring attention to the "excessive" images of violence on enslaved female bodies that emerge in the debates to abolish the slave trade and contemplate the aurality of pain as a way to consider the rhetorical demands of otherwise anonymous historical subjects.

Over two decades of scholarship on the social histories of gender and slavery and theoretical work on the politics of the archive serve as the foundation for this book's emphasis on historical production and the archives of enslaved women in Caribbean slavery. These social histories of enslaved women's everyday lives allow me to focus specific attention on the questions of archival fragmentation and historicity without reproducing their labors on the historical, social, and economic circumstances of slavery in the Atlantic world.[7] Driven by questions of historical production in the context of archives that are partial, incomplete, and structured by privileges of class, race, and gender, my work follows the path-breaking scholarship of Deborah Gray White, Jennifer Morgan, Camilla Townsend, and Natalie Zemon Davis, who found ingenious ways to use known biases within particular archives to ask seemingly impossible questions of subjects whose presence, when noted, is systematically distorted. Scholars in the fields of colonial slavery and women's history more broadly understand and contend with scant sources from the enslaved perspective, and this is particularly true in the colonial British Caribbean.

This study also draws attention to the nature of the archives that inform historical works on slavery by employing a methodology that purposely subverts the overdetermining power of colonial discourses. By changing the perspective of a document's author to that of an enslaved subject, questioning the archives' veracity and filling out miniscule fragmentary mentions or the absence of evidence with spatial and historical context our historical interpretation shifts to the enslaved viewpoint in important ways. As previous scholarship has generated substantial knowledge about how enslaved women made meaning in their lives despite commodification and domination, my book does not simply seek to recover enslaved female subjects from historical obscurity. Instead, it makes plain the manner in which the violent systems and structures of white supremacy produced devastating images of enslaved female personhood, and how these pervade the archive and govern what can be known about them. Rather than leaving enslaved women "vulnerable to the readings and misreadings of whoever chooses to make assumptions about them,"[8] my book probes the construction of enslaved women in the archival records, using methods that at once subvert and illuminate biases in these accounts in order to map a range of life conditions that profoundly challenge assumptions about the "slave experience" in Caribbean systems of domination.

What would a narrative of slavery look like when taking into account "power in the production of history?" That is, how do slaveholders' interests affect how they document their world, and in turn, how do these very documents result in persistent historical silences?[9] What would it mean to be critical of how our historical methodologies dependent on such sources often reproduce these silences? There is not a paucity of sources about slavery in the Caribbean from the words and perspectives of white authorities and slave owners. In fact, there are vital archival materials that describe the contours of enslaved women's work and reproduction in the Caribbean. Using sources such as probate records, inventories of property, and descriptions of punishment and profit, scholars have mined the words and worlds of colonial authorities for clues to how the enslaved lived, worked, reproduced, and perished. Indeed, there are few if any new sources in this field; and *Dispossessed Lives* uses some of these same records but draws different conclusions by productively mining archival silences and pausing at the corruptive nature of this material.[10] The objectification of the enslaved allowed authorities to reduce them to valued objects to be bought and sold, used to produce profit and to retain and bequeath wealth. It also made the enslaved disposable when they could no longer labor for profit. This same objectification led to the violence in and of the archive. Enslaved women appear as historical subjects through the form and content of archival documents in the manner in which they lived: spectacularly violated, objectified, disposable, hypersexualized, and silenced. The violence is transferred from the enslaved bodies to the documents that count, condemn, assess, and evoke them, and we receive them in this condition. Epistemic violence originates from the knowledge produced about enslaved women by white men and women in this society, and that knowledge is what survives in archival form. With sole reliance on the empirical matter of the eighteenth-century Caribbean, we can only create historical narratives that reproduce these violent colonial discourses. The work of this book is to make plain how and why this knowledge was created and reproduced, and to employ new methodologies that disrupt this process in order to illuminate subjugated, "marginalized and fugitive knowledge [and perspectives] from," enslaved women.[11]

In each chapter I contend with the historical paradox and methodological challenges produced by the near erasure of enslaved women's own perspectives, in spite and because of the superabundance of words white Europeans wrote about them. By applying theoretical approaches to power, the production of text, and constructions of race and gender to the written archive, I question historical methods that search for archival veracity, statistical substantiation, and empiricism in sources wherein enslaved women are voiceless and objectified. The subjects in this study, the laborers, the enslaved women, men, and children, lived their "historical" lives as numbers on an estate inventory or a ship's ledger and their afterlives often shaped by additional commodification. The very call to "find more sources" about people who left few if any of their own reproduces the same erasures and silences they experienced in the eighteenth-century Caribbean world by demanding the impossible. Paying attention to these archival imbalances illuminates systems of power and deconstructs the influences of colonial constructions of race, gender, and sexuality on the sources that inform our work. This enables a nuanced engagement with the layers of domination under which enslaved women and men endured, resisted, and died. This is a methodological project concerned with the ethical implications of historical practice and representations of enslaved life and death produced through different types of violence.

Violence pervades the histories of slavery and this book. The violence committed on enslaved bodies permeates the archive, and the methods of history heretofore have not adequately offered the vocabulary to reconstitute "the depth, density, and intricacies of the dialectic of subjection and subjectivity" in enslaved lives.[12] A legible and linear narrative cannot sufficiently account for the palimpsest of material and meaning embedded in the lives of people shaped by the intimacies and ubiquity of violence. Therefore, this book dwells on violence in its many configurations: physical, archival, and epistemic. The most obvious instances are physical—the ways violence inflicted on enslaved bodies turned them into objects in slave societies. Chapter 5 features and reproduces the inordinate accounts of enslaved women's beatings in the records of the slave trade abolition debates. This reproduction brings to the fore how the excessive nature of such images works to silence these violent experiences beneath the titillated gazes of white men, abolitionist sensationalism, and historiographical skepticism, as well as our unavoidable complicity in replicating these accounts in order to historicize them.

Violence, then, is the historical material that animates this book in its subtle and excessive modes—on the body of the archive, the body in the archive and the material body.[13] Focusing on the "mutilated historicity" of enslaved women (the violent condition in which enslaved women appear in the archive disfigured and violated), this book shows how "the violence of slavery made actual bodies disappear."[14] For example, Chapter 4 assesses execution records of enslaved women and men to challenge our understanding of colonial laws. In a system that forbade the enslaved a legal voice, the arbitrary and capricious nature of enslaved "crime" and punishment comes to the fore and challenges our readings of enslaved resistance. It also explicates the reach of these laws, which in 1768 demanded that the bodies of executed slaves be weighted down and thrown into the sea to prevent the enslaved community from rituals of mourning. Colonial power subsequently made the archive complicit in obscuring the offenses committed against the enslaved through the language of criminality. My work resists the authority of the traditional archive that legitimates structures built on racial and gendered subjugation and spectacles of terror. This violence of slavery concealed enslaved bodies and voices from others in their own the time and we lose them in the archive due to those systems of power and violence. Each chapter contends with these circumstances and uses different methods to draw out the link between violence, archival disappearance, and historical representation in the fragmentary records in which enslaved women materialize. The nature of this archive demands this effort.

Dispossessed Lives uses archival sources at times "for contrary purposes."[15] I stretch archival fragments by reading *along the bias grain* to eke out extinguished and invisible but no less historically important lives.[16] In Chapter 3, for example, I use the court case of sexual entanglement between two white men and a married white woman to discuss the ways the presence and expectations of enslaved women in Bridgetown gave white women particular forms of power. Beliefs about enslaved women also enabled a young enslaved boy, owned by one of the men in the case, to dress as a woman in order to access public spaces without being perceived as a threat. Here the absence of explicit representations of enslaved women does not mean they have no bearing on the subjectivities and possibilities for other people in this society. I purposely fill out their absence as one way to address the above methodological questions. *Dispossessed Lives* demonstrates what other knowledge can be produced from archival sources if we apply the theoretical concerns of both cultural studies and critical historiography to documents and sources. It is an argument that history can still be made, and we can gain an understanding of the past even as we consciously resist efforts to reproduce the lived inequities of our subjects and the discourses that served to distort them.

Within the scope of this book I make two interventions into the extant literature on slavery in the Atlantic world. First, I argue that close attention to the specificities of urban slavery challenges scholarly representations of plantation slavery as more violent and spatially confining than slavery in other locales.[17] To do this, I map how urban slave owners constructed and used architectures of terror and control on this seemingly mobile enslaved population through imprisonment, public punishment, and legal restrictions. Second, much of the previous historical scholarship on slavery influenced by the crucial Civil Rights and Black Power activism of the 1960s and 1970s focuses on enslaved resistance, a vital (and decades long) effort to gain insight into the "agency" of enslaved people and to refute earlier depictions of the enslaved as passive and submissive.[18] The agency of enslaved and free(d) people of color, however, was more complex than the "liberal humanist" framework allows.[19] We need to examine the excruciating conditions faced by enslaved women in order to understand the significance of their behaviors within the confounding and violent world of the colonial Caribbean. Finally, the centrality of gender in this study illuminates how African and Afro-Caribbean women experienced constructions of sexuality and gender in relation to white women and, as important, how enslaved women's subaltern positions in slave society shaped the ways they entered the archive and, consequently, history.

A significant amount of scholarship on Atlantic slavery necessarily highlights life in the sugar plantation complex.[20] Certainly, the majority of enslaved Africans and Afro-Caribbean people lived and died producing sugar for mass exportation from the Caribbean. But a focus on the rural conditions of slavery leaves the urban context underexamined and too easily subject to generalizations. Scholarly distinctions between rural and urban slavery tend to create a rigid dichotomy between the violence of rural slavery and the mobility and less arduous conditions of urban life, ignoring systems of surveillance and control in urban architectures and spaces. In addition, the predominantly domestic labor performed by enslaved women in towns might be read as less dangerous than field labor. To be sure, the enslaved who worked in sugar production were more vulnerable to early deaths, lack of sustenance, and the terror of plantation punishments. However, this did not mean that domestic or urban labor was necessarily easier and less constraining or violent. *Dispossessed Lives* reconsiders these assertions by examining the continuities and distinctions of violence from the planation to the urban complex. I explore the mechanisms and technologies created and employed by colonial authorities to control an enslaved population outside the confines of a plantation or the surveillance of an overseer. Although not large in terms of area, nor as densely populated as other Caribbean towns, Bridgetown sustained a significant population of urban slaves who labored under the duress of strict laws limiting their movement and architectures—both the structures of policy and the built environment—that ensured their confinement and punishment. Moreover, the surplus enslaved and female population of this town allowed slaveowners to turn enslaved women into sexual objects for incoming soldiers and sailors, a lucrative informal economy for their owners. Examining the degree to which colonial authorities utilized public punishments and structures of confinement complicates discussions of the possibilities of freedom and mobility in urban enslavement.

Since the late 1990s, scholars from a range of fields, including history, have challenged and refined the concept of agency as it applies to enslaved people. In her now definitive book, Saidiya Hartman argues that agency connotes the idea of "will" and "intent," both of which were foreclosed by the legal condition of chattel slavery.[21] Walter Johnson contends that agency as a trope originated from noble origins in the Civil Rights era but should be carefully interrogated for the conflation of its meaning with resistance and humanity in slavery scholarship.[22] These scholars argue that the issue of "redress" is inescapable in writing histories of black life as the legacies of racism, racialized sexism, and poverty continue to haunt our present. In this effort, Hartman's concerns shed light on the contradictions, exclusions, and demands of black people in post-emancipation liberal humanist discourses of rights and duties.[23] She asks us to consider to what extent our work on the past is in service of redress and therefore what is the historian's relationship to her subjects? To what end do we write these narratives?[24]

At stake here are the ways in which scholars, working within the paradigm of traditional African American historiography, insist that agency—akin to resistance—is still the most appropriate lens through which to examine slave life.[25] Stephanie Camp contends that "slave resistance in its

many forms is a necessary point of historical inquiry, and it continues to demand research."[26] Camp recognizes that studies of resistance have changed
but, she argues, we "need not [abandon] the category altogether."[27] The present study troubles similar tropes of agency in Chapters 2 and 3 by examining
the lives of white and free(d) women of color whose social and economic
power relied on patriarchy and slave ownership.[28] In Chapter 2 I address this
issue in relationship to Rachael Pringle Polgreen, a mixed-race slave-owning
woman in Barbados.[29] Using the scholarship of Michel-Rolph Trouillot and
Saba Mahmood, I question the application of sexual agency to enslaved and
free(d) women's sexual relations with white men in the context of this slave
society where many enslaved and free women were subjected to unequal
power relations and violence. Focusing specifically on women also deconstructs "resistance" as armed, militaristic, physical, and triumphant—a vision
of resistance particularly resonant in the Caribbean with its histories of large-
scale uprisings.

In counterpoint to definitions of agency, the concept of "social death" addresses how the enslaved were constrained by law, commodification, and
subjection. In recent years, scholars have expanded on Orlando Patterson's
pivotal text *Slavery and Social Death* (1982), detailing the process by which
Africans were made into property and how the condition of slavery in the
past adversely affects how they can be accounted for historically. Still, promi-
nent scholars reassert the imperative of resistance studies. In Vincent Brown's
important analysis of social death, he urges us away "from seeing slavery as a
condition to viewing enslavement as a predicament, in which enslaved Africans and their descendants never ceased to pursue a politics of belonging,
mourning, accounting, and regeneration."[30] Chapter 4, however, reminds us
of the extent of power wielded by authorities and how the enslaved were subjected to arbitrary executions at the caprice of their owners and colonial officials, therefore limiting their strategies of mourning and shaping the
perceptions of enslaved humanity and resistance.

Arguably, as many have noted, concepts of agency, resistance, and social
death, perhaps even more than in other historical fields, continue to influence the ways we write and think about the enslaved and about systems of
slavery and domination. *Dispossessed Lives* maintains that these historiographical debates are as important as illuminating the actions of the enslaved,
because they have implications for what we have come to know and the limits
of what we can know about the history of slavery. While the majority of studies of slavery have focused on the antebellum U.S. South, the British

Caribbean offers a different tale, one in which slavery depended on a factory of violence in sugar production unsurpassed in North America. Life spans for most of the enslaved were brief and the physical distance from imperial control allowed particular types of atrocities on their bodies. On an island like Barbados, where sustained or permanent flight was nearly impossible, "rival geographies"—spaces created by the enslaved in defiance of the restrictions of plantation life—were threatened by surveillance, dangerous waterways, and deplorable material conditions.[31] This study does not suppress the historical efforts of enslaved people to resist their circumstances. Rather, it presents the agonizing decisions they made in the face of violent retribution from colonial authorities. Dwelling on these uncomfortable junctures in history highlights the messy and contradictory behaviors of enslaved people. This book's theoretical underpinnings at once read along the bias grain of the archive[32] and against the politics of the historiography to gain nuanced understandings of what Avery Gordon calls "complex personhood" and the minute details of fragmentary lives that are challenging for historians to access.[33]

The fields of women's and gender studies and black feminist theory give significant attention to knowledge production and the intersectional experiences of women; and these fields frame the questions with which I approach this history and these enslaved female subjects. This study argues that there was something particular about being enslaved and female in slave societies even as it resists more traditional concepts of gender; it dwells purposely on feminist epistemological questions concerning how (historical) knowledge is produced about enslaved female subjects through the archive. I draw on a range of interdisciplinary black feminist scholars, including historians, cultural studies scholars, and novelists who interrogate how black women have been represented historically and contemporarily; their sexual violations; and their hypersexualized images.[34] Moreover, these scholars use analyses of race and gender to destabilize the power of dominant knowledge and representations of women of the African diaspora. My focus on the centrality of enslaved women to the project of slavery follows in the wake of such work and elucidates the manner in which their specific sexualized identities and social constructions placed them in particular roles and positions in Caribbean and Barbadian slave societies. It also demonstrates how gender and sexuality were shaped and produced in a society where white and Afro-Barbadian women outnumbered men. Building on Jennifer Morgan's scholarship, which illustrates how reproduction signified a central experience for enslaved women, I consider the ways in which sexuality was inhabited, performed and consequential for urban female slaves.

Finally, this book examines our own desires as historical scholars to recover what might never be recoverable and to allow for uncertainty, unresolvable narratives, and contradictions. It begins from the premise that history is a production as much as an accounting of the past, and that our ability to recount has much to do with the conditions under which our subjects lived. This is a project concerned with an ethics of history and the consequences of reproducing indifference to violence against and the silencing of black lives. Our responsibility to these vulnerable historical subjects is to acknowledge and actively resist the perpetuation of their subjugation and commodification in our own discourse and historical practices. It is a gesture toward redress.

CHAPTER 1

Jane: Fugitivity, Space, and Structures of Control in Bridgetown

Black women's histories, lives, and spaces must be understood as enmeshing with traditional geographic arrangements in order to identify a different way of knowing and writing the social world and to expand how the production of space is achieved across terrains of domination.

—Katherine McKittrick, *Demonic Grounds*

The body African henceforth inscribed with the text of events of the New World. Body becoming text. In turn the Body African—dis place—place and s/place of exploitation inscribes itself permanently on the European text. *Not* in the Margins. But within the very body of the text where the silence exists.

—M. NourbeSe Philip, *A Genealogy of Resistance and Other Essays*

Jan 13, 1789
RUNAWAY: A short black skin negro woman named JANE, speaks broken English, has her country marks in [sic] her forehead and a fire brand on one of her breasts, likewise a large mark of her country behind her shoulder almost to the small of her back, and a [stab] of a knife in her neck. Whoever will bring the said negro to the subscriber in Bridge Town shall receive 20 shillings . . . JOHN WRIGHT

—*Barbados Mercury*

In a typical late eighteenth-century advertisement for the return of "lost property," Jane, an enslaved woman who survived the Middle Passage, stumbles into history. In her brief encounter with the "official" record, Jane emerges in the archive disfigured by her capture, captivity, enslavement, and the power of her owner in this written document. The scars on enslaved women's "flesh" as described in runaway advertisements disclose more than who owned them, what they wore, and to whom they might have run even as they limit their historicization. The very description of this wounded "flesh" represents one of the points at which black bodies became racialized objects, and their scars produce multiple axes of meaning.

Contradictions between Jane's constructed humanity as an enslaved "negro woman" and the memory of a time before enslavement in Barbados play out in the descriptions of her textualized flesh. The "country marks in her forehead" exemplify the temporality of her life, a time before captivity when she belonged to a kinship.[1] The "firebrand on one of her breasts" marks not only her capture and objectification, but also the violation of bodily exposure at the time of her branding.[2] The advertisement re-exposes her body to history. "A large mark of her country behind her shoulder almost to the small of her back" may be from another kinship ritual performed, or a mark of abuse in the moment of her capture in West Africa. "A stab of a knife in her neck" exemplifies the extreme peril and powerlessness of her captivity. It may have happened in a moment of defense in the process of capture or on board the ship across the Atlantic. These scars turn into enslaved women's stories—symbols of the deep penetration of violence that mark the relationship between the body of the archive, the body in the archive, the material body, and the enslaved female body in space.

Jane materializes briefly in a runaway advertisement from a condition of trauma describing all that her owner wanted the public to know about her—scarred and running—in a few sentences. With this scant accounting we must write her history. Jane's language, possible ethnic origins (although dubious in this description by her owner), history of violence, and the crisis of her condition as an enslaved subject are herein revealed.[3] Her subjectivity, constituted through theft from Africa, violence marked on her flesh, and her unrecorded suffering "is a life that [had] to be lived in loss."[4] Tragically and perversely, her flesh and her bodily movements in flight to "freedom" become her archive.

Enslaved women interacted with local urban spaces and their bodies became concentrated sites of meaning that in turn represented their inhumanity to owners or other whites and their predicament to other slaves. The public discourse of runaway advertisements exposed their private scarred bodies even as they were concealed in fugitivity. Thus, the condition of slavery permeated all spaces; and where slavery existed, "there is no place that is wholly liberatory" not even the archive, itself layered with "geographies of domination" and violence.[5] Attention to how power was mobilized and deployed through space—urban space, body-space, archival space—and how colonial authorities confronted, confined, and distorted mobile enslaved bodies complicates what was possible in the alternative spaces created by the enslaved. As Katherine McKittrick argues, dwelling on the relationship between bodies and space also "reveals that the interplay between domination and black women's geographies is underscored by the social production of space."[6] The archive encompasses another space of domination in this configuration and represents the link between the objectification of enslaved women and historical dispossession.

The following discussion utilizes a methodological practice that aims to subvert the archival discourse that filters the past only through white (male and female) voices by dwelling on the scars of other fugitive women. Close readings of scarred enslaved bodies in runaway ads alongside analyses of urban space—the built environment—and theoretical scholarship concerned with black women's bodies as sites of meaning demonstrate how enslaved women encountered and were configured by urban slavery and the difficulties constituent to their historical narration.[7] In the subsequent section we will follow Jane through the streets of Bridgetown. Jane's movement through the town maps the sensorial and architectural history of slavery in this urban site from an enslaved woman's perspective. Experiencing Bridgetown from Jane's view—emanating from the silences within the runaway ad—the historian's focus is redirected to the sensorial perspective of the historically disempowered enslaved woman. After Jane's flight through town, a detailed chronology of Bridgetown's history illuminates the vulnerability of slaves in an urban environment with the port town's exposure to natural disaster, disease, and invasion. In addition, the layout and geographical particularities of Bridgetown embody the confluence of urban space and enslaved punishment.

Fugitive Women: The Body in the Archive

As identifying marks, the scars on enslaved bodies signified different meanings for various groups of people within Barbados slave society. For the colonial authorities they served as punishment for the victim and terror to the
enslaved population. For the enslaved they confirmed one's condition of captivity and this "body memory"—the permanent marks and meanings inscribed on the body—also transferred knowledge of enslavement to future
generations.[8] An enslaved child would come to understand that the scars on
her caregivers represented pain and unfreedom. Put another way, the scars
became a different type of "country mark," produced by a ritual of violence
that identified a person to other enslaved people not by their "ethnic" origin
but by their dishonored condition that branded them as commodities.

Hortense Spillers makes an important intervention in understanding the
distinction between the "enslaved body" and "flesh" "as the central one between captive and liberated subject-positions," which is helpful in reading
scars on enslaved bodies and to account for their multiplicity of meanings.[9]
Spillers argues that the human body is a site imbued with cultural significa-
tions (race, gender, sexuality), but it is the violence upon the flesh of African
captives—"its seared, divided, ripped-apartness, riveted to the ship's hole,
fallen, or 'escaped' over-board"[10]— that is the point at which African captives
became differentiated from human subjects and made into commodified objects.[11] Consequently, in runaway ads the flesh is the site of objectification
that becomes the material from which the enslaved, in this case fugitive enslaved women, come into what I call a *mutilated historicity*. This term refers
to the violent condition in which enslaved women appear in the archive disfigured and violated. Mutilated historicity exemplifies how their bodies and
flesh become "inscribed" with the text/violence of slavery.[12] As a result, the
quality of their historicization remains degraded in our present attempts to
recreate their everyday experiences. The infliction of scars, lacerations, burns,
and wounds of captivity reproduce African captive objectification and display as a "social hieroglyph" that communicates enslaved status to others—
enslaved and free—and these flesh injuries are the remains with which we
must construct their history.[13]

All Jane's probable movements, the impetus of her flight and experience
in *fugitivity*, are unknowable in the existing archive. The publicity and intention of the runaway ad challenges her concealment and freedom. Fugitivity

in this context denotes the experience of enslaved women as fugitives—both hidden from view and in the state of absconding. It also signifies the fragile condition of runaways who came into visibility through runaway advertisements. If fugitivity is "the artful escape of objectification"[14] (racial, commodified, legal/political), Jane's disappearance was a defiant act against these constraints. The fugitive slave subverted the very paradigm of enslavement—immobility, disembodiment, violation—and created an alternative self in what Stephanie Camp terms a "rival geography."[15] Yet, the discourse of runaway advertisements remained an ever looming and corporeal threat for the absconding slave. This discursive power combined with the legal right of whites to interrogate, inspect, probe, and detain any black suspect made fugitivity both an insecure and defiant status.[16] Jane's owner conjured an image of her body that enabled others to access her through their surveillance and her bodily exposure.[17] As the earliest slave laws of Barbados indicated, the fear and reality of rebellion and maroon resistance in the mid-seventeenth century made running away punishable by death if the slave had been captured after one year.[18] These laws lasted into the mid-eighteenth century.[19] Fugitivity then, embodied both a critique of slavery and the precarity of the fugitive condition.[20]

Jane was one of many fugitive women who may have run to Bridgetown and were then described by their scarred flesh.[21] On 5 April 1783, Harrison Walke of St. Peter placed an advertisement in the *Barbados Mercury*: "Runaway . . . a negro wench named SARAH CLARKE, about forty-five years old, she is a stout woman, very bandy legged, and has a large scar between one of her shoulders and breasts, she is supposed to be harboured in Bridge Town, and employed in the occupation of washerwoman, having been [seen] there several times with a tray of clothes on her head."[22] Sarah Clarke's flight reveals multiple aspects of her life. That she ran away as an older woman is notable though not unusual, according to the collection of late eighteenth-century runaway advertisements.[23] Clarke also ran several miles from her owner to Bridgetown, when Speightstown and its free black population might have offered an easier journey. She therefore traveled as far away from her owner as possible. In addition, Sarah Clarke was marked by the whip. Her "escape," whether temporary or permanent, carries a scar that that provides evidence of endured brutality as well as a certain identification to those who sought her apprehension.

An enslaved woman named Affey was similarly described by marks on her skin. Affey was "about forty odd years of age; . . . is a little [pitted or

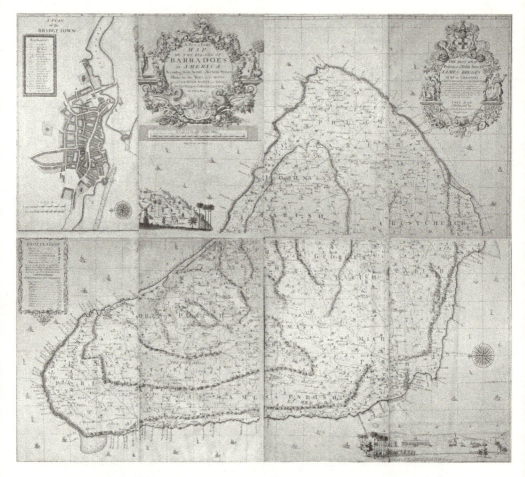

Figure 2. A new & exact map of the island of Barbados in America according
to survey made in the years 1717 to 1721, by William Mayo. Courtesy of the
Barbados Museum and Historical Society.

pecked] with the small pox, and has a remarkable scar under the calf of one
of her legs, the size of the palm of a hand, about five feet six inches high, is
well know[n] in Bridge Town, and has comrades in different parts of the island."[24] Daphney, listed as "a mulatto woman," had been "branded in the face
with the letters H.L." She had been seen in Bridge Town among the Barracks
and at other sites.[25] The man who claimed ownership of her body hailed from
St. Lucy, the northernmost parish and at least twenty-two miles away from
Bridgetown. Daphney also bypassed the closest urban space of Speightstown

to seek escape. In the weeks of 9 through 22 November 1788, an advertisement sought a woman named Joney who had part of her ear missing and a
"scar on her underlip."[26]

More than a year before Joney's escape, Pothenah ran away in August
1787. She was sought by a subscriber to the newspaper, who offered a reward
of five pounds "for apprehending a stout yellow skin negro woman . . . has a
mark from the lash of a whip across her stomach, and two others on one of
her sides."[27] During the month of September 1787, Mary escaped her owner.
She was described by a proximity to a working animal, "between a black and
yellow complexion, stout limbed, is marked in the forehead near the form of
a horse shoe and marked on her stomach, she had a mark of a whip on one
eye," and her owner noted that she "speaks tolerable good English."[28] Enslaved women often ran toward town and to the military barracks in hopes of
hiding themselves or earning money working for the soldiers. Other enslaved
women were hired out to soldiers and officers as part of an informal sexual
economy.[29] Their networks across the island demonstrate the distances across
which the enslaved maintained kin and communal ties, whether family or
friend.

But Daphney, Joney, Pothenah and Mary also carried their flesh wounds
and the memories of their infliction into hiding. They could not escape the
fact of their objectification nor the precarious status stemming from perpetual enslavement. Their scars would always be associated with slavery.
The society in which they lived made it impossible to change the meaning
of their mutilations even if they did find freedom. Although many enslaved
women ran away, sometimes great distances from their owners, what they
could not escape, even in death or hiding, was the violence of their condition and material lives. And, this remains the condition in which we find
them in the archive and from where we must attempt to recount their
stories.

Barbados developed into a lucrative colony from its establishment in 1627
until Jamaica surpassed its economic significance by the mid-eighteenth century. Bridgetown, the capital "city," was for the late seventeenth and early eighteenth centuries the preeminent entrepôt for British Caribbean colonial
production and profit.[30] This profit, directly linked to the rise in sugar production, manifested itself in concerted urban building projects that supported the
intensive shipping and trade industries.[31] Corresponding to this expanded architecture was the influx of thousands of Africans brought into the colony to
sustain sugar production on hundreds of plantations throughout the island.

Urban planning began as early as 1657, when an "Act for ye appointing and nomination of Streets, Lanes Alleys, Wharfs and other passages convenient in and about ye towne of St. Michael" passed for building the streets, government buildings and infrastructure that would support a rising merchant class.[32] Planters, merchants, and widows who initially populated the town of St. Michael, as it was first named, brought and purchased slaves who worked to support their owners' increasingly opulent urban lives. To focus solely on profit, development, and trade in colonial urban sites elides a central facet of the economy and this urbanization—that British colonists built into the landscape spatial features, both material and symbolic, to control and terrorize a growing enslaved population over the course of the eighteenth century.[33] One crucial element is the violent tactics employed by urban slave owners, legislators, and colonial governments in an effort to regulate enslaved bodies in a physically porous environment where the mobility of the enslaved and free threatened colonial power. Therefore, enslaved people experienced surveillance and spectacles of violent punishments as they went about their daily work.

Attention to how urban colonists consciously developed structures of confinement and punishment discloses a strong link between physical space, slavery, and enslaved bodies. It also indexes the specificities of unfreedom and fear in urban enslavement that have remained unremarkable compared with the violence of the sugar plantation complex.[34] Here we also see that the transition from private owner punishment to state punishment that has typically characterized the historiography of post-emancipation societies was not the reality for West Indian slave societies. As Diana Paton reminds us, punishment "was carried out on the authority of the state both before and after the end of slavery . . . and that slave holders made direct use of imprisonment, both on and off their estates."[35] There was a marked transition after the British Abolition Act that took away the ability of slave owners to punish black bodies and shifted this authority to the state.[36] However, state authority to punish was always present in urban contexts, and the regimentation and standardization of punishment, including laws of flogging, were practiced much earlier than post-emancipation legislation would suggest.[37] Without the definable constricting geography of the plantation landscape—its "Great House," sugar fields, provision grounds, and slave villages—the colonists residing in Bridgetown constructed markers and holding cells and enacted spatial punishments on enslaved bodies limiting enslaved movement, congregation, and other group activities. In addition, the enclosing space of

Barbados as a small non-mountainous island limited possibilities for pro-longed escape. There was generally no sustainable maroon community to run toward after the seventeenth century, nor an easily accessible neighboring colony that might offer slaves freedom for loyalty against a colonial enemy. This landscape was essentially finite.[38] Yet, over time and precisely correlated to the influx of Africans into the colony, Bridgetown council members, as-sembly, and vestry men ordered and paid for structures like the Cage and the gallows to serve as a constant reminder to the enslaved laborers who tra-versed the town that their lives were bound to perpetual servitude violently enforced. One way to consider this historical experience of urban enslave-ment is to follow fugitive bodies moving through the space of Bridgetown as they encountered various spatial reminders of the looming violence of slavery.

Jane's Flight: The Fugitive Body in Space

From her runaway advertisement it is unknown whether Jane spent her life in town or the countryside, but she shared with many enslaved women the desire to run toward Bridgetown to conceal themselves in a dense and more diverse population. Demographic statistics for the eighteenth century are sparse, but by 1774 the enslaved population of Saint Michael's Parish num-bered 12,268 to 5,105 white inhabitants.[39] These numbers included both rural and urban parts of the parish in which Bridgetown was located.[40] Wherever Jane originated on the island, she would have entered a town still rebuilding from "the worst hurricane in historic times," which in 1780 wiped out half the houses, buildings, and wharves and the infrastructure that sustained this bustling Caribbean port town.[41]

Constructed around swamps and a landscape of mangroves, Bridgetown suffered from damp and humid conditions and the streets were strewn with animal and human waste. Richard Ligon, a seventeenth-century visitor, de-scribes the town as being "ill scituate" and that it was built

> upon so unwholesome a place for the spring Tides flow over [the banks], and there remains, making a great part of that flat, a kind of Bog or Morass, which vents out so loathsome a savour, as cannot but breed ill blood, and is (no doubt) the occasion of much sickness to those that live there.[42]

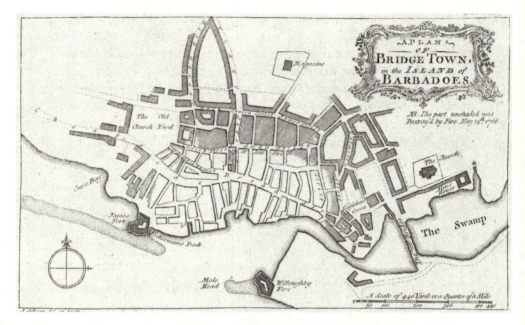

Figure 3. A Plan of Bridge Town in the island of Barbadoes, by John Gibson
(London: Gent. Mag., c.1766). Courtesy of Harvard University.

Just five months before John Wright placed the notice in the paper for Jane's
(re)capture, Mr. John Crawford, a Bridgetown surveyor, also complained of
the inhospitable conditions of Bridgetown:

> dung heaps had been accumulated to such a number and those so
> large as to render many of the Alleys & narrow Streets almost impass-
> sible which was a nuisance of so intolerable a nature as to render the
> Houses in the viscinity scarsely habitable from the stench, and from
> the Air being impregnated with such noxious particles as could
> scaresly fail to injure the health of the Inhabitants.[43]

The unhealthy conditions of town were manifold, and enslaved people,
tasked with the most degraded jobs, cleaned and carried household and animal waste into the streets. One historian notes that, "[the enslaved] emptied
chamber pots of their owners, sometimes going no further than the street
gutter to do so, disposed of their garbage in vacant lots or threw it into the
streets or the sea."[44] Indeed, Crawford recognized that the enslaved were

responsible for waste disposal and recommended that the parish officer should "oblige the Negroes to deposit what they had taken from the Houses in [appointed] places only."[45] Other early modern European towns suffered from similarly polluted conditions and certainly the poor took the jobs of handling household waste. In the context of West Indian slave societies, however, the enslaved performed the most degrading and dangerous work. Many white visitors to Bridgetown remarked on the splendors of buildings and the opulent hospitality of the white residents. In the early eighteenth century visitor Pierre Baptiste Labat commented on the beauty and grandness of the town. Labat remarked on the well-set streets and the "English style" houses, that "have an air of propriety, politeness and opulence, that does not exist in other islands, and would be difficult to find elsewhere."[46] In contrast, enslaved women and men navigated an intimate proximity to the waste and excrement of urban slavery—the byproduct of capital accumulation—and their proximity to refuse exemplified their historical expendability.[47] If enslaved lives were linked to waste and garbage, the authors of archival documents did not record the experiences of the enslaved as historical actors. They were often evoked in relation to filth.

Whether Jane arrived during the day or night there would have been people about—merchant and government men attending their affairs, meeting in government offices on the east end or the multiple taverns throughout the town. The streets would also be filled with "jobbing" slaves, poor white and black hucksters and free people of color going about their work, opening shops, and setting up stands to sell their goods. Walking from the eastside to the west, Jane would have passed Egginton's Green, a piece of land close to an acre in area that made up the "front yard of [Jeremiah] Egginton's grand mansion ('the finest house in town').[48] In the late seventeenth century the Bridgetown courthouse and town hall were located in Egginton's Green. For a period of time the Barbados House of Assembly met in these buildings. In addition, before the completion of James Fort in western Cheapside in 1701 many slaves were punished for various legal offenses at Egginton's Green, which contained stocks and a whipping post.[49]

Jane might also have walked close to the careenage where small skiffs came in and out, returning with goods and people from the larger merchant ships anchored in the large natural harbor of Carlisle Bay just west of town. Dr. George Pinckard, a late eighteenth-century English visitor described the heavy maritime traffic:

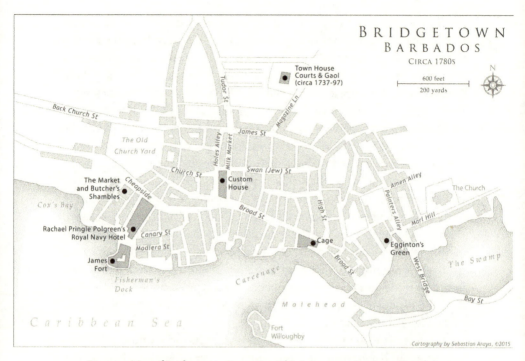

Figure 4. Map of Bridgetown circa 1780s. This is a composite map using data
from Denise Challenger, Luther Johnson, John Bannister, and Arlene Water-
man, "The Streets of Bridgetown Circa 1765," *Journal of the Barbados Museum
and Historical Society* 45 (1999): 77–87, and Martyn Bowden, "The Three
Centuries of Bridgetown: An Historical Geography," *Journal of the Barbados
Museum and Historical* 49 (November 2003): 1–137. The locations on this map
are an approximation based on the above data to provide a sense of the spatial
layout of the town by the late eighteenth century. Courtesy of *Journal of the
Barbados Museum and Historical Society.*

Carlisle Bay is become quite the busy Thames of the West Indies. English ships of war, merchantmen, and transports; slave ships from the
coast of Africa; packets; prizes; American traders; island vessels, pri-
vateers, fishing smacks, and different kinds of boats, cutters, and lug-
gers are among the almost hourly variety.[50]

This geography of Carlisle Bay as an accommodating and large harbor was
likely one factor in making Bridgetown the economic capital of Barbados instead of Speightstown, Holetown, or Oistins. With calm waters, small boats

easily navigated to and from the larger merchant ships carrying goods in both directions. The wharves on the careenage always teemed with enslaved men and women, the former who worked loading the small boats with casks of sugar or rum and the latter huckster women selling produce, meat and household wares to the passersby. In November 1757 the Barbados Council debated a bill "to Remedy the Mischief & Inconveniency arising to the Inhabitants of this Island from the Traffick of Huckster Slaves. . . . Committed in any of the Harbours, Bays, Rivers, or Creeks or upon the Coast of this Island."[51] Similar laws were proposed throughout the eighteenth century as colonial authorities attempted to regulate enslaved movement and commerce.

Walking along the careenage, Jane would smell the seawater, mixed with the sour and dank smells of too many people in too small an area, and if she passed by the Cage, which held captured runaways, she would have seen the sweat and sensed the fear of the occupants inside. Enslaved people were no longer executed for running away by the time Jane made her escape, but the return to an angry owner offered no solace to the captured fugitive, as whipping or some form of bodily mutilation followed capture.[52] James Fort, both a structure of official government business (completed in 1701) and by the mid-eighteenth century a common site, as Governor James Spry stated, "where Slaves have frequently Suffered Death,"[53] sat on an out-cropping on the south west of the Bridgetown waterfront.[54] Execution sites in Barbados towns were centrally located, and slaves were often hanged, gibbeted, or burned to death in front of large audiences. For example, in 1768 an enslaved woman named Molly was executed in Speightstown for allegedly poisoning John Denny Esqr., while a crowd of slaves gathered to bear witness to colonial violence.[55] Similarly, Jane might have heard the beating of drums announcing new acts passed for the "governing of negroes" or overheard conversations about a recent burning alive of enslaved men who were falsely accused of murdering a white doctor just three years before her escape.[56] One of the accused, an elderly black man, likely named Nick, raised the stake to which he was tied with his bound body, in an effort to escape the terror of being burned alive. The authorities instantly struck the stake farther into the ground and increased the wood to intensify the flames that eventually ended his life.[57]

If Jane continued west she would see balconied two and three story houses, only a few of which were still made of wood after the fires of 1757 and 1766.[58] The fires of May and December 1766 destroyed 70 percent of the houses, storefronts, and warehouses throughout the town.[59] The minutes of council records for the period describe the destruction: "The fire broke out

May 14th, at 11 O' Clock at night, at a house in High Street. Four hundred & eighteen principal houses, independent of lesser buildings, stores, & sheds were burnt. The rents of the houses burnt, by the Church Books, amounted to £15, 442 Per Annum."[60] Accounts and statements from the governor's council included the conflation of fire with the surreptitious activities of the urban enslaved. In 1757, a speech given by Governor Charles Pinfold clarified the continued objective of slave control and confinement. Imploring council members to convene committees to force residents to rebuild in brick and stone and not timber, Pinfold makes explicit reference to the increased regulations on urban slaves,

> [Infesting] Your streets . . . their Lust for Revenge, the great Advantage they have Reaped from the two late fires, I am under the Greatest Apprehensions, that unless prevented by Your Care and prudence they may by such favourable Opportunitys for theft and plunder be tempted to renew your misfortunes.[61]

In 1771 Governor Spry, still responding to the devastation of property from the 1766 fires, wrote to the Board of Trade and Plantations concerning the most pertinent issues consuming council members in the legislature: "some Bills for the Improvement of our Internal Police: The Preservation of the Town from future Accidents by Fire—And the better Government of the Negros."[62] Despite the evidence presented to the Board of Trade that the 1766 fire in Bridgetown "was started by the Carelessness of an Apprentice Boy who fell asleep & left a lighted Candle too near some loose Flakes of Cotton,"[63] the enslaved remained criminal suspects and subject to restrictive legislation curtailing their movements and regulating enslaved gatherings throughout the town.[64] Colonial authorities in Barbados were responding to the history of attempts and conspiracies to revolt in the seventeenth century and the recent large-scale and deadly wars the British fought with the maroons in Jamaica in the early eighteenth century, including Tacky's revolt in 1760, in which over a thousand slaves rose up against the British on that island for more than a year.[65]

As Jane made her way west she might have caught a glimpse of newly arrived Africans or "seasoned" creole slaves being sold in various storehouses throughout the merchant district and in the Molehead warehouses across the careenage from the mainland.[66] On 2 August 1783, for example, the *Barbados Mercury* announced for sale, "At public Vendue at the store of James Beaumont Evans & Co. on the wharf Eighty Seasoned Negroes."[67] Lacking a central marketplace for the sale of slaves, slave merchants constructed make-shift spaces for the auction of African captives. These warehouses lined the waterfront and also housed bulk export items such as sugar, ginger, rum, and molasses for the wealthiest planters and merchants on the island.[68] Con-structed of wood or stone and close to the waterfront, they sweltered in the heat of the day. The threat and reality of pestilence from incoming ships, foul air and insects, and human bodies packed dangerously tight rendered the con-ditions inside the warehouses a constant peril and extended the mortal condi-tions of the Middle Passage onto shore. Merchant companies, townspeople, and planters all advertised sales of the enslaved. One such advertisement reads:

Dec 29th 1787
Just imported in the ship FANNY. Jenkins Evans, Co. from the Coast of Africa, and to be sold by the subscribers. A remarkable fine cargo, consisting of One Hundred and Eighty Five, prime young healthy SLAVES, which will be exposed to sale at the yard of Mr Thomas Grif-fith, on Monday the 7th of January early in the fore noon.
GRIFFITH and APPLEWHAITE[69]

The language of "exposure" and "fine cargo" describes the process of com-modification and "black dispossession."[70] The African captives in this in-stance were removed from the ship's hold to another pen in the warehouse district or the yards of merchant businesses, where they waited a week for their impending sale. Likely suffering from loss of shipmates during the jour-ney, and other archivally invisible horrors, these men, women, and children faced new threats as they stood in Griffith's yard where planters and towns-people, men and women, crowded around to inspect their potential invest-ment. At the same time, the sight of newly arrived Africans being moved from the ship *Fanny* docked in Carlisle Bay reminded creole slaves of their denigrated position whether remembering their own moment of disembarka-tion and sale or the repeated terror of witnessing frightened captives led into a life of perpetual bondage and violence.[71] In 1789, the year Jane became a fugi-tive, debates raged in the British Parliament about the cessation of the slave trade. It would not end in the British Empire for another eighteen years.[72]

The volume of Bridgetown's slave trade and its convenient geographic lo-cation frequently lured purchasers from the French or Spanish colonies or even Europe. In late June 1773, a Spanish ship from Cadiz but bound for Ha-vana entered Carlisle Bay. The captain, Don Ramon de la Hera, was ill with a fever and the crew asked local authorities for a few days berth. Another man from the ship, Don Heronimo Enrile, "Director for the Company of Asiento of Negroes," purchased African captives with a "considerable sum of money . . . which sum was delivered to Messrs. Stevensen and . . . British Merchants Established here."[73] The Spaniard received slaves and provisions from the same. Stifling captivity, then, did not end in the dungeons of Cape Coast or in the holds of ships during the Middle Passage. From the layout of the town and the circumstances of slave trading, merchants and planters likely held many African captives for extended periods as they awaited sale in the warehouses lining the wharves.

To the north of the wharves and above the main thoroughfare of Broad Street, Jewish families, descendants of those who fled Dutch Brazil in the mid-seventeenth century, occupied Swan Street (formerly Jew Street), with shops of hardware and other goods.[74] The former Quaker meeting house and the Milk Market dominated by enslaved and free hucksters and poor whites was not far from Swan Street to the west.[75] Farther west Jane would meet the fish market and butchers' shambles, where goats, cows, chickens, and pigs were slaughtered and fish was sold by the enslaved for dinner tables through-out the town.[76] Jane may have known and made her way to the great market in Cheapside, to ask the huckster women for a place to hide, or a job where she might blend in with the twelve thousand or so enslaved people who worked in domestic capacities or on the docks. The great market, largely pop-ulated by enslaved women, was a place where runaways could gain informa-tion, hear news, and grasp a sense of the new dangers of town life. If Jane had run away on a Sunday, she would mingle with many enslaved people given day travel passes and wearing the required metal collar to sell goods in town.[77] On 6 January 1708, an act passed, "to prohibit the Inhabitants of this Island from employing, their Negroes or other Slaves, in selling or bartering." The authorities had difficulties enforcing this so added a provision, "That all such Negroes and other Slaves who are employed in selling Milk, Horse-meat, or Fire-wood shall have at all such times . . . a metaled Collar locked about his, her, or their Neck or Necks, Leg or Legs."[78] It is unclear to what extent owners complied with this provision, and although white residents at-tempted in various ways over the eighteenth century to curtail the commerce of huckstering slaves, they nonetheless persisted in their market activities.[79]

Across the water from Cheapside market and butcher's shambles lay a swamp on the Molehead. This land was considered "unproductive" by the white townspeople and was often flooded by torrential rain or the tidewater brought in by hurricanes. If Jane was out at night she may have heard the sounds of song and mourning from a group of her fellow slaves interring a deceased friend or kin in this marginal land.[80] She might have passed Rachael Pringle Polgreen's infamous "Royal Navy Hotel" on Canary Street near the careenage, peopled by enslaved women who provided sexual services to the many sailors and military officers briefly in port.[81] During the night there were also white watchmen patrolling the streets for suspect activity, black bodies out of place or engaged in illegal behavior.[82] However, perceptions of enslaved women as public, mobile, and accessible provided some a useful disguise. On an October evening in 1742 an enslaved boy dressed as a woman walked across Bridgetown and was caught with a concealed sword at a home to which he was not bonded. Although he was following orders from his master, who was having an affair with the woman of the house, any efforts to explain himself were unrecognized by the law. Only white men decided the "guilt" or "innocence" of the enslaved. The law did not permit slave testimony.[83]

From a single runaway advertisement we cannot know Jane's ultimate fate—whether she was harbored by friends, relatives, or strangers, caught, or continued her journey in danger. Left only with the newspaper trace of her scarred body, we lose her alongside "all the lives that are outside of history."[84] By subverting the discourse of the runaway ad and the gaze of her white male owner, we shift the epistemological weight of the archival document. Using maps and first-hand descriptions, we can reconstruct Bridgetown's topography and visualize the historical experience of the enslaved in an urban context in a way that does not reinscribe the violence of the archive and erase the enslaved women who were a significant presence. Traveling through Bridgetown guided by Jane's sensorial insight, we imagine the embodied experience of the enslaved, even if the record insists on reproducing the commodification and objectification in the descriptions of her scars and the reward offered for her return. Moreover, this method points to the tensions inherent in fugitivity between the rejection of the notion of being owned as property and the tenuous position of moving through public space. Violent punishment inevitably followed capture; well into the eighteenth century mutilation and death were commonly inflicted on runaways.[85] Indeed, after a 1675 insurrection plot was discovered, the Barbados legislature revised existing laws in a 1676 act to include the death penalty for runaways.[86] Yet, over the course of the eighteenth century, Bridgetown and other urban sites endured as a destination for runaways hoping for a permanent or temporary reprieve from their captivity. Whether enslaved in town or coming from the country to sell provisions, enslaved women and men became familiar with the urban landscape they traversed. Jane's body, marked from the violence of enslaved captivity, would have also been a common corporeal topography to enslaved and free alike. Colonial power was mapped onto enslaved bodies through physical punishment and displays of public violence, and these modes of production developed early in step with the growing investment in a sugar economy. From its earliest development Bridgetown became a focal point for the production and exchange of commodities, colonial power, and the precarious lives of the enslaved.

Emergent Bridgetown:
The Material Body and Spatial Control

Fueled by the growing significance of sugar, late seventeenth-century Bridgetown's development demanded a growing enslaved African population.[87] The geography, economy, and coastal location of the town facilitated significant human and maritime traffic, exposing the urban population to threats of war from rival colonies, disease, and natural disasters. Conscious of their own vulnerability to an increasing majority African and island-born enslaved population, colonial authorities erected the Cage, gallows, and stocks within town to discourage rebellion and revolt.[88] These factors, explored in detail below contributed to the hazards of urban enslaved life in unique ways.

Settled in 1627, Barbados became one of the first and most economically successful early modern British colonial projects in the Caribbean.[89] This success developed slowly over time from dozens of Englishmen experimenting with tobacco, cotton, and livestock in the early years of settlement to the introduction of sugar by the Dutch in the mid-seventeenth century.[90] Situated in a strategic geography that isolated the island from its neighbors, and as the most easterly of the Caribbean islands, Barbados grew in significance in the sugar and slave trades, both of which expanded exponentially. Over the course of the seventeenth century, the island boasted an elevated status in the British Empire as a lucrative sugar producer in addition to being a transportation hub of commodities, including captive Africans, shipped throughout the Americas.[91] The first recorded settlement in the area of Bridgetown dates back to 1628 and was financed by James Hay, earl of Carlisle, who initiated the first group of settlers into the "Indian Bridge Town" named for an early Amerindian bridge that connected two parts of town over "Indian River."[92] Bridgetown developed haphazardly and slowly over the late seventeenth century.[93] Located on the southwestern coast of the island, it boasted a natural harbor in Carlisle Bay that would become important to the shipping trade for the entire island colony. Large portions of St. Michael's Parish remained rural in the seventeenth, eighteenth, and nineteenth centuries while Bridgetown had increased its urbanity and density consistently since the initial settlement. Speightstown on the northwest coast and Oistins on the south both developed distinct urban communities during this period, the former with a substantial free community of color into the nineteenth century.[94] However, similar to Holetown, neither town became as important in terms of business, shipping, and colonial administration as Bridgetown. Indeed, Bridgetown was established as a rival town to Holetown, the first English settlement on the island.[95] By the late seventeenth century, Bridgetown emerged as the island's governmental and economic center, eclipsing Holetown in significance. The town arose around a substantial mangrove swamp where settlers claimed lands, built homes, and used natural bridges and harbors to establish their port. In the 1650s, directly related to the agricultural transition to sugar production, rudimentary cart roads gave way to trading infrastructures, warehouses, and wharves lining the waterways of the town and a usable port.[96] Supplementing the creation of an infrastructure supporting sugar production, "the town also had a jail, stocks, pillory, whipping post, and dunking pool for thieves, fugitive slaves and servants, and the gangs of drunken seamen who frequently disturbed the peace of the town's citizens."[97] Central to the project of a slave economy, the government of Barbados constructed these instruments of torture to subjugate disorderly black and white bodies publicly and persistently. Moreover, many of these technologies were specific to this urban context and increasingly reserved for the enslaved population.

By the 1680s, with its population of some 3,000 residents, Bridgetown was larger and more populated than all British American towns except Boston.[98] During the sugar boom of the 1640s through 1660s, the Atlantic slave trade brought in tens of thousands of Africans, most of whom labored on the plantations strewn throughout the island colony. And by 1715, enslaved women outnumbered men. Similarly, from 1715 to the end of the century Bridgetown's enslaved population grew substantially, from 13,000 to 17,000.[99] Over the late seventeenth and early eighteenth centuries, Bridgetown became the epicenter of British profit in the Caribbean. The growth of the sugar trade spurred the large-scale importation of Africans from west and central Africa. Combined, these economic factors made Barbados the most profitable colony in the region until the 1720s, when it was surpassed in exportation by Jamaica.[100] Between 1707 and 1726, the board of trade and plantations listed 49,594 Africans brought into the colony.[101] Destined for the fatal conditions associated with sugar cultivation, the majority were sold to planters across the island. Others were sold to neighboring colonies and a few remained to labor in town. Early Bridgetown was a central hub in this slave trade, and the Royal African Company of slave traders maintained an office on Tudor Street from 1671–1721.[102] With no central market site for sales, a variety of urban spaces became flesh markets, further implicating this town in the violence of slavery. African captives were sold in several ways. A "vendue," public auction, or "outcry" usually involved a financially distressed or liquidated estate. In the British Caribbean, captives also experienced sale through a "scramble," wherein buyers raced around a holding yard or on a ship grabbing as many captives as they could afford within a designated timeframe marked with a bell.[103] Other captives were sold individually within the ships by which they were transported.

From the late seventeenth century on, Bridgetown grew in density in people and buildings as well as in susceptibility to the elements, disease, and world affairs. Though disease, war, and natural disasters affected the entire population, slaves living in town acutely felt the brunt of incoming plagues, thinning provisions, and destruction of shelters. Since the late seventeenth century, Bridgetown had been known as "being by far the unhealthiest place on the island," with a constant influx of diseased and transient sailors in addition to the African captives sickened by the Middle Passage.[104] Epidemics killed hundreds of people in this society; in 1694 yellow fever killed 354 people in Bridgetown alone. Into the late eighteenth century governors wrote to England about the periodically high mortality of all the inhabitants.[105] On 13 April 1776, for example, Governor Hay wrote the Lords of Trade and Plantations about "a Calamity . . . that has reigned in the Island for these three or four [Monthes], which is the Small Pox, attended with a putrid fever; Some Hundreds of People have been carried off by this disorder, particularly White Children and Negroes."[106] Living in a dense urban environment where the enslaved moved through town in ways not possible on plantations still left them exposed to the rapid spread of disease from a constant influx of people from abroad. Incoming ships brought decimating illness to the inhabitants of the town, and captive Africans remained the most predisposed to disease and

death. In February 1782, slave trader Captain Coleman "of a Liverpool Guin-
eaman" ship petitioned Governor James Cunninghame "for leave to land his
Slaves in order to inoculate them for the small Pox, some few of them having
caught the infection from the [West African] Shore."[107] In the late eighteenth
century, Surveyor Crawford remarked to the St. Michael's Parish Vestry that
"In every populous Town such as this it will be ever found impossible to [in-
force] that law so effectually as to prevent the accumulation of dirt in different parts of the Town, and from that accumulation, together with the [pudles]
formed in broken parts of the Streets, I am perfectly persuaded many diseases especially [epidemic] Sore Throats and Fevers originate."[108] Both white
and black residents suffered from the unhealthy conditions of urban life and
disease, but Richard Dunn points out that both groups' survival rates differed
resulting from the general maltreatment of the enslaved: "the blacks were
overdisciplined and underfed, while their masters were underdisciplined and
overfed."[109] The opulent lifestyles of the planter class existed in distinct contrast to the conditions in which enslaved people lived and worked.

In times of war these differences proved stark. The architecture of militia
and military fortifications served as powerful symbols of the strength of colonial power and as crucial sites for controlling the enslaved throughout
Bridgetown. Situated the farthest east of the Caribbean islands, Barbados
benefited from its relative isolation in cases of hostility from rival and neighboring colonial powers. Still, occasional threats between and during war-
time kept Barbados colonists in a state of readiness, particularly from their
tense relationship with the French and Spanish.[110] A militia established by
the mid-seventeenth century helped prepare the island for foreign invasion.
By 1680 about 5,588 men served in this unit, which also functioned as a defense against threats of slave rebellions in the same period.[111] Bridgetown
did not host the British Caribbean's largest military fortifications until the
late eighteenth century, but as early as 1650 Needham's Point's fortifications
were built for the protection of Carlisle Bay.[112] In 1705 Barbados officials
commissioned St. Ann's Fort in the area on the southeast edge of Bridgetown that would be occupied by the garrison military buildings in the late
eighteenth century.[113]

Barbados colonists often recruited enslaved men in the building and defense of the colony when it served their interests. The enslaved, therefore,
were particularly threatened at times of invasion. During a conversation in
the Barbados Assembly in 1740 about raising money to build fortifications, a
list of expenses exemplified the peril to which the enslaved were subject and

the significant attention given to the building of forts, accumulation of ammunition, and arming of magazines. The list reads as follows:

> The Orders that the Governor or Commander in Chief with the Consent of the Council may issue without an Address from the Assembly are:
>   1. Value of Negroes lost in the Publick Service
>   2. Value of Negroes set free for Gallantry [opposing] the Enemy.
>   3. Value of Negroes kill'd at the Time of Invasion or Appearance of the Enemy.
>   4. Gunners and Matrosses Sallarys
>   5. Master Gunner and Matrosses of Artillery
>   6. Captain and Men at the Magazine
>   7. Certificates from the Commissioners for repairing the Fortifications[114]

Noted for their bravery, enslaved men served as armed soldiers when it suited colonial interests, and some were freed for their "loyalty."[115] However, they had no choice in the matter of protecting and serving the public, and many lost their lives in the front lines of conflict.[116] Enslaved men were also made to build and repair roads, public buildings, bridges, military fortifications, and other urban infrastructures that served to control their mobility.[117] Slave owners benefited from payment from the public treasury for their slaves' work, including a sum of twenty-five pounds if the slave died during this public labor. This financial reimbursement to slave owners for loss of their slaves in service revealed another level of enslaved objectification—their retained value as commodities in death and expendability, in physical harm from invasion, or the dangers of public works projects.

The enslaved population in Bridgetown also suffered acutely from interruption of trade during extended warfare. For example, without the provision grounds typical on plantations, urban slaves struggled for sustenance during the American Revolution. While anticipating a trade embargo from England due to the war with its North American colonies, Barbadian planters seemed to have prepared more provision grounds and "increased their imports to stock up Barbadian warehouses as much as possible."[118] However, Governor Hay proved overconfident when allowing the Royal Navy to provision Boston out of Barbados stocks. A year after the trade embargo of September 1775 supplies were depleted in Barbados to a dangerous degree.[119]

During a political conflict between Governor Hay, who continually denied the lack of supplies, and the Barbados Assembly, who sent their complaints directly to the king, the danger of food shortages continued. Historian Karl Watson remarks that "the urban white poor were the greatest sufferers" in such conditions because they could not plant food crops as their peers in the country.[120] Despite the political disagreements between the governor and the assembly, with the governor denying the veracity of food scarcity claims, it was clear that the urban enslaved would also be susceptible to dwindling food supplies.[121] In a letter from Governor Hay to the Lords of Trade and Plantations on 24 March 1776, he suggests that the Assembly's complaint of the scarceness of Guinea Corn and Indian corn, the main staple for slaves, was overblown.[122] This letter was followed by an address from the assembly to the Lords complaining that the distress from want of provisions to feed the poor and slaves was not exaggerated as the governor claimed.[123] Without significant demographic statistics for the period, Watson asserts that "the situation [of scarcity of food] with respect to the slave population is less clear," but one can surmise that when the "urban poor" suffered, the urban enslaved enjoyed no better conditions, given the deeply stratified social conditions in which the enslaved occupied the lowest status.

While slave owners might have wanted to keep their investments in human property alive, when forced to choose between their own lives and the lives of their slaves one can assume they chose themselves.[124] This is evident in the general maltreatment of slaves throughout the islands, slave laws demanding mutilating punishments for alleged crimes, the dangerous tasks they were assigned in times of war and disaster, and travelers' and locals' observations during the eighteenth century on the depraved appearance of enslaved people in town.[125] William Dickson, a resident of Barbados in the late eighteenth century, described "several worn out and leprous negroes, who frequented the more public parts of [Bridgetown], especially the market and both the bridges." His recollection included "a most miserable and leprous woman . . . in the alley parallel to and between, Broad street and Jew Street," and another "negro" woman whose "naked and extenuated corpse [was] . . . surrounded with ordure and vermin."[126] Enslaved people past their productive labor were sometimes left to fend for themselves, and Bridgetown became frequented by those destitute from lack of food and shelter and ill from disease.[127]

The urban slaves' susceptibility to danger was likewise acutely visible in times of natural disaster. One of the most devastating events in Barbados history occurred on the morning of October 10, 1780, when a colossal hurricane struck the island and its neighboring colonies, including Jamaica far to the north.[128] This notorious hurricane produced volumes of desperate correspondence from officials and residents describing ruin beyond anything previously experienced. Even the governor and his family were forced into the open as the roof of their home tore away.[129] Bridgetown felt the force of the storm. Several witnesses, including colonial officials, described the extreme destruction. One resident wrote, "Scarce a house is standing in Bridgetown; whole families were buried in the ruins of their habitations."[130] Governor Cunningham reported, "Bridge Town our Capital is now a [heap] of ruins, the Court House & Prisons, where criminals & Prisoners of War were confined, lies open, therefore the Prisoners of all kinds are at liberty."[131] Although some enslaved might have been inadvertently set free, they likely did not survive for long due to the food shortages and destruction of homes. Many witnesses and victims wrote in apprehension of the sight and sounds of death throughout the towns and countryside. Several men of the Barbados Council wrote an address to King George III declaring their horror of hearing "the dying groans of a very considerable number of the inhabitants, who lay expiring in the streets of the towns . . . a circumstance too shocking to even mention."[132] Significant attention in the written reports also focused on slaves, noting their lack of shelter and impending starvation.[133] A Barbadian planter wrote about ships being sent to North America to secure provisions, "without a supply of which numbers must die of famine: 1000 negroes have perished that way since the hurricane for want."[134] All inhabitants suffered from the 1780 hurricane, but evidence illuminates the particular hardships endured by the enslaved.[135]

John Gay Alleyne, speaker of the House of Assembly and a wealthy planter, expressed concern for his prospective loss of property in dying slaves. Alleyne implores, "The King's Most Excellent Majesty . . . we dread a scarcity of [Indian corn] . . . for the subsistence of our negroes, and that a famine will complete that misery which the tempest may then seem only to have begun."[136] The limited diet of the enslaved made them incredibly vulnerable to any threats to these sources of sustenance. In contrast to the quality of food to which planters and slave owners had access to during disasters, the enslaved either starved or struggled to survive the diseases that spread across the island following hurricanes.[137] Meanwhile colonists scrambled to prevent their loss of profits. Authorities feared not only famine and the death of their enslaved but also unrest and revolt due to the chaos after disasters.[138]

Evidence of colonial authorities' fear and their efforts to exert control can be read in the technologies and architectures they developed to confine the urban enslaved population before and after the hurricane of 1780.

Architectures of Control

There was an obvious link between enslaved bodies in urban space and architectures of control. White supremacy was expressed in ideology, physical exertion, and inanimate symbols of power to the enslaved population with structures such as the common gaol, the execution gallows, or the Cage. These architectures served as stark reminders of the consequences of resistance to the enslaved even as they grafted a criminal identity onto their bodies.[139] In Barbados the concentration of power was expressed through the organization of labor, punishment, and space. Barbados slave owners and the colonial government built and maintained urban carceral sites and practiced the spectacle of mobile punishments—whipping the same enslaved body in different locations—to (re)produce and exercise the forms of discipline that were found on plantations.

The control wielded by slave owners, overseers, and drivers on plantations was shared with constables, magistrates, jumpers, and executioners in urban areas.[140] On the plantation, punishment for most offenses committed by the enslaved, whether purposely or in self-defense, remained in the hands of the planter, overseer, or driver. These men used the whip and other physical forms of discipline at their discretion with little, if any, regulation from colonial authorities. In town, however, in the absence of a "gang" of laboring workers and the urban reality of more individualized tasks, the white men appointed as constables and watchmen served as representatives of the urban slave holder, non-slave holders, and the larger white population and were given authority to mete out punishments on enslaved bodies.[141]

Power to inflict physical punishment extended to the judiciary as well as magistrates, who could order a whipping at their discretion, even if the slaveholder was not present or aware that the slave had been taken up by a constable. For instance, an Act passed in January 1708 allowed any justice of the peace to order "one and twenty stripes," of the whip on any slave caught selling allegedly stolen goods.[142] The slaveholder was required to pay for both the captivity of his/her "property" and the whipping, illustrating the extent to which control of "slave behavior" was enforced from many areas of urban society and was distinct from plantation discipline.[143] Punishments on enslaved bodies included public displays of colonial power, and Bridgetown contained several spaces that invoked fear in the absence of the spatial confinement of the plantation complex. These spaces reproduced criminal identities, racial terror, and mortal confinement in urban Barbados.

An enslaved woman walking from one end of Bridgetown to the other would pass scenes and "visible symbols" of public punishment reinforcing the threat of violence as well as her own racial and gendered status.[144] Such sites included the Cage, James Fort, the Custom House, taverns, brothels busy streets, and the commercial warehouses that lined the active wharf. Seemingly neutral sites occupied by enslaved women engaged in economic endeavors, such as the Milk Market or Great Market, were also spaces of terror since punishments were often meted out in different locations. For instance, Grigg and Bess were prosecuted for the theft of a cow in February 1743. This felony conviction carried the sentence of death. While Bess's sentence of guilt was reversed, Grigg was ordered to be whipped by the town "jumper." The order stated specifically that he be released from incarceration once "The Gaoler or his Deputy See . . . that [Grigg] first receive 39 Lashes on his bare back (vizt.) 13 at the Roebuck 13 at the Cage and 13 at the Custom House."[145] "The Roebuck," or Roebuck Street was a busy district of shops and foot traffic and largely occupied by free(d) people of color by the end of the eighteenth century.[146] Indeed, even the free population of color suffered the proximity to the violence of slavery. Likewise, the Custom House sat in the center of town where Grigg's punishment would be witnessed by many enslaved and free(d)men, women, and children. The Custom Houses, a relic from Europe, were prevalent in many port towns across the Atlantic. Its purpose was to regulate and account for the import and export of trade goods. Not surprisingly, by linking punishment of slaves to the structure of the Custom House, the authorities reinforced enslaved commodification and objectification while setting an example of deterrence to the enslaved population. The Custom House's location in the center of town and as a common site of whipping exemplifies the deliberate linking of the punishment and subjugation of black life and the consolidation of white supremacy in urban spaces. The other significant intention of such punishment was to make the spectacle visible to the greatest number of enslaved people.

The Cage, another physical representation of colonial power, was a gaol building originally erected for the confinement of riotous sailors in the mid-seventeenth century. Prior to 1657, there was a Cage located farther northwest at the intersection of Milk Market and Jew Streets. Situated between the courthouse and the main town market, this pre-1657 Cage held unruly indentured servants and "riotous sailors" after an incident in 1654.[147] In 1657 a new Cage was completed on the southeastern public wharf, where Broad Street meets White Street, next to a public jail and near the State House. This new Cage was at the turn of the nineteenth century surrounded by open land that bordered a public "boardwalk" lined with pedestrian "stepping stones," from which the walkway received its name.[148] The Cage appears to have faced the busy Broad Street, although it could have been open to both the street and the wharf on the rear.[149] From its early use for the confinement of white seamen and indentured servants, the new Cage's purpose quickly shifted to that of a holding cell for runaway slaves, "a poignant symbol of the new stresses of the sugar era."[150] Captured runaways confined in the Cage waited there until they were claimed by their owners or tried.

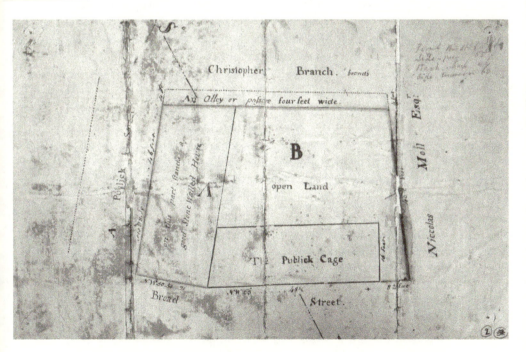

Figure 5. Plan of the Publick Cage, drawn by John Atwood, c. 1830. Courtesy of the Barbados Museum and Historical Society.

Directly related to the surveillance and confinement of the ever-increasing enslaved population, this shift in the use of the Cage from riotous white sailors to the confinement of black bodies signaled a critical shift in colonial priorities. Shortly after the sugar boom in the mid-seventeenth century, controlling the urban slave population was the most important aspect of enforcing white colonial power. Located on Broad Street and facing the careenage or public wharf the Cage was in the midst of busy maritime and foot traffic.[151] As early as 1688 an Act "For the Governing of Negroes" specifies that "Negroes or Slaves So brought [to Bridgetown], shall be kept in the Cage at the Stepping-Stones, by the Provost Marshall, and not in the gaol; which said Cage is always to be kept in sufficient repair, at the public charge of this Island."[152] By this edict it appears the gaol was primarily reserved for white criminals and debtors representing the segregation between slaves and whites and reinforcing the special category in which the enslaved were held. In 1762, "An Act to impower the Justices of the Peace at their respective Quarter Sessions, to appoint Constables for the Several Parishes of this Island; and also for the appointment of Watches to be in the respective Towns of this Island" was passed.[153] It authorized the justices of the peace to divide the town into districts and appoint "twenty-eight Watch-men, who with the Constable of the night to be deemed as two men, shall watch every night within the said [Bridgetown], from the hour of nine o'clock at night, till five o'clock the next morning."[154] The Justices directed each Watch-man to be armed and a Cage built, "and stocks kept in good order."[155] This law created a vast system of surveillance throughout the town and seems to suggest that in addition to the main Cage near the main bridge in the eastern region, many Cages would be built, one in each district. Although there are no surviving records that referred to the actual existence of multiple Cages throughout the town, these edicts expose a careful plan of confinement and control aimed at enslaved people.[156]

Enslaved women like Jane who ran away for thirty days or more and were caught would have likely been held in the Cage until their trial and execution.[157] Such occurrences were not rare. Prior to the 1750s, if a woman "absented" herself above thirty days, the law directed conviction and execution following her capture. For instance, on 27 October 1702, George Sharpe Esq. submitted a petition to the Barbados Council for the value of "a Negro Wooman of his, who was Executed for running away and absenting herself from her Masters Service for about one whole Yeare."[158] Execution records for the course of the eighteenth century reveal that enslaved men and women were condemned for running away as late at 1759.[159] In later years, likely due to the impending abolition of the slave trade to and from Africa rather than humanitarian concerns, colonial authorities changed the terms by which runaways would be punished in the latter eighteenth century.[160] But the Cage(s) and other sites of punishment remained the literal and symbolic material of colonial power and the consolidation of white supremacy into the nineteenth century.

The Cage's deadly conditions proved distressing not only to the slaves confined within but an affront to the respectability of the residents of Bridgetown into the nineteenth-century who complained of it as "disgusting to Humanity and at first view disgraceful to the Age in which we live," and as a "Nuisance to its Neighborhood."[161] In 1810, an enslaved man died while being held in the Cage and the Assembly and Bridgetown magistrates investigated the causes of his death.[162] The construction of the main Cage purported to hold no more than twelve persons, yet, as the Barbados Minutes of Assembly reported, "[in] this wretched and miserable hole, shocking to relate, eighty-five persons have been confined at one time. If they lay down at all, they must have lain tier upon tier, at least four deep."[163] Similar to conditions of the Middle Passage, the confining spaces of an urban slave environment served not simply to hold fugitives in captivity but to symbolically reinforce the legal status of chattel and the disposability of black life. The Barbados Council met in the middle of December 1810 to hear the investigations by the Assembly and Bridgetown magistrates and to consider requests to remove the Cage, "as far as can be . . . from the principal & public Streets of the Town."[164] The Assembly, magistrates and Council ultimately agreed that the fatal conditions of the Cage stemmed from two main issues. First, the enslaved suffered from insufficient provisions because the keeper of the Cage took a third of their allotted daily corn in exchange for providing them with meals and water.[165] Additionally, Bridgetown slave owners, or "proprietors" of slaves confined their slaves for punishment which was an, "illuse, the Cage being intended for the Confinement only of runaway and disorderly Slaves," the latter of which were taken from the streets and held overnight.[166] Consequently, the residents' concerns were not resolved for seven years. A deed poll of 1818, contesting the ownership and transfer of the land upon which the Cage stood, describes the site as still located within the "most public and populous street in the town" and reports the "Cage unwholesome to the slaves confined therein."[167] It was in 1818 that the Barbados government acquiesced to the white residents and moved the cage to the

Pierhead (Molehead) until it was finally eradicated in 1838 after Emancipation in the British Caribbean.[168]

However, despite the threat of "unwholesome" conditions, it is evident from the records that some women were repeatedly confined within this prison. If captured and confined in the Cage, the enslaved were stripped of clothing by the guards and their owners in order to identify them by the scars on their bodies. Descriptions of burns and whip marks brought them out of hiding and into public exposure: the private concealed black female body made public and legible. In October 1787, two enslaved women, Molly and Bessey, ran away from their owners in the southeast part of the island. Bessey, "has frequently been taken up and confined in the Cage," according to her owner Elizabeth Pollard.[169] On December 20, 1788, Jonathan Perkins also advertised for the return of four enslaved women. Ambah was fifty years old, African born, and "[had] lost the forefinger from her left hand."[170] Ambah disappeared with two of her daughters, Quasheba (thirty) and Betty (thirteen). All were said to be "so well known in and about Bridgetown (where they lived for many years) as to require no further description: [they were] perfectly well known to Mr. Gooding, of the Cage and his attendants."[171] Others fought their way out in order to escape the suffocating environment. On 25 October 1788, *The Barbados Mercury* reported that "fourteen of the negroes confined in the Public Cage in this town made their escape; having filed the lock from the bolt to which it was fastened, they opened the door and got out."[172] Risking further punishment, including death, the enslaved confined in Bridgetown's Cage sometimes made desperate efforts to break free.

Enslaved women who ran away did so at great risk to themselves. Even if they managed to avoid capture, they risked manipulation by people who sought to exploit their dangerous situation. Some no doubt worried about the fate of children or family members left behind. Those who ran with their children had to find ways to feed and shelter them. And of course, if caught, they would be immediately confined and possibly sentenced to death.[173] The threats of capture and punishment made fugitivity a fraught choice. The repetition in the advertisements of women who ran from the far corners of the island to town reflects their understanding of Bridgetown as a possible hiding place. Some had relatives and friends in the town and may have had knowledge of networks along the way. But even fugitive women without such ties or knowledge may have viewed urban spaces as offering the best chance of hiding in plain sight among the large enslaved and free black population.

These urban spaces also demonstrated the control of the authorities to impose their will on slave owners, since owners lost valuable property when police or magistrates chose to charge one of their slaves with a crime. With no legal defense to oppose mistreatment, enslaved people remained at the mercy of their owners' ability to argue for their innocence. Occasionally slave owners successfully managed to overturn death sentences for their con- demned slaves. However, if the Council overturned a conviction, the enslaved were rarely released without punishment. Most often, like Grigg, their sentences were reduced from death to multiple whippings at symbolic and hyper-visible sites. For example, on 16 February 1748, Christopher Moe submitted a petition "to Reverse the Sentence of Death against a Negro Man called Somers" to the Court of Errors presided over by the Governor and Council,

> Whereupon the Errors assigned by the Petitioner for Reversing the said sentence were Confessed by the Solicitor for the Prosecution Robert Leader . . . And thereupon [His Excellency] & all the Council were pleased to alter the said [Judgment] of Death; & to order that the said Negro Man Somers receive 13 Lashes before the Custom House; 13 in the Market Place; & 13 before Eldridge's Tavern before he is Discharged.[174]

Although the case was dismissed, a public example was made of Somers and he did not escape punishment. Indeed, the authorities retained their ability to make a spectacle of Somers's tortured body. The records do not indicate the crime for which Somers was accused of or if the confession of errors by the prosecutor exonerated him from the crime. Nevertheless, it appears that the accusation was enough for Somers to be whipped several times around Bridgetown.

Witnesses to punishment recalled the specific exposure town slaves suffered in public displays of humiliation. Evidence from travelers on the display of urban enslaved bodies to strangers and the ways that the sounds of inflicted pain traveled through town illuminate how the seemingly fluid nature of urban space was actually inherently physically intense and specifically violent. Distinguishing between country and town punishments, Captain Cook of the 89th Infantry of Foot explained that in the country "the mode of flogging these Negroes is by laying them upon their bellies, with a Negro at each extremity to raise each hand and foot from the ground, this is the general mode of flogging them in the country."[175] "But in the towns," he continued, "their method is more horrid and shameful, the poor wretch is obliged to stand bare in the open streets, and expose his posteriors to the jumper."[176] In order to assert control in a context where the enslaved often moved through town independently, the authorities purposely conducted punishment so that it was highly visible to the other enslaved people walking around.

Captain Cook remembered an instance where he, "was once particularly shocked at the sight of a young girl, a domestic Slave of about sixteen or seventeen years old, running about on her ordinary business with an iron collar with two hooks before and behind, projecting several inches, and this in the streets of Bridge Town."[177] Enslaved women may have seemingly "enjoyed autonomy" by controlling the informal market economy in produce and other goods and certainly predominated the market place. But the market, like other sites of bodily disciplining—the Cage, the Custom House—also reproduced colonial power and reinforced social, racial, and gendered hierarchies.[178] Authorities in Bridgetown created symbolic boundaries of control with ritual punishments throughout the town that were visible to enslaved people carrying out their daily labors, and each architectural site embodied or produced social relationships based on colonial power, terror, and control. Even if, as one historian states, "urban slaves did not work under the constant threat of the whip which faced rural workers . . . there was the constant reality of living in a slave society" and constant spatial representations of the threat of violence.[179]

As the production of sites of confinement in urban spaces provided colonial authorities the means to terrorize an urban enslaved population, so too do the discursive spaces within the archive confine enslaved women in disfiguring historical representations. These marks and the brutality of slave laws also follow enslaved women into the archive. Indeed, descriptions of their scarred bodies and the acts passed that subjected them to instruments of torture are the primary content of the documents on which we must base their narratives. The fragmentary nature and format of runaway ads confine enslaved women in a depiction of violence and commodification from the perspective of the slave owner and other white authorities. In other words, combining the study of the body of the archive, bodies in the archive and the bodies in space, in the historical analyses of enslaved women in this context sheds light on the multiplicity of forces simultaneously at play in their subjugation. Narrating fugitive enslaved women's stories from these records requires subversion of archival intent through a methodological practice that approaches these documents from the gaze of enslaved women and takes on power in the production of subaltern historical knowledge and the spatial terrain of urban slavery. This epistemological shift reorients historical inquiry to consider the workings of power on the bodies and historical afterlives of the enslaved to produce new knowledge about their lives from the records left by the regime of power.

Interrogating the use and production of spaces and technologies of control on urban enslaved women's bodies and within the archive also makes clear the important differences that shaped enslaved life within towns and plantation complexes without assuming that one was less brutal than the other. It also articulates how central enslaved black bodies were to the production of urban and domestic spaces. As the case of Bridgetown demonstrates, urban life proved equally distressing for the enslaved living there and those laboring on sugar plantations throughout the islands. Moreover, urban life proved fraught with danger for the enslaved who were especially subject to the violence of urban life whether by means of colonial authorities, natural disaster, disease or serving in the informal sexual economy. Enslaved women suffered in particular ways within the confines of Bridgetown as their gendered labor in the domestic realm forced them into close intimacies with their owners, many of who were white and free women of color. A careful interrogation of the brothel as a site of urban confinement reveals the complex intra-gendered relationships of enslaved women and their female owners and provides new insight into the troubling domestic spaces enslaved women occupied. It also exposes how narratives of economic success tragically and historiographically obscures the violence of sexualized labor in slavery and in freedom.

CHAPTER 2

Rachael and Joanna: Power, Historical Figuring, and Troubling Freedom

Scandal and excess inundate the archive . . . The libidinal investment in violence is everywhere apparent in the documents, statements, and institutions that decide our knowledge of the past.

—Saidiya Hartman, "Venus in Two Acts"

[H]istory reveals itself only through the production of specific narratives. What matters most are the process and conditions of such narratives. . . . Only through that overlap can we discover the differential exercise of power that makes some narratives possible and silences others.

—Michel-Rolph Trouillot, *Silencing the Past*

Item it is my Will, and I do hereby manumit and set free my negro Woman named Joannah from all Servitude whatsoever, and for compleating that purpose I do hereby desire my Executors herein after named to pay all such Sums of money and Execute such deeds as are necessary about the same:—And I do give, devise and bequeath unto the said woman Joannah, her child Richard, and a negro Woman named Amber, with her future Issue and Increase, to her the said Joannah and her heirs forever.

—Will of Rachael Pringle Polgreen, 1791

The great hurricane of 1780 destroyed lives, homes, and businesses, and free people of color felt acutely the tenuous nature of their freedom in Bridgetown. On 20 July 1793, Captain Henry Carter and William Willoughby—two white men—swore under oath that Joanna Polgreen, "a certain negroe or mulatto woman," had been freed in 1780 but had lost her manumission papers in the storm.[1] Carter and Willoughby testified that Joanna was once owned by Bridgetown hotelier Rachael Pringle Polgreen, but Rachael sold her to a soldier named Joseph Haycock who promptly freed her from slavery. After her successful reclamation of her freedom Joanna enters another document into the archive, this time a deed wherein she frees her son Richard Braithwaite, "for the natural love & affection which She hath to [him]."[2]

Joanna's quest for freedom for herself and her son involved a long journey from slavery in a brothel to freedom and back, and has until recently remained in the shadows of Rachael Pringle Polgreen's sensational narrative of infamy and fortune.[3] Drawing Joanna's story from underneath Pringle Polgreen's dominance as a historical agent allows us to reconsider the terms of agency and sexuality in this slave society. We also gain insight into the dynamics between women of color and enslaved women in the context of a sexual economy in an urban slave society. Deconstructing Pringle Polgreen's historical narrative ultimately exposes the power of certain narratives to obscure the politics of representing success, the violence fundamental to slavery, and the lives relegated to historical anonymity. The challenge, then, is to track power in the production of Pringle Polgreen's history while recognizing that her historical visibility is also an erasure of the lives of those she enslaved. Doing so reveals, for the first time, the story of Joanna's struggle and determination in freedom and the limits of freedom, sexual commerce, and agency in eighteenth-century Bridgetown.

Rachael Pringle Polgreen, Historicity, and Liminality

It may be precisely due to Rachael Pringle Polgreen's "exorbitant circumstances"[4] during her life as a free(d) woman of color in late eighteenth-century Bridgetown that historical narratives about her life have not changed since she appeared in J. W. Orderson's 1842 novel, *Creoleana*.[5] Apart from an important critique by Melanie Newton of the political and historical context of Orderson's novel, Polgreen's life story—her triumphs, extraordinary relationships, and visual depictions—has not altered since the nineteenth century. Thus both the archive and secondary historical accounts beg reexamination.

Polgreen was a woman of color, a former slave turned slave owner, and many stories circulate that she ran a well-known brothel without much controversy.[6] Persistent representations of Polgreen's life draw from an archive unusual for women of color in eighteenth-century slave societies. She left a will, and her estate was inventoried by white men on her death—a process used primarily by the society's wealthier (white) citizens. Her relationships with elite white men and the British Royal Navy are well documented in newspaper accounts and, most significantly, in the nineteenth-century novel by a Bridgetown resident who was likely well acquainted with Polgreen. In the 1770s and 1780s, this female entrepreneur appears in Bridgetown's tax records as a propertied resident, and her advertisements in a local newspaper allude to the importance she placed on property. From a caricatured 1796 lithograph to the folkloric accounts of Prince William Henry's (King William Henry IV's) rampage through her brothel, Polgreen's story has in many ways been rendered impermeable, difficult to revise, and overdetermined by the language and power of the archive.

Yet the archive conceals, distorts, and silences as much as it reveals. In *Creoleana*, a "complete" dramatized life story of Polgreen is narrated; it provides a tantalizing but fictional solution to gaps and uncertainties for scholars who struggle with the fragmented and fraught records of female enslavement marked by the embedded silences, commodified representations of bodies, and epistemic violence. However, for Polgreen, it is perhaps her hypervisibility in images and stories that continues to obscure her everyday life, even when the archive appears to substantiate certain aspects of that life. Such powerful narratives, visual reproductions, and archival assumptions erase the crucial complexities of her personhood and obfuscate the violent and violating relationships she maintained with other women of color in Bridgetown's slave society.

In the scholarship of slavery and slave societies of the Caribbean, Polgreen and other free(d) women of color are centered in narratives about business acumen and entrepreneurship. Several historians discuss the significant role prostitution played in the local and transnational market economy.[7] Indeed, in many eighteenth-century Caribbean and metropolitan Atlantic port cities prostitution was rampant and served a significant mobile military population as well as providing local "entertainment." During the 1790s, "the symbol of non-white business success in Barbados was the female hotelier."[8]

A number of free(d) women found slave-owning and prostitution economically viable routes to self-sustenance, since they and other free(d) people of color were systemically excluded from most occupations and opportunities.[9] Bridgetown's white female (mostly slave-owning) majority, however, tended to own more women than men and set the precedent for selling and renting out enslaved women for sexual purposes.[10] Moreover, without the possibility of employing their enslaved laborers in agricultural pursuits, urban white women profited from the surplus of domestic workers by hiring them out to island visitors.[11] It is in this environment of slaves, sailors, Royal Navy officers, and other maritime traffic in Bridgetown's bustling port that Rachael Pringle Polgreen made her living.

However, Polgreen's seductive narrative too often eclipses and silences the experiences of other enslaved and free(d) women who lived during her time. This chapter revisits her story to analyze how material and discursive power moves through the archive in the historical production of subaltern women.[12] Reexamining the documentary traces of Polgreen's life and death illuminates several contradictions and historical paradoxes that make it problematic to characterize Polgreen or enslaved and free(d) women's sexual relations with white men as unmediated examples of black female agency. How does one write a narrative of enslaved "prostitution"? What language should we use to describe this economy of forced sexual labor? How do we write against historical scholarship, which too often relies on the discourses of will, agency, choice, and volunteerism that reproduce a troubling archive, one that cements enslaved and free(d) women of color in representations of "their willingness to become mistresses of white men"?[13] If "freedom" meant being free from bondage but not from social, economic, and political degradation, what did it mean to survive under such conditions?

In the 1770s and 1780s, Bridgetown's free population of color remained relatively small, but it experienced significant growth by the turn of the nineteenth century.[14] This group of "free colored" women and men survived through store-keeping, huckstering, ship-building, prostitution, and a small range of other trades. The Royal Navy's military infrastructure perpetuated the demand for an informal sexual economy that was not fully met by the efforts of white slave owners in Bridgetown. For former slaves like Polgreen, who had certainly witnessed white owners profiting from sexual violations of black women, it was possible to imagine hiring enslaved women out for similar purposes. And, if it is true that Polgreen's original owner was her own father, then the sexual dynamics of her life and her business become even more complex.[15] Women comprised a majority of slave owners in Bridge-town, some of them women of color. Therefore, female slave owners like Polgreen comprised an important part of the urban landscape. However, Polgreen's business of brothel keeping diverged sharply from the public economic pursuits of most white female slave owners. Although many white women engaged in "hiring-out" their female slaves for sexual purposes, there is no evidence suggesting that they engaged in running houses of prostitution in Bridgetown.[16] While Polgreen's ability to accumulate wealth was comparable to that of her white counterparts, her avenues for profit restricted her to an arena that would likely have been shameful and disreputable for them.

For studies focused on Barbados specifically, Jerome Handler's two publications, *The Unappropriated People: Freedman in the Slave Society of Barbados* (1974), and "Joseph Rachell and Rachael Pringle-Polgreen: Petty Entrepreneurs" (1981), laid the foundation for later discussions of Rachael Pringle Polgreen, free(d) women of color and prostitution.[17] Handler's discussion recounts Polgreen's enslavement by William Lauder and her freedom and rise to "business" woman—a story drawn directly from the nineteenth-century novel *Creoleana*. Understandably, subsequent historical work has drawn extensively on Handler's authority on Polgreen and free(d) people of color in Barbados.[18] Consequently, several texts mention Polgreen's property accumulation, her relationships with white male elites, her shrewd business management, and her demurring yet assertive challenge to the prince of Britain.[19] One historian of Barbados contends that property ownership by free(d) women of color, "managed [to] challenge the economic hegemony of whites."[20]

Polgreen was part of a "colored elite" who owned property—including slaves—and were able to maintain a standard of living comparable to their white counterparts. But focusing on economic prosperity alone obscures the coercive nature of the enterprise of enslaved prostitution. When concentrated on the economic possibilities for enslaved and free(d) women of color, it is easy to equate black female agency with sexuality without critically examining some of the violating attributes of this labor. Discussions of black women, free(d) or enslaved, using white men as an avenue to freedom often erase the reality of coercion and violence, and the complicated place of black women in this system of domination. Indeed, attention only to opportunities for material benefit suggests that women of color wielded an inordinate amount of power in these sexual encounters. How then, do we tease out the ways narratives of "resistance," "sexual power," and "will" shape our understanding of female slavery? Is will, as Hartman asks, "an overextended approximation of the agency of the dispossessed subject/object of property or perhaps simply unrecognizable in a context in which agency and intentionality are inseparable from the threat of punishment?"[21] The power gained from slave ownership and enslaved prostitution benefited slave owners while leaving enslaved women in a position in which they could not refuse this work. Polgreen herself was dependent on this system of exploitation that left few other avenues for economic prosperity. This reality, and the archive that documented these circumstances, shaped the way her history has been written, leaving the lives of the vast majority of exploited enslaved women virtually invisible.

Michel-Rolph Trouillot writes of historical power, arguing that history represents both the past (facts and archival materials) and the stories told about the past (narratives).[22] Polgreen's archival remains and the histories written about her clearly represent this interaction between the processes of historical production and her limited power of self-representation, as well as the ways authors who narrated her life represent her agency through her material success. Throughout her life and afterlife, Polgreen served the agendas of divergent political discourses. In the nineteenth century, she was used as a motif to remind white society that black women's sexuality must be contained; for the postcolonial Barbados elite, she exemplified loyalty to Britain, accommodation, and peaceful negotiation. In more recent scholarship dating to the 1980s, Polgreen and women of color represented successful challenges to colonial domination.

The documents and processes used to fashion "truths" about Polgreen's experiences represent material accumulation as a triumph over adversity. Polgreen's inner self—her fears and confidences—remain impossible to retrieve using documents produced in a slave society limited by capitalist and elite perspectives.[23] A critical reengagement with the sources elucidates the complexities and contradictions she embodied. Although no birth record survives, historians contend that Rachael Pringle Polgreen was born Rachael Lauder sometime around 1753.[24] Her burial was recorded on 23 July 1791 at the Parish Church of St. Michael.[25] At her death, her estate was worth "Two Thousand nine hundred & thirty Six pounds nine Shillings four pence half penny," an amount comparable to a moderately wealthy white person living at the same time.[26] According to her inventory, along with ample material wealth in the form of houses, furniture, and household sundries, Polgreen owned thirty-eight enslaved people: fifteen men and boys and twenty-three women and girls.[27] In her will she freed a Negro woman named Joanna and bequeathed to her an enslaved Negro woman named Amber. Joanna was also given her own son Richard, who was still enslaved. Polgreen also freed a "mulatto" woman named Princess and four "mulatto" children (not listed in familial relation to any "parents"). Polgreen ordered that the rest of her estate—including William, Dickey, Rachael, Teresa, Dido Beckey, Pickett, Jack Thomas, Betsey, Cesar, a boy named Peter, and nineteen other enslaved people—be divided among William Firebrace and his female relatives, William Stevens, and Captain Thomas Pringle, all white people with whom she had social ties. This bequest—giving away the enslaved as property—was to them and "their heirs forever."[28]

The above information survives precisely because of the value placed on property. Produced through her material wealth, Polgreen's archival visibility relies on the logic of white colonial patriarchal and capitalist functions, reproducing the terms of the system of enslavement. Her burial in the yard of the Anglican Church of Saint Michael's Parish did not, as a triumphal narrative might argue, exemplify transcendence over racial and gendered systems of domination. Rather, it illustrates the power of her social connections, without which permission for a church burial would not have been granted. We may speculate that the limited degree of Polgreen's integration into the white Anglican religious community of Bridgetown granted her unusual status given her profession as a brothel owner, even as we acknowledge that her participation in, even acceptance of, the economic and social circles of white slave owners granted her unusual power.

Beyond her will and estate inventory, another remarkable document has survived: a lithograph produced by British artist Thomas Rowlandson and printed in 1796.[29] It pictures a large and dark-skinned Rachael Pringle Polgreen seated in front of a house purported to be her "hotel." Her breasts are revealed through a low-cut dress as she sits open-legged and bejeweled. In the background of the lithograph are three other figures, a young woman and two white men. The young woman is similarly dressed, with a bodice cut even lower than Polgreen's. She stares, almost sullen-faced, at a large white man appearing in the rear of the picture in a tattered jacket and hat.[30] Observing the young woman from the right side of the picture is a younger white man wearing a British military uniform. He is a partial figure, shown in profile only. A sign posted behind Polgreen reads: "Pawpaw Sweetmeats & Pickles of all Sorts by Rachel PP."[31]

In 1958, an anonymous editorial preceded the first "scholarly" article

Figure 6. Illustration by Thomas Rowlandson, published by William Holland (London, 1796). Courtesy of the Barbados Museum and Historical Society.

about Polgreen in the *Journal of the Barbados Museum and Historical Society*. The editorial reads the image as a narrative about her life, contending that "a gifted [caricaturist] such as Rowlandson would not . . . have placed as a background to the central figure of Polgreen in her later and prosperous years characters such as "a tall girl in a white frock," etc. and an officer looking through a window, which had no relation to her or to her career."[32] In the writer's view, the figures in the background represent a young Polgreen, averting the repulsive advances of her master/father. The young military man represents her "savior" Captain Pringle, the man credited with granting her freedom. Deduced from the most pervasive narrative about her life,

Polgreen's name came from Pringle after the captain who allegedly purchased her from her father/master William Lauder (d. 1771). After settling Polgreen in a house in Bridgetown, Pringle left the island to pursue his military career, and in his absence Rachael Pringle added the name Polgreen.[33]

The editorial does not, however, consider the explicit sexual tone of the sign posted above Polgreen. "Pawpaw, Sweetmeats & Pickles of all Sorts" advertised more than the culinary items available for purchase. Free(d) and enslaved women in towns played a significant role in the informal market economy, selling a variety of ground provisions to locals and incoming ships, and the sign above Polgreen clearly situates her within a well-established economic system. She can easily assume the part of a market woman seated outside her "shop."[34] However, the artist's phallic references on the sign also allude to sexual services offered. The language of "sweetmeats and pickles" worked to both mask and advertise the sexually overt activities within the tavern. At the same time, the image reinforces the positionality of enslaved black women as sexually available, consenting, consumable, and disposable. Many of Rowlandson's works depict London and other maritime scenes and are filled with sexual references. These include sailors and prostitutes in various sexual acts and stages of undress. It may not be surprising, then, to find him dedicating an entire collection to what was then described as "erotic" art.[35] Rowlandson's caricature of Rachael Pringle Polgreen depicts an extravagant woman of color in various stages of her life. In this single frame, she is racialized, discursively and visually sexualized, and carried across her lifespan from a younger, lighter self to an older, darker, larger self. This visual production intertwines Polgreen's race, gender, and sexuality with a complete narrative of her life story as the artist imagined it. The material fragments of Polgreen's existence evident in her will, inventory, and the lithograph exemplify Trouillot's concept of archival power.[36] Operating on two levels, it influences what it is possible to know or not to know about her life. In the first instance, power is present in the making of the archival fragments during her lifetime. Her will, recorded by a white male contemporary, only leaves evidence of what was valued in Polgreen's time—the material worth of her assets in property. She left no diary or self-produced records.[37] Second, illustrated by the lithographic representation, Polgreen's image and life history were imagined by a British man whose own socioeconomic and racial reality limited and informed what he produced about a woman of African descent.

In 1842, nearly fifty-one years after Polgreen's death, *Creoleana, or Social and Domestic Scenes and Incidents in Barbados in the Days of Yore*, written by

J. W. Orderson, was published in London. Orderson was born in Barbados in 1767 and grew up in Bridgetown. His father John Orderson owned the *Barbados Mercury*, a local newspaper, and J. W. became its sole proprietor in 1795.[38] Thus, he would have been a teenager when many of the events he wrote about in *Creoleana* occurred, although he wrote about them when he was seventy-five. It was likely, as evidenced in the numerous newspaper advertisements Polgreen placed in his paper, that J. W. Orderson knew the female hotelier.[39] It is important to read *Creoleana* as a "sentimental" novel of its time, for the historical context in and the literary conventions with which the novel was written are as pertinent as Orderson's characterization of Polgreen. The novel was, as Newton suggests, both "a revision of slavery and a moral reformist tale to guide behavior in post-emancipation society."[40] Slavery and apprenticeship had officially been abolished in Britain's Caribbean colonies by 1842, only four years prior to the novel's publication. Orderson was clear about his nostalgia for a time in which the enslaved were "happier" in their bondage than in freedom.[41] The consequences for Polgreen's historical reproduction are clear, as Melanie Newton notes in her critical reading of the novel:

> In the post-slavery era, as had been the case during slavery, stereotyped and sexualized representations of women of color, especially the "mulatto" woman, often served as the means through which white reactionaries expressed both anti-black sentiment and fear of racial "amalgamation."[42]

Acknowledging the pro-slavery project constituent to such representations raises questions about how to use a text like *Creoleana* as a primary source for Polgreen's historical "reality." This is not to dismiss entirely the novel's potential to historically inform readers or scholars, but rather to offer insight into its distorting representations of Polgreen. At the moment when the British and North American anti-slavery movements were storming across the Atlantic and into the Caribbean, Orderson articulated his pro-slavery beliefs while condemning the "perversion" of inter-racial sex.[43] In a pamphlet published in 1816, Orderson responded to British Parliamentary debates concerning the illicit international trade in Africans and the gradual abolition of slavery in their colonies, but his remarks center specifically on the growth of the free population of color in Bridgetown. Using less symbolic language than the novel to describe his abhorrence of inter-racial sex and unions, Orderson explicitly expressed his opinions guided by his own "moral"

ideologies. Beyond even his disapprobation for the public display of inter-
racial coupling between military men and women of color, he remarks on the
moral decline of white society through this "licentious intercourse" with
women of color:

> I would, however, clearly be understood as deprecating in the highest
> degree every attempt to introduce such connections between [free(d)
> women of color] and the white inhabitants; for here, I own, the West
> India prejudice is sufficiently implanted in my mind to render such a
> connection, not only repugnant to my feelings, but contrary to my
> ideas of morals, religion and polity.[44]

It was precisely Orderson's disapproval of inter-racial sexual and social relations that led, ironically, to his contention that free(d) people of color should
be awarded rights in Barbados society. He argued that if they were given social
and economic rights, thus removing the incentive for material rewards with
white men, women of color would return to seeking legitimate relationships
among their own. More important, Orderson's claims served to silence any
coercion on the part of the white men he accused of contributing to the society's moral decline. He essentially erased sexual coercion from the relations
between women of color and white men, eradicating even the possibility of
their violation. Orderson's investment in pro-slavery and "anti-black" discourses shaped his representations of women of color, whether in political
statements or fictional portrayals. Our own reproductions of Polgreen's historical experiences from his texts must be critically situated in such analyses.

The novel, *Creoleana* centers on the lives of two white characters, Jack
Goldacre and Caroline Fairfield. A young "mulatto" girl named Lucy is a
shadow character of Caroline, whose tragic death resulted from her "voluntary" sexual encounter with an Irishman. Lucy's story remains encapsulated
in an oft-reproduced trope of the virtuous white woman and the "tragic mu-
latta" (read as illicit inter-racial sex, immorality, and death). Although Polgreen is not a main character in the novel, Orderson includes a brief life-sketch
of her bondage, abuse, humiliation, redemption, and "triumph." ' "Miss Rachael' . . . [was] the daughter and slave of the notorious William Lauder, a
Scotch schoolmaster, and an African woman he owned."[45] Orderson described how Polgreen was frequently abused by her owner/father, a result of
her physical "charms that touched not the heart, but awakened the libidinous
desires."[46] The author imagined Lauder's many "unsuccessful attempts on her

chastity" and recounted his resort to public punishment by the town "jumper" for her disobedience.[47]

Interrogating the possibilities of Lauder's sexually violent relationship with his own "daughter" exposes the absence of previous scholarly attention to these incidents. Her incestuous experiences have remained encapsulated within a novel (and perhaps Rowlandson's lithograph), but consequently outside the historian's critical gaze. This narrative of incest shows Orderson's "libidinal investment" in Polgreen's "history," the depths of her subjection, and the erasure of her African mother. Orderson regards the act of incest upon one's family member as the point at which the brutal nature of slavery is illuminated:

> Lauder's conduct to his offspring, is a damning proof how debasing to the human mind is the power given us over our fellow creatures by holding them in bondage! The ties of consanguinity were all merged in the authority of the master, and he saw but the slave in his own daughter![48]

The legal parameters of slavery and the violence that protected its existence severed the ties of "family" for the enslaved.[49] Elucidating a complicated formulation, literary scholar Hortense Spillers touches upon the nature of female enslavement, sexual violation, and the disruption of the "family" in slavery. The act of incest relies on a recognizable and legal biological bond that the laws and logic of slavery make impossible.[50] The role and relationship of the "father" to the "daughter" in this instance, Lauder to Polgreen, are confused and denied. Essentially, incest performed or threatened in a system of slavery with "its imposed abeyance of order and degree" cannot really exist. Or, in Spillers's contention, this moment can speak for or illuminate the extant "losses" of family and "confusions" of the status of the enslaved person as both object and subject—person and property.[51] Polgreen was at once nonhuman, daughter, woman, chattel, and sexual object. Ultimately, it is only through the revelation of her abuses and the desecration of her body that Polgreen becomes a subject through a sentimental novel. Thus, the act of incest provokes recognition of Polgreen's humanity that is at the same instant destabilized by the laws of slavery.[52]

Immediately following Orderson's discussion of incest, his sensational account of Polgreen's whipping sexualizes her body, connecting it to her rescue by a white seaman:

She was already "tucked up," in the indecorous manner of those days, and the brutal hand of the mercenary whipper, armed with the fatal "cowskin," stretched forth to lay on the unpitying merciless lash, when a British tar! A gallant seaman rushed on the relentless executioner, seized the whip from his grasp, and rescuing his panting victim, carried her off in triumph amidst the cheers of a thronging multitude![53]

Orderson ends Polgreen's story with the visit of Britain's Prince William Henry to the island in 1789.[54] As Barbadians celebrated the prince's presence by illuminating the town with lights, he used Polgreen's Hotel as the base from which to make his rounds dining with various planters and merchants. During his visit, the prince led a regiment on a drunken rampage through Polgreen's hotel, destroying nearly all her property by "breaking the furniture, &c., . . . the very beds [were] cut up, and their contents emptied into the street, and the whole neighbourhood strewed with feathers."[55] As a final act, epitomizing the pinnacle of colonial power, "he bid [Polgreen] 'good night,' and to crown his sport, upset her and chair together, leaving her unwieldy body sprawling in the street, to the effable amusement of the laughing crowd."[56] Polgreen's supposed response, through Orderson's ventriloquism, leaves her in her place, "calling out in her sweetest dulcet tones, 'Mas Prince! Mas Prince; you come ma-morning, to see wha' mischief you been do!'"[57] In closing, Orderson describes Polgreen's industriousness as she took immediate account of the damage to her property and sent a bill to the prince on his departure from the island—"which was duly paid."[58] Not allowing the reader to remain long with her humiliation and abuse, Orderson's narrative forces Polgreen into an embodiment of triumph and guile. Through *Creoleana*, he produces a distorted, disfigured, and largely silenced Polgreen, creating an almost unchangeable snapshot of her (imagined) intimacies by fixing her into a bounded frame of identity. For historians this novelistic representation has forged the central understanding of her identity—its narrative power so pervasive as to inform most other historical representations of her life.[59]

The "completeness" of Polgreen's narrative in *Creoleana* has proven so seductive that several attempts have been made to historicize Polgreen's encounter with the prince. An editorial published in the *Barbadian* (1842) by Abel Clinkett, editor of that paper, acknowledged the publication of the novel, and provided circumstantial evidence to support its depiction of events.[60] Yet, he powerfully (re)fixes Polgreen's bodily image within the text of the newspaper and into the nineteenth century:

Many of the scenes [Orderson] has remarked we have a distant recollection of. We well remember the wild frolics and pranks of Prince William Henry . . . who probably little thought that one of the Barbadians would, at this distant period of 55 years, amuse the world with his mischievous tricks at old Rachael Lauder's alias Rachael Pringle. We perfectly recollect this immense mass of flesh (she was nearly as big as a sugar hogshead) walking with the Prince, actually leaning on the Royal Arm, and accompanied by other Naval Officers, and a host of mulatto women.[61]

Here, Clinckett reproduces Polgreen's troubled archive through an editorial. Polgreen is referred to as "an immense mass of flesh," and commodified in the language of "sugar hogshead." Her postmortem dehumanization translated into mythohistory and the despicable captivation she inspired in Barbadian lore implacably passes through time. Transparently despised in this moment of recollection, "actually leaning on the Royal Arm," Clinckett degrades the memory of Polgreen. He shifts our understanding away from Orderson's victim-to-trickster representation to a woman whose arrogance and audacity violated nineteenth-century mores.[62] Aghast at the possibility that a woman of color would take such liberties with Royalty, the editorial caricatures Polgreen and implicitly disempowers her in relation to the late king. Moreover, in this nineteenth-century moment, Polgreen's body is aged and reduced to mere flesh, "as big as a sugar hogshead," refiguring the terms of her commodified captivity—literally and symbolically. Reducing Polgreen to an object of commerce, Clinckett deconstructs Orderson's representation of Polgreen as embattled yet empowered.

Another documentary trace that unsettles Orderson's novel as mere fiction is revealed in an advertisement Polgreen had placed in the *Barbados Gazette* from 31 January to 4 February 1789:

Lost by subscriber, a small filigree waiter, scalloped round the edge, and bordered with a vignette, seven silver table spoons, seven teaspoons; marked S.B. in a cipher, also two dessert spoons marked R.P. in a cipher. Whoever had found the same, and will deliver them to her or the printer of this paper, shall receive FOUR MOIDORES reward, or, in proportion part. Silver-Smiths and others are requested to stop the above articles if offered for sale.

RACHAEL-PRINGLE POLGREEN[63]

This archival fragment coincides with Prince Henry's 1789 visit and according to Barbados historian Neville Connell, may represent the "contents emptied into the street," during the prince's violent sweep through the hotel.[64] On
closer scrutiny Polgreen's advertisement troubles a triumphal narrative of
compensation from the prince. Merely being compensated for damage did
not, it would seem, completely satisfy the hotelier's sentimental attachment
to certain items. Furthermore, her call to the public for assistance in recovering these items makes clear that the damage and theft lingered beyond the
alleged compensation.

Tracing the manner in which Polgreen enters the historical record, and
accounting for the power with which her story is reproduced, enables an understanding of the productive nature of history—and illuminates what is silenced in the process. While *Creoleana* remains the major source for scholarly
portraits of Polgreen, other archival sources—mostly fragments—exist, created in the midst of the trans-Atlantic abolition movement and while debates
over ending the slave trade raged in the chambers of the British parliament.
In an interview between a British Military Officer named Captain Cook and
members of the Privy Council taken in 1791 a harrowing image of Polgreen
appears. It reads:

> [Captain Cook, of the 89th Regiment of Foot, called in; and examined]
> *Were you ever in the West Indies?*
>
> Yes.
>
> *When, and in what islands?*
> In the years 1780 and 1781, in Barbados, St. Lucia, St. Christopher's &c.
>
> *Did the Negro Slaves in general appear to you to be treated with mild-
> ness or severity?*
>
> In the towns I thought with very great severity.
>
> *Do any particular instances occur to you of [slaves] being treated with
> severity?*
>
> Many; one was an instance of a female Slave belonging to a woman
> named Rachael La[u]der, who I saw beat in a most unmerciful man-
> ner; She beat her about the head with the heel of her shoe, till it was
> almost all of a jelly; she then threw her down with great force on a
> child's seat of a necessary, and there attempted to stamp her head
> through the hole; she would have murdered her had she not been

prevented by the interposition of two officers. [The girl's] crime was, not bringing money enough from aboard ship, where she was sent by her mistress for the purpose of prostitution.[65]

Although gathered during these debates in England in which abolitionist literature generated at the time often sensationalized violent acts on enslaved women's bodies, this account is crucial in illuminating the dynamics of intra-racial and intra-gendered power wielded by that small class of black, and in this case female, owners, and the violence against enslaved women in urban spaces.[66] The system of slavery in which Polgreen operated granted her the power to enact violence on the bodies of those she enslaved. Yet this incident described by a British naval officer reveals both Polgreen's power and its limits. It is not known whether she was indicted for beating this woman, but the toleration of "prostitution" in the town and her position as a slave owner supports the assumption that she retained a form of power over her slaves similar to that of white owners. From the details Captain Cook provides about a "child's seat of a necessary [toilet]" and the fact that two military "officers"—not the town's constable—intervened, it is likely that this violent scene occurred in Polgreen's hotel. The officers, like Captain Cook—all of whom were likely patrons of the brothel—were struck by the brutality Polgreen committed against this unnamed woman and eager to recount the story. The intensity of the beating also suggests a passion that went beyond financial concerns, because Polgreen seemed willing to murder a woman whose productive value she relied on. Generally, violence against one's own property was not punishable by law. Her power to mortally punish her slave originated in the Barbados Slave Act of 1661 "for governing negroes" which states, "that if any Negro under [punishment] by his Master or his order for [running] away or any other Crime or misdemeanour towards his said Master shall suffer in Life or in Member no person whatsoever shall bee accomptable to any Law therefore.[67] The law continues in the next few sentences seemingly to attend to slaves who were killed by the "wanton cruelty of their master," that the master would pay the colonial treasury "three thousand pounds of sugar," but this was revised in the 1688 Act reducing the fine to fifteen pounds. There is no evidence that any slave owner was punished in this way. Moreover, the law was left ambiguous and slave testimony was not permitted, leaving the owner with the benefit of the doubt.

But like other women of all races Pringle was also vulnerable to the law, as she could not vote or hold office. And as a woman of color she remained particularly disadvantaged from laws originating in 1721 and 1739 that prevented people of color from testifying in court.[68] Restrictions aimed at free(d) people of color curtailed their freedom and added to their political, economic, and social vulnerability into the nineteenth century.[69] Conversely, this incident also reveals the nature of Polgreen's agency, which depended on the subjugation of others. Through the enslaved women she owned, Polgreen amassed a small fortune. Her "production of pleasure" for the sailors and military men she entertained, as well as the sexual labor she demanded from her slaves, hint at the many layers of her agency. If we consider the brothel as a microcosm of racial and gendered social relations of eighteenth-century Barbados, we can analyze it as a site where varying degrees of power played out. Polgreen inhabited a liminal space within the larger Bridgetown society. Though free, she was a woman of color whose racial, gendered, and sexual markers confined her to a particular economic function. She could have never inhabited the role of "wife" as did white women of her time, and she sustained a vulnerability to whites' legal and social regulation and control of black bodies. Through her will, we understand she made connections with elite white males and their families and acquired the means to survive at a higher economic level than many of her free(d) peers. This too depended on her buying into a system of slavery from which she was not far removed. Within her brothel then, racial and gendered meaning (that is, hierarchies based on race and gender) sustained her liminal place within Bridgetown while further subjugating the women and men she owned. The women she owned were forced into an "economy of enjoyment" that they did not control. The performative nature of such an economy—"pleasurable" sexual service—must be carefully interrogated.

In a gesture toward an alternative understanding of Polgreen's constructed history, we might ask if this fragment draws us nearer to the otherwise invisible women she owned. What then, are the configurations of enslaved prostitutes' sexual labor—their particular enslavement tragically recounted by this military man? The woman beaten by Polgreen was required to find transportation (most likely by rowboat) to the unknown lawless space of whatever ship was in harbor, in order to secure a willing white patron who would pay for sexual acts.[70] Satisfying the patron meant putting oneself at the mercy of sailors or officers who had often been at sea for an extended period, who were likely drinking heavily while in port, and who probably considered enslaved prostitutes less than human. The enslaved woman on board would not necessarily be in a private space during the sexual acts and would be subjected to the taunts and jeers of other men on board. She might be passed around among different men or forced with only one, and in any of these encounters mortal violence was always possible, especially for someone who had no rights or recognition of humanity within the law. Enslaved women forced to prostitute were also vulnerable to venereal disease, which at the time could have debilitating effects.[71] Not satisfying the owner, by returning without the expected compensation, was also clearly dangerous. Moreover, due to her enslaved status, this beaten woman could never guarantee payment for her services, so that she might be both sexually abused by a "client" who refused payment and then beaten by her owner. The nature and labor of her slavery required daily and threatening access to her sexualized body.

Henri Lefebvre argues, "the city and the urban cannot be understood without institutions springing from relations of class and property."[72] Thus, the brothel cannot be imagined as a space where enslaved women were empowered by the mode of (sexual) production outside the constraints of the system of slavery. Imagining the space thus extricates both the site of the brothel and the women who labored therein from the social and racial hierarchies that made the brothel possible in the first place. These relations between enslaved sexual laborers and their patrons depended on hierarchical racial and gendered codes that placed enslaved women in subjugation and rendered them lascivious, sexually deviant, and whoreish.[73] Moreover "sexual intercourse, regardless of whether it is coerced or consensual, comes to describe the arrangements, however violent, between men and enslaved women."[74] Yet in much of the historical literature, sexual intercourse becomes the means by which enslaved women are ascribed power and/or agency.[75]

The trans-Atlantic context of prostitution illuminates the expectations of the men who employed enslaved and free(d) women in sexual services. By the late eighteenth century, prostitution was widespread in British port cities such as London and Liverpool.[76] The men sailing to the West Indies carried expectations of paid sexual services from experiences with prostitutes in British cities. Most of the women who worked as prostitutes in Liverpool and London, however, were white, lower-class free women. They, too, performed pleasure to the expectations of their patrons. But the nature of enslaved prostitution is strikingly different. Racial slavery kept them in a particularly subaltern position. Sexual acts reproduced not just an unequal relation of power, but one that reinscribed the larger framework of owner and owned. The men who purchased sex from Polgreen's enslaved women purchased the illusion of consent—an imaginary erotic of mutuality that was performed in spite of their enslavement and powerlessness. In essence, enslaved women forced to prostitute for the pleasure of white males (re)produced degrading and brutalizing forms of racialized inequality. For the enslaved black women forced to labor in this particular manner, their "personal desire or erotic interests" could not exist.[77] It forced enslaved women to serve the desires of the paying male without compensation and without a guaranteed avenue to "freedom." It is precisely the type of labor extracted from an enslaved female body that denies the possibility of pain or pleasure, rape and violence. Thus we cannot simply collapse this particular form of sexualized labor into contemporary definitions of "prostitution." Even as we search for "in-between" categories inhabiting space between rape and consent, we are in effect reinscribing the very terms that fundamentally fail to account for the sexual experiences of these enslaved women.

Silences in the archive of women of color in slave societies bury narratives of the most subaltern. Overshadowed by Polgreen's metanarrative of material success, nearly all the women she owned disappear as quickly as they are mentioned in her will. However, evidence from late eighteenth-century deeds enable a fuller revision of Polgreen's narrative by shifting the focus to a woman she owned. As stated previously, in her will Polgreen requested that four women be freed on her death. Joanna (who was given her own son still enslaved, and also a woman named Amber) appears in succession several times in the register of deeds for this period. There are many aspects of Joanna's and Amber's lives we will never know. Indeed, Amber disappears completely from the historical record. These fleeting glimpses from a historical aperture that closes too fast make it nearly impossible to string together events into a neat narrative. Nevertheless, the information in these documents and the time frame of their production allude to Joanna Polgreen's destitute circumstances in "freedom," her complicated labor negotiation and relationship with her former owner, the role of the military in the support and perpetuation of brothel culture, and the vulnerability of free(d) people of color to white legal and economic power.

On 20 July 1793, two years after Rachael Pringle Polgreen's death, Captain Henry Carter (Mariner) and William Willoughby (Gentleman) gave a deposition affirming that in 1779 or 1780,

they knew a certain Negro or Mulatto Slave named Joanna who had been the property of Rachael Pringle Polgreen & by her Sold or conveyed to one Joseph Haycock who was a Servant to General Ackland or Soldier in the Regiment . . . And that the Said Joseph Haycock did manumit and set free by Deed of Manumission the Said Joanna now known by the name of Joanna Polgreen.[78]

The purpose of this deposition by Carter and Willoughby was to act as witnesses to Joanna's freedom as "they have heard & been told by the Said Joanna Polgreen that it is alleged that her manumission was lost in the Hurrycane" of October 1780, and so "at her particular request the Deponents came forward to prove and maintain the freedom of the Said Joanna Polgreen."[79]

At first glance this deposition appears to support the narrative of enslaved women and their "room to maneuver" toward freedom in an urban slave society.[80] Consistent with the literature on the military and the informal sexual economy in Barbados, Haycock likely met Joanna in Polgreen's brothel and arranged for her purchase.[81] Joanna's agency here might easily be linked with her ability to achieve freedom through her sexual interactions with white men. However, another deed recorded earlier complicates what "freedom" actually meant for many black women and reveals the cost of their survival in this society. On 3 December 1783, three years after her freedom was "secured," Joanna set her mark of X to a deed asking Rachael Pringle Polgreen to legally and formally honor a contract of indenture while supplying Joanna with food, drink, and clothing:

I the underwritten do by these Presents Bind myself in the Capacity of an apprentice for and during the term of Twelve years from the date hereof unto Mrs. Rachael Pringle Polgreen . . . to be in her Service and Direction. . . . And the Said Rachael Pringle Polgreen do by these presents for the respect She bears [Joanna] do hereby agree for her better maintenance to find her Victual, and Drink & [a] couple Suits of Decent apparel for her.[82]

Based on this evidence, we must assume that if Haycock did in fact free Joanna he apparently did not provide for her maintenance, and the newly emancipated woman must not have been able to survive on her own. The dates of these documents and the time frame of their production allude to Joanna's destitute circumstances in "freedom," forcing her to commit to an unusually long indenture again to Polgreen. We can speculate that Joanna's use of this legal avenue stemmed from a mistrust of Polgreen's verbal promises. The language, "for the respect she bears for her," appealed to Polgreen's conscience to honor Joanna's request for material support. That it was necessary to ask for clothing and food forces us to consider whether Polgreen adequately provided for her slaves. It is curious, too, that Joanna took Polgreen's last name, perhaps to establish her status as a free black woman. However, Joanna Polgreen's short-lived "freedom" (1779/1780–1783) and her "voluntary" indenture challenges narratives of the success and privileges afforded to free(d) women of color in the urban context.

In his short biography of Rachel Pringle Polgreen, historian Jerome Handler describes Joanna's relationship to Rachel in the following terms: "two other slaves [Richard and Amber] were bequeathed to a slave woman [Joanna] who won her freedom under the terms of Rachael's will."[83] But these additional sources show that Joanna's freedom was not so easily "won" or retained. What then, did "freedom" mean in such a society? Joanna sought to indenture herself in 1783 for a period of twelve years. Polgreen died before the end of Joanna's contract and in her will freed "my Negro Woman Joanna" with vague language regarding the nature of her "apprentice's" status. Her will stipulates, "I do hereby manumit and set free my negro Woman named [Joannah] from all Servitude whatsoever, and for compleating that purpose I do hereby desire my Executors herein after named to pay all such Sums of money and Execute such deeds as are necessary about the same."[84] The ambiguity in this language resides in the requirement that manumitting a slave from slavery required fifty pounds be paid to the churchwarden of the parish vestry, some of which would be used for the annual maintenance of the freed person. While Joanna may have been entitled to some sort of "freedom dues" by finishing her contract of indenture, it is unclear what they would consist of or whether she ever received any, aside from Amber, the enslaved woman Polgreen bequeathed to Joanna.[85] As Joanna's liminal status was negotiated, she also became a slave owner herself within this tangled logic of slavery. Amber's life of slavery presumably continued. Just as troubling, Joanna sought to substantiate her freedom based on circumstances outside Polgreen's will— her manumission by Joseph Haycock circa 1780. Had she secured freedom through Polgreen's will, there would have been no need for Joanna to elicit the testimony of two white men in an effort to prove her free status—a status always under suspicion and under the threat of being stolen. If the executors of Rachael Pringle Polgreen's will had in fact performed her bequests, then Joanna would have been freed (again) in 1791, thereby terminating the labor contract she had negotiated in 1783.

A final document further complicates Joanna's story. In a deed dated 1800, Joanna frees her "mulatto" son Richard Braithwaite.[86] This important record documents Joanna's relationship to her son and the years she likely labored in order to free him. We do not know Richard's age at this manumission, but Joanna became his legal owner through Polgreen's 1791 bequest. There are many ways to speculate on the circumstances of Richard's status, but none provide a certain answer. It is possible that Joanna's self-indenture to Polgreen in 1783 was also to remain near her son, who was still enslaved at that time, or her son may have been born during Joanna's indenture contract between 1783 and 1791. From Polgreen's 1791 bequest Joanna was given her son still enslaved and another enslaved woman named Amber. Although less likely, Joanna could have sold Amber to pay for her son's manumission or hired her out to raise money for this transaction.

Given Joanna's complicated labor negotiation and relationship with her former owner, the role of the military in perpetuating the enslaved brothel culture, and the vulnerability of free(d) people of color to white legal and economic power, it is important to reexamine what it means to valorize Polgreen's "successes." This is true in the face of the violence she endured in slavery and certainly in the the violence she perpetuated. Planters, merchants, white elites, and the British colonial government created a system of economic development that set the terms of success in Barbados: slave ownership and material accumulation based on white supremacy and the bodily exploitation of people of African descent. This system also depended on a systematic sexual exploitation of enslaved women. The military complex, sustained by the Royal Navy, whose presence in the eighteenth-century West Indies protected British economic and political interests, was serviced by the informal sexual economy of enslaved prostitution.

Central to debates on "enslaved agency" and resistance in contemporary scholarship are the gendered and sexualized examples of enslaved women and women of color wielding their sexual relations with white men to gain opportunities or advantages.[87] Even dominant feminist concepts of agency as resistance might be revised if we focus specifically on Rachael Pringle Polgreen. Polgreen's status rested on the axis of different types of power. First, the archive that produced her material life was created and sustained by white colonial power. This power is replicated in subsequent narratives of her lived "experiences" in the secondary literature. In addition, the power attributed to Polgreen as slave holder and brothel keeper must be understood within the context of the processes (techniques, mechanisms, and strategies) that enable a formerly enslaved woman to own other women of similar racialization and to coerce them into a sexual economy from which the benefits were not necessarily freedom and economic independence.[88] We cannot, of course, separate Polgreen from the system of racial and gendered domination in which she lived. Instead, we need to examine the particularities of that system, which rendered her choices and the limits of her actions therein. A look back at the system of slavery operating in eighteenth-century Bridgetown reveals the racial and gendered hierarchies in place (where white male supremacy dominated and black women were at the bottom), and the implicit (white) societal desire for white men, both resident and transient, to enjoy sexual freedoms with women who could not refuse them. Understanding the system in which the economic and social possibilities for Polgreen were created means also a reexamination of the concept of agency as attached to notions of subversion or resistance. Saba Mahmood's scholarship usefully deconstructs the concept of agency in order to articulate the actions of her own scholarly subjects who "behave in ways that confound our expectations."[89] Drawing on Michel Foucault and Judith Butler, Mahmood argues, "power is to be understood as a strategic relation of force that permeates life and is productive of new forms of desires, objects, relations and discourses," and that power and agency "are not the residue of an undominated self that existed prior to the operations of power but are themselves the products of these operations."[90] Therefore, in the context of eighteenth-century Barbados, "the abilities that defined Polgreen's economic and social power—her modes of agency," were produced by the system of slavery in place and were not harnessed by her in an effort to subvert that system.[91] Free(d) and enslaved women tapped into the power of others to gain material privileges. This possibility existed because it was created and sustained by the system of slavery in place. Rather than being "radically liberatory," these situations allowed enslaved and free(d) women of color a mode of survival that kept structures of inequality and denigration in place. Certainly, Rachael Pringle Polgreen was an iconic figure whose life story, most explicitly her material success as a businesswoman, has captivated historians' attention into the twenty-first century. Yet understanding how she came by her "success" is just as important as the unusual position she occupied in eighteenth-century Bridgetown—a quintessential slave society ruled by the commodification of black bodies. If the nature of her success depended on slave-owning and the forced sexual labor she demanded from the women bound to her, then those enslaved women's stories are also vital to understanding the nuances of gender and power in slave societies. Knowing more about Rachel Pringle Polgreen's relationships with women whose labor she owned changes the way we imagine her and also questions narratives of black women's "success" in slave societies. But even more, unraveling Polgreen's seemingly unyielding story forces us to also reconsider how we produce histories of enslaved and free(d) women of color in the Atlantic world using archives that significantly limit our efforts to access their lives. Their core experiences, shaped by sexual violence and impossible choices, are not fully elucidated by progressive notions of agency. Without discounting the imperative in historical scholarship since the 1960s to recover enslaved agency—especially against attempts to render the enslaved passive and utterly dominated—scholars nonetheless need to consider what other facets of enslaved lives we can discover beyond heroic tales of resistance and survival. Agency cannot be examined outside the constraints of slavery's systematic mechanisms of domination. Joanna's desperate circumstances, read in tandem with Polgreen's success, make it difficult to write of this iconic free(d) woman separately from her troubling power. Despite the effort to recover enslaved women from Polgreen's probate documents, those most disposable in their exchangeability and commodification—the thirty-seven other men, women, and children owned by Polgreen at her death—remain confined by the violence of slavery's archive.

Rachael Pringle Polgreen and Joanna Polgreen's stories cannot be separated from those of the thousands of other enslaved women laboring in towns who were also subject to specific types of sexual exploitation and were publicly exposed in multiple ways. Their narratives also provide another way to understand the structure of white households as shaped by the material and sexual economy of slavery and the urban brothel, as we shall see in the next chapter. Whether white domestic spaces were controlled by white female slave owners or patriarchs, the relations of slavery—of sexual identities and the commodification of enslaved female bodies—determined the character of intimacy, subjection, and sexuality for the slaveholding class as well. Viewing white households through the prism of Rachael Pringle and Joanna Polgreen and the urban brothel, reframes our ideas of white female identities and (sexualized) power and demonstrates how white women were intricately and intimately enmeshed within the sexual relations of slavery.

CHAPTER 3

Agatha: White Women, Slave Owners, and the Dialectic of Racialized "Gender"

To Sum up the character of Jamaican ladies, I shall conclude
with this remark; that, considering the very great defects in
their education, and other local disadvantages, their virtues
and merits seem justly entitled to our highest encomium;
and their frailties and failings to our mildest censure.
                    —Edward Long, *The History of Jamaica*

[The] said Dudley Crofts came up to her said Father's house
[her father being off the island] . . . and after dinner he the
said Dudley Crofts claimed the promise which the said
Deponent had before made to him and which promise this
Deponent then very unhappily complyd with by suffering
the sd Dudley Crofts then to commit adultery with this
Depont. And which he afterward from time to time
repeated with this depnt as they had convenient
opportunities.
                    —Agatha Moore, Deposition, 1743

The reason which induced [me] to demand such a
recognizance was because [of] a complaint made to [me] by
the sd Daniel Moore against a Negro of [Crofts]. The negro
[sic] had taken his Masters Sword which [Crofts]
acknowledged to [me] he had directed him to take and went
the proceeding night therewith disguised in womens Cloaths
to the house of Thomas Withers Esqr where Mr Moore lived

and where the Criminal Correspondence between [Crofts] &
the wife of the sd Mr Moore was carried on.
—Hon. Thomas Harrison, Deposition, 1743

On a night "between October 2 and 4, 1742," an enslaved boy left his owner's
house alone, dressed as a woman and armed with a hidden sword.[1] He headed
toward High Street to the unhappy house of Daniel Moore and his wife Agatha.[2] Agatha Moore was engaged in an adulterous affair with Dudley Crofts,
the enslaved boy's master. Perhaps Dudley Crofts ordered the boy to go to the
Moore residence to kill Daniel Moore, the cuckolded husband. Daniel's wife,
Agatha may have urged Crofts to get rid of her husband so she and Crofts
could marry. It is unknown what time the boy arrived at the Moore residence
or whom he met when he reached the tree in the garden. It could have been a
nurse residing with the Moore family or another male slave named Toney.[3]

We will never know the exact circumstances of his discovery, but the danger of being caught armed with a lethal weapon must have been terrifying.
Attempts to harm a white person, instigate or participate in a revolt, or otherwise enact one's will often led to a death sentence. Execution was usually
painful and slow.[4] Soon after the boy's arrival to the Moore household, he was
caught by someone and arrested. He may have spent at least a few days in the
Cage awaiting trial by three freeholders and two justices of the peace, all
white men. Always crowded, the Cage was dank in the tropical October of
Barbados, but he would at least have been in the company of other slaves
awaiting similar fates. If the Cage once held riotous sailors, it was now reserved exclusively for the enslaved.[5] Perhaps these slaves consoled each other
inside the cell; maybe they fought for space. Few conversations among the
enslaved reached the archive in seventeenth- and eighteenth-century Barbados, much less the intimate exchanges of those confined in the Cage. No records of the boy's trial exist. Although he would be asked to answer for his
presence at a household to which he was not bound, his words and name
were not recorded in the archive. In the Bridgetown "slave court" he would
be surrounded by white men, some of whom spoke on his behalf, and others
against him. The legal system in Barbados did not allow any slave to testify or
defend him/herself in a court of law.[6] He was not allowed to testify or offer a
defense. Yet the court acquitted him of all charges.[7]

Crofts Versus Harrison

The apprehension of the armed boy disguised as a woman brought the domestic woes of Agatha and Daniel Moore into public notice and subsequently to the Governor's Council, the highest court of appeals in this British colony. Agatha Moore's illicit liaison with Dudley Crofts had begun at least as early as July 1740. They were discovered in May 1741 when Daniel Moore, who had been sleeping upstairs in his own home, caught Crofts and his wife together downstairs.[8] To aggravate matters, in the midst of the affair, on 3 May 1742, Agatha Moore gave birth to a daughter whose father was possibly not her husband.[9] What ensued from these circumstances was a multifaceted legal web of petitions, criminal trials, and countersuits as the Governor's Council tried to sort out what, if any, crimes had been committed by the parties involved, and who would ultimately pay recompense for any damages incurred.

The Honorable Thomas Harrison, a justice of the peace for the precinct of Bridgetown, sat at the heart of this legal chaos. He presided over the investigation against Dudley Crofts for the "crime" of adultery and the separate case against the slave boy for purportedly conspiring to murder. And it was Harrison who was eventually held (ir)responsible for his handling of the proceedings.[10] Gathering several witnesses to testify against Crofts for both alleged crimes, Harrison presumed Crofts' guilt and imposed on him over ten thousand pounds in security bonds. In retaliation, Crofts petitioned the Governor's Council for redress from financial and character damage. On 4 October 1743, the Governor and Council held a ten-hour session to review all depositions, petitions, and complaints related to Crofts' plea of redress and Harrison's statement defending his own actions.[11] Among the pieces of evidence gathered and read during the council meeting was a full deposition by Agatha Moore discussing her role in the affair. In addition, several other witnesses commented on whether Dudley Crofts purposely sent his armed and disguised enslaved boy to his rival's house or whether a member of the Moore household summoned the boy.

This chapter closely analyzes the legal deposition of a white adulteress and scrutinizes the movements of an enslaved boy in gendered disguise. Examining the domestic space of a white household, and the events of the Crofts versus Harrison case itself, allows us to historicize and theorize white female power and sexuality in this time and place. The gender and sexual economy governing the brothel analyzed in the previous chapter also shaped dynamics within and legal judgements about this white household. Examining Agatha Moore through the optics of the brothel and enslaved women's experiences as sexualized laborers elucidates how the material and sexual economy of slavery shaped white domesticity. Both the testimonial depictions of the enslaved boy's movements and Agatha Moore's language describing her illicit sexual behavior reveal how discourse, prevailing racial and gendered ideologies about black women, and (ab)uses of power produced the violent sexual realties enslaved women and men experienced in colonial Caribbean slave societies. Put differently, I show how Agatha Moore's story cannot be separated from Rachael and Joanna Polgreen in Chapter 2: each powerfully informed and shaped the other.

Demography, Domesticity, and Sexual Dialectics

In eighteenth-century Bridgetown, like many other Caribbean port towns dependent on domestic work, enslaved women were in the demographic majority.[12] Although population statistics are rare for this period, Jerome Handler estimates that in 1786 there were approximately 62,115 slaves, 16,167 whites, and 838 free(d) people of color living in the colony.[13] No census data exist after 1715 that would provide population numbers; but Pedro Welch has detailed percentage estimates of Bridgetown's enslaved population relative to whites and free(d) people of color before the nineteenth century.[14] According to Welch, during the eighteenth century the enslaved population of Bridgetown remained relatively stable at about 16.5 percent. The free(d) population of color gradually rose from just over 20 percent in the 1740s to near 40 percent in 1812.[15] In addition, the gender demographics of Barbados' white population were unique for a Caribbean colony. Unlike Jamaica and the Leeward Islands, Barbados sustained a slight majority of women within the white population by the early eighteenth century.[16] In comparison to Jamaica, where white women never exceeded more than 40 percent of the white population into the late eighteenth century, by 1715, "white women outnumbered white men in Barbados by one percent, and by seven percent in 1748, leveling off at about fifty-two percent female for the remainder of the slavery period."[17]

In Bridgetown, these black and white female majorities influenced the sexual-cultural character of urban slave society. For example, Hillary Beckles's scholarship challenges Caribbean historiography that focuses on the planter "patriarch" by showing that "58 per cent of slave owners in [Bridge-town] were female, mostly white . . . [and] women owned 54 per cent of the slaves in town."[18] Furthermore, he points out that "white women also owned more female slaves than male slaves."[19] The relatively smaller population of white women in Jamaica and the Leewards shaped their economic, social, and sexual opportunities in a distinctly different way than for white women in Barbados.[20] The demographic majorities of black and white females in Barbados makes consideration of relationships *between* women crucial to understanding the nature of slavery, the cultural constructions of sexuality, and the economic and sexual power of white women in this town. These issues together shaped both perceptions and the daily lives of urban enslaved women.[21]

Over the last few decades, scholars of slavery and the Atlantic world have turned their attention to the role of white women of various classes in plantation economies from the early modern era through the antebellum period of the United States.[22] This focus has most recently included white women in the colonial British Caribbean.[23] Revising an older historiography that positioned white women as victims of patriarchal colonial societies under slavery, new scholarship interrogates white women's power in and support of the Atlantic slave economy. These studies range from the Caribbean to England, North America and intercolonial networks, and from the colonial era through the antebellum United States.[24] Given Bridgetown's demographics, a close analysis of the records white women left behind conveys how integral and intertwined they were in the relations and production of slavery as well as what benefits they reaped from racial and gender privilege. Cecily Jones delineates throughout her work "that slaveownership directly and indirectly provided white women with wealth, social status, and a measure of power."[25] Pervasive race privilege also afforded poor white women elevated social status above women of African descent.[26]

The following discussion also builds on a foundation of feminist scholarship on gender and slavery. Scholars have illustrated how integral enslaved women were to the reproduction of enslaved labor.[27] They have also shown how early modern Europeans used their ideas about African women to objectify and abuse their bodies through hard labor and sexual exploitation.[28] As recent work on colonial Barbados explains, analyzing the raced and gendered constructions of white women indicates how they, too, were implicated in and influenced by the production of slavery.[29] For example, probate records of white women in the seventeenth and early eighteenth centuries demarcate how white women and their female relatives reproduced wealth by bequeathing slaves to daughters, nieces, and female friends.[30] From their economic participation in slavery—their ability to own, exchange, and bequeath enslaved people—and despite the social and legal limitations, white women gained power: economic, social, racial, and sexual.

Agatha Moore's case offers an opportunity to expand analyses of both gendered and "genderless" female bodies by illuminating the relationship between white women and enslaved women's gendered positions. As white women accumulated racialized and gendered power through slavery, enslaved women were relegated to "genderless" objects by the hegemony of "ethnicity." This hegemony became the primary means through which black bodies were captured for slave ships and the mode by which they were exchanged.[31] If we follow Hortense Spillers's conceptualization, in this historical moment gender was a privilege of the dominant (white) class and produced in the domestic sphere of family, motherhood, and patriarchal and patronymic structures. Spillers argues that the theft of African bodies "severed the captive body from its motive will, its active desire," losing gendered distinctions through the project of commerce in human flesh.[32] Moreover, in the system of racial slavery and the dehumanization that accompanied this condition "the [black] female body and the [black] male body become a territory of cultural and political maneuver, not at all gender-related, gender-specific."[33] In this way, she argues, enslaved women became genderless. Notwithstanding the ways in which African captives made meaning of their varied and complex ethnic identities,[34] the imposition of "externally imposed meanings and uses" during the process of capture and commodification turned captives into sexual repositories, objects of commerce, and relentless, destructive desire.[35]

Slavery permitted the redefinition of enslaved women by dominant groups; the power of white supremacy depended on the dialectical contours between whites and the enslaved. Through objectification, "the captive body translates into a potential for pornotroping and embodies sheer physical powerlessness . . . resonating through various centers of human and social meaning."[36] This "pornotroping" and "sheer powerlessness" of enslaved women and men—that is, the fungible, hypersexualized, and infinitely breachable black body—can be read in dialectic relation to white women as wives, slaveholders, sexualized, and racialized beings. These conditions become particularly visible through the enslaved boy disguised as a black woman. His performance as a black female, I will show, enabled white men and women to act out their transgressive desires and disrupt the codes that constructed the gendered dichotomy between white women and black women without accompanying racial denigration. Ultimately, white women served an important function in Bridgetown and gained racial and gendered privilege through exclusion of enslaved women from the "benefits of *patriarchilized* female gender."[37] This term refers to gender constructed under dominant (white) patriarchy, in which the female should be a submissive, protected, nurturing, and virtuous mother. The highly sexualized social context of this slave society in which enslaved women were rented out for sex, violated by their male and female owners, and sold as real estate, enabled a woman like Agatha Moore to capitalize on the benefits of patriarchilized gender in significant ways.

White women in slave societies caught disrupting normative gender, racial, and sexual expectations could also deploy rhetorical strategies to challenge the ideologies of ruin and shame attached to their actions, and thereby assert their racialized gendered power.[38] More significantly, analyzing the sexual behaviors of a white female adulteress through the lives of enslaved women exposes the complexity of white female domesticity and sexuality. Patriarchy may have tethered white women to an ideology of virtue and submission, but the reality of Agatha Moore's behavior demonstrates that the white household was not itself exempt from licentiousness and sexual desire outside of traditional white marriage arrangements. Certainly, white men forced their extramarital sexual desire on enslaved women without social stigma. Existing gender ideologies regulated white women's sociosexual behavior in relation to white men, black men, and black women. The legal structure also delimited that white women could reproduce freedom. *Partus sequitur ventrum*, a law that made children's status heritable through the "mother," simultaneously cast white, enslaved, and free(d) women of color in different but related roles as producers: white women made free humans and enslaved women birthed other slaves.[39] This law, of course, benefited the slave-owning class in myriad ways, as enslaved women were the only ones in society who could reproduce slave status. For white women, however, this meant that scrutiny of their sexual comportment sought to prevent the birth of free black or illegitimate children who could not be heirs. To be sure, the rigid gender and sexual expectations governing white women constrained their lives. But this did not destroy their sexual agency.[40] The agency available to white women in the social shaming following nonconjugal sex rested in their ability to make certain claims about their inviolability despite "consenting" to transgressive sexual acts. They achieved this by claiming to consent to sexually illicit acts "unhappily" or "against better judgment" in order to maintain their reputation of virtue. Sexual inviolability and consent represent agential acts and subjective statuses to which black women in the same society had no access.

Discourses of sexual behavior, whether the "virtuous comportment" of white women or the "lasciviousness" of black women, dictated the nature of sexual performance publicly and privately. As Natalie Zacek argues, "in order for a white woman to be put on such a pedestal, black and mixed-race women, both enslaved and free(d), had to assume the blame for all varieties of sexual immorality, to be denigrated universally as libidinous creatures whose innate depravity enticed white men into vice and degeneracy.[41] I build on the existing scholarship concerning white women in the British Caribbean and colonial North America in analyzing the case of *Crofts v. Harrison*. This case shows how white women deployed diffuse forms of power—not just physical modes—to negate enslaved women's sexualities and leave them vulnerable to sexual violence. We know that repeated acts of violence and terror maintained racial and gendered subjugation of enslaved men and women.[42] Gender and racial hierarchies in slave societies required constant (re)articulation because slave resistance rendered them unstable.[43] These reiterations of power (that is, the ways white patriarchal power reasserted itself in the face of challenge or instability) took place during the commodification process on slave ships, at the auction block, through the force of the whip and law, and, most important here, in the realm of sexuality, sexual behavior, and sexual violence.[44] One way to pinpoint these instabilities and demarcate the reiteration of patriarchal and white supremacist power in slave societies is to track the moments of identity crisis. As the court case *Crofts v. Harrison* indicates, seemingly "stable" gender and racial identities could and did falter. Agatha Moore's deposition and the boy's female apparel and mobility permit us to map the ways white female (sexual) identity might be reaffirmed, especially in a situation that could bring them social shame. Furthermore, the power to "reaffirm" white female identity both shapes white female sexual agency and illuminates the negation of enslaved women's sexual power.

Enslaved women are explicitly and notably absent from the incidents and the surviving documents surrounding this case. Nonetheless, this chapter shows how their experiences can—and need—to be distilled from the archive representing the affairs and entanglements of white Barbadians Agatha and Daniel Moore, Dudley Crofts, Judge Thomas Harrison, and an unnamed enslaved boy. Scholars often "read against the grain" of archival documents to fill out the silences inherent to the archives of slavery.[45] Here the scholar attempts to subvert archival power to narrate the experiences or recover the voices of enslaved people depicted in commodified terms. Rather than reading against the grain, mining this court case for traces of enslaved women when they are not explicitly represented requires reading *along the bias grain*.[46] Like cutting fabric on the bias to create more elasticity, reading along the bias grain expands the legibility of these archival documents to accentuate the figures of enslaved women present in the society who are a spectral influence on the lives of white and black men and women. Approaching the archive in this way allows an expansive interpretation of the records while retaining the historical integrity of the documents. This expanded interpretive space articulates how the sizeable presence of enslaved women and the property relations intrinsic to slavery in Bridgetown influenced the actions of the white men and women, and the enslaved boy implicated in these events, even as enslaved women are not the subjects of this archive. Similar to fugitive Jane's journey in Chapter 1, imagining the boy dressed in women's clothes, walking alone at night, illuminates the significant sociodemographic presence of enslaved women in Bridgetown and the expectations of and assumptions about their bodies, public sexualities, and vulnerabilities as they moved around town. Returning to the disguised enslaved boy at the end of the chapter will further elaborate the subjection of enslaved women, the complexities of white domestic spaces, and the crisis of "gender" in this historical moment and context.[47]

"The Mistress/Slave Dialectic"

In G. W. F. Hegel's famous "Master/Slave dialectic" in the *Phenomenology of Spirit* (1807), he argues that the master and slave were constituted as subjects relationally.[48] Orlando Patterson extends Hegel's theory to the operations of slave societies, ancient and modern. He argues that a master gains his power and honor from "the subjection of his slave."[49] The concept of honor, he contends, was central to the master/slave dialectic.[50] It was the slave's dishonor that "came in the primal act of submission. This was the most immediate human expression of the inability to defend oneself or to secure one's livelihood."[51] In contrast and in relation to a slave's dishonor, "what the captive or condemned person lost was the master's gain . . . the honor of the master was enhanced by the subjection of his slave."[52] Patterson explains, "the key [to enslavement] is the total absence of any hint of 'manhood,' which in turn is a perfect description of the dishonored condition."[53] In a clearly masculinist reading of the relationship between masters and slaves, Patterson resolutely denies the existence of the female "master" or slave owner, her power in Caribbean slave society, the avenues by which she acquired and reproduced socioeconomic freedom, and what sociosexual identity she drew from selling enslaved women's sexuality. His analysis also masks the privileges white women enjoyed by not being sexually commodified in the same manner as enslaved women.[54]

What then, constituted honor for slave mistresses? Patterson offers that "[more] often than not, the mistress of the stone hovel that passed for a great house in the Caribbean was herself a slave. Since there was no one to confirm honor, it was simply thrown to the winds."[55] More recent scholarship refutes Patterson's easy dismissal of slave mistresses as powerless "slaves."[56] In fact, honor was an important aspect of freedom for white and slave-owning women. As one scholar argues, white women, "profited from slave labor and like their male counterparts sponsored an ideology which was designed to buttress the class structure."[57] To elaborate on this configuration, the notion of honor, linked to white women's sexuality, was connected to both perceptions and expectations of their virtue and their ability to commodify another's sexuality and reproduce freedom.[58] Patterson ignores how enslaved women were dishonored and disempowered through violence, commodification, and sexual coercion, as well as their necessity to reproduce slavery. These identities—racial, gendered, social, and sexual—of white and enslaved women were mutually constitutive. More than the economic power free(d) women of color gained from slave ownership, white women accumulated sexual and racial power through the exchange of enslaved women's bodies and passed this power onto their relatives.[59] Power to engage in the circulation of enslaved bodies and the ability to secure capital and manipulate legal structures to secure their family's future enabled white women to contribute to and benefit from a gendered white supremacy in Caribbean slave societies.[60] Elite white women also gained power through laws protecting them from nonmarital rape.[61] Of course, free(d) women of color also acquired power through the commodification of enslaved women's sexuality and reproduction, but the benefits they accrued from participating in the marketing of slaves remained distinct from those of white women.[62] Many free women of color were previously enslaved or had enslaved relatives in close proximity, thereby risking the degradation of their social status.[63] The eighteenth-century ideologies of sexually available and promiscuous women of color, free or enslaved, meant that they were susceptible to racial and gendered denigration based on their constructed sexualities. As noted in the previous chapter, free(d) women of color purveyed enslaved women in brothels, an occupation deemed shameful to most white women in Barbados.[64] Edward Long, who held particularly racist and animalistic views of women of color, comments that, "they are lascivious."[65] Consequently, he assumed that this led to the degeneration of their reproductive capacities. He claimed,

> Some examples may possibly have occurred, where, upon the intermarriage of two Mulattos, the woman has bourne children; which children have grown to maturity: but I have never heard of any such an instance; and may we not suspect the lady, in those cases, to have privately intrigued with another man, a White perhaps?[66]

The privileged position white women acquired through the exchange of enslaved women's bodies resulted in a "reputation" of their own virtue compared to those of mulatto and black women.[67] As one scholar argues, "in the West Indies . . . all white women, regardless of class origins, were elevated to a superior 'respectable' status."[68] White women's honored reputation rested on the subjugation of enslaved women as sexual objects and this reputation was constituent to their ability to commodify slaves and be themselves perceived as in need of protection. Closer scrutiny of Agatha Moore's deposition in the *Crofts v. Harrison* case enables an elaboration of the parameters of sexual culture in eighteenth-century Barbados, thereby elucidating the limits and domination of black female sexuality at the same time.

Agatha Moore: Deposed

On 11 October 1742, Judge Harrison took a long statement from Agatha Moore regarding her role in the sexual liaison with Dudley Crofts. Neither Agatha Moore's husband Daniel nor Crofts seemed to object to this action; Crofts was invited to cross examine her but did not show up.[69] In her deposition, related by Harrison in the third person, Agatha explains how Crofts began his seduction of her:

[Deponent] positively says that she never gave the said Dudley Crofts any hints or signs to encourage him to endeavor to seduce her . . . the said Dudley Crofts very much importun'd her to commit adultery with him which she then refused declaring she could not consent to his desires as it would be cruelly injuring to her Husband and she could not answer it on any account but he then very much pressing that the next time they had a convenient opportunity she would give him her promise she was prevailed on by him to promise she would.[70]

Her deposition continues to recount the several sexual encounters she had with Crofts:

In the said month of July in the said Year one thousand seven hundred and forty [when] her Husband the said Daniel Moore being gone to Scotland [district][71] the said Dudley Crofts came up to her said Father's house [her father being off the island] . . . and after dinner he the said Dudley Crofts claimed the promise which the said Deponent had before made to him and which promise this Deponent then very unhappily complyd with by suffering the sd Dudley Crofts then to commit adultery with this Depont. And which he afterwards from time to time repeated with this depnt as they had convenient opportunities.[72]

Crofts and Agatha Moore were eventually caught together by her husband in May 1741, and subsequently Agatha was discovered writing a letter to her lover. She admitted through carefully crafted language that although she left the island after discovery by her husband, when she returned she continued to correspond with Crofts by letter. She then admitted that "having acquainted him of her Husband [soon] being gone, the said Dudley Crofts came up to this . . . house & then & there committed adultery with her, which he has never done since."[73] She ends her remarkable statement saying that she wrote to Crofts asking him to cease writing to her, "for that if her said Husband died, she would perform the Promise or Oath she had made to him, that she would marry the said Dudley Crofts."[74] In the midst of the affair Agatha Moore gave birth to a daughter whose paternity is uncertain given the circumstances of her sexual liaison with Crofts.[75]

Governor Thomas Robinson, who made the final decision in such cases, deemed Agatha's deposition unusual, declaring, "it does not appear that any good or Lawful use could be made of so extraordinary [a] Deposition [by Agatha Moore] which his [Excellency] said he [believed] was without Example."[76] Agatha Moore was certainly a victim of patriarchy in this case. Her testimony relegated to supportive evidence, Agatha Moore remained peripheral to the case's main concerns. The juridical decision hinged on which white man involved suffered the most dishonor. All the white men in the proceedings, as plaintiffs or defendants, more or less reclaimed their lives and redeemed their reputations.[77] The Council censored Judge Harrison for unfairly punishing Crofts for actions that were not against the law, and forced Harrison to resign all public positions except his elected seat of vestryman of St. Michael's Parish. Crofts paid a two hundred pound fine for immoral behavior, but the Council vindicated him of any alleged criminal conduct and Daniel Moore resumed his business as a merchant.[78] In contrast, Agatha Moore disappears from the Barbados archive and possibly escaped further embarrassing publicity on the island.[79]

The deposition disempowered Agatha Moore on multiple levels, most strikingly in how it stated what the "deponent" said, but never in her own words or through direct quotes. The traditional legal format distorted her testimony by filtering what she actually said through Judge Harrison's third person interpretation of her testimony and transcribed by a clerk. Additionally, her physical absence from the Governor's Council meeting, a space predominantly for propertied white men only, left her without the ability to clarify and defend herself against the language of "whoredom" which permeates this historical record.[80] Agatha Moore was likely socially ruined, despite her "honesty," and leaving the island was probably her only recourse. Yet, on further examination of her language and position, it is clear that she was not necessarily destitute.[81] The resources she managed to access in her exposed sexual conduct demonstrate her ability to harness a type of power which enslaved and free(d) women could not.

When Agatha Moore came of age, she inherited property in houses in Bridgetown from her maternal grandmother.[82] Cecily Jones details the property laws relative to different categories of white women including married, single, and widowed. The laws in Barbados subjected white women to similar property restrictions as their peers in England, but demographic and social conditions required some legal flexibility allowing white women new economic avenues.[83] Coverture laws transformed married white women into the status of *femes coverts* and required that they surrender their property to their husbands on marriage.[84] This status erased wives legal visibility, "her property rights, down to the ownership of her petticoats, passed to her husband."[85] As widows, white women reverted back to *femes soles* and regained the same rights to property and legal transactions as men and unmarried women.[86] Although primogeniture laws existed in which the children (usually sons) inherited the majority of the estate, Barbados laws from the mid-seventeenth century ensured that wives were not abandoned in their husbands' wills.[87] Most important, many factors including high mortality rates forced the Barbados legislature to accommodate married women's property claims.[88] Married women employed premarital contracts, gained their husband's permission to create their own wills, sued for annuities in the case of separation, and fought in court to secure their ownership of slaves.[89] The probate records left by Barbados widows demonstrate both their ability to retain some property through their marriages and their attempts to circumvent the laws by giving property in trust to a male friend to avoid having it seized by marriage.[90] If Daniel Moore forced Agatha to flee Barbados, she likely took with her material resources to support herself including clothes, jewelry, and possibly slaves. In addition, Agatha Moore utilized rhetorical strategies in her deposition to appeal to the patriarchal system in place, denying her own agency in order to recoup her gendered and racial standing, while, at the same time, subtly pronouncing her free will.

Claiming "seduction" by Crofts, Agatha Moore disputes her consent (and will) in the affair. She states that, "she never gave the said Dudley Crofts any hints or signs to encourage him to endeavor to seduce her" and that "[she] unhappily complyd . . . by suffering the sd Dudley Crofts then to commit adultery with this Depont."[91] Moore deployed this language to elicit sympathy from the judge and council in claiming that she unwillingly participated in "immoral" behavior. Putting on record that she did not initiate the affair or the advances from Crofts allowed her the discursive room to claim innocence and a certain type of victimization through a "[discourse] of seduction." The concept of "seduction is a meditation on liberty and slavery; and will and subjection in the arena of sexuality."[92] "Discourse of seduction" refers to the ways in which the planter class represented enslaved women as always willing in sexual encounters, despite the fact that their status as enslaved persons and the punishments that would follow disobedience toward a white person prevented their refusal.[93] In other words, enslaved women as objects and commodities could not legally consent or deny unwanted sexual relations, and thus "rape is unimaginable."[94] Conversely, for Agatha Moore, a discourse of seduction becomes the means through

which she can claim victimization. In her case, Agatha Moore projects seduction onto the white male perpetrator, as she claims she was seduced by
Dudley Crofts.[95] Moreover, Agatha Moore's defense coalesces around the
issue of consent. Her claims that she was "importuned" and "unhappily
complied" implied she did not consent to the affair, even as she did not claim
she was raped.[96] Her racial and gendered subjectivity as a white woman be-
stowed her with the power to consent or refuse sexual relations with men
other than her husband. Enslaved women could not legally make such decisions with respect to their own bodies. These divergent meanings of discourses of seduction enacted on white and black female bodies mark precisely
the relational or dialectical sexual configurations of female sexualities in Barbados society. The fact that Agatha Moore could speak about her "unwilling-
ness" to engage in transgressive sexual acts and blame her "seduction" on
Crofts, delimits the significant schism/chasm between the sexual subjectivities of white and enslaved women. White women could defend their "honor"
in moments of domestic crisis, while enslaved women, as property (a status
that implied their sexual availability to men), could neither give nor withhold
consent.

Yet confounding her denial of sexual agency (elite white women were
certainly not meant to assert sexual agency in the traditional sense), Agatha
Moore then admits to informing Crofts of "convenient" moments when they
might have sex undisturbed and promised she would marry him if her husband died.[97] This latter point lends evidence to the possibility that Crofts sent
his slave boy to murder her husband to hasten the process by which he might
possess Agatha Moore, thus implicating her in a deadly scheme.[98] Equally
important are the ways she inhabited a status of privilege allowing her a range
of discursive options to defend herself in the face of social ridicule. These
options spoke to a specific type of subjection that both oppressed her as a
woman and empowered her as a white woman. Unpacking the relationship
between discourses of sex and power relations illuminates critical questions
related to Agatha Moore's testimony in this case. As Michel Foucault asks,
"[in] a specific type of discourse on sex, in a specific form of exhortation of
the truth, appearing historically and in specific places . . . what were the most
immediate, the most local power relations at work? And, how were these discourses used to support power relations?"[99] Ideology and discourse shaped
the life conditions and experiences of freedom and enslavement for everyone
in slave societies. Combined, the discursive power of racial ideology worked
to subjugate, mark as deviant, and make sexually accessible black women's

bodies for public consumption at the same time and in relation to the ways white women were protected via law, gender, race, and sexual norms.

Prevailing ideas and expectations of sexual behavior, for both white women and women of color, enslaved and free(d), influenced the treatment and avenues of privilege for these different groups of women. Agatha Moore's deposition and her language in it represent the rhetorical space white women could exploit to feign innocence. Beyond mere rhetoric, in this moment her (sexual) subjectivity comes clearly into view. Her ability to claim seduction and disempowerment ironically spoke to her empowerment within the existing racial hierarchy. Contrary to the ways the concept of agency is used in most scholarship on slavery—as resistance to domination—Agatha Moore denied her agency, appealing to patriarchal norms of white female submission and honor in an attempt to rescue her innocence and sexual virtue. Moore thus reproduced the "discourses used to support power relations" in Barbados slave society; her innocence/guilt and her ability to speak on her own behalf expose the more subtle forms of power available to white women beyond the economic.[100]

Agatha Moore's "shame" in her transgressive behavior meant she inhabited a position of status from which to fall. This status, although tenuous, gave her a position of power over enslaved and free(d) women in the same society. Of course, if she had been caught having sex with a black man, free(d) or enslaved, her power to evoke "unwilling consent" would be greatly reduced. In all likelihood, her ruin would have been unrecoverable unless she claimed rape. However limiting the double standard of interracial sex was for white men and women in Caribbean slave societies, a white woman's recourse to claiming rape elaborates not only her power but also the powerlessness of enslaved men, whose imminent execution followed any such encounter by the eighteenth century. All these strategies—these avenues that bespoke her status, subjectivity, and placement in the racial/gendered hierarchy—were possible because of the subjugation of black women.

Beyond the discursive strategies available to white women caught in nonconjugal sexual relationships, white women's ability to market enslaved female sexuality in the context of urban slavery further subjugated enslaved women. Aliyyah I. Abdur-Rahman explains that "ideologies of white womanhood were articulable and meaningful only in relation to slave women's experience: forced physical labor, "natal alienation," reproductive exploitation, necessary dependence on extra-familial networks, enforced prostitution, and enslavement."[101] Just as white men controlled access to enslaved women's bodies, white women's participation in the "jobbing" slave market—slaves hired out by task or hour—allowed them a significant degree of social and economic mobility in Bridgetown. Whether selling weaned enslaved children or their mothers' sexual services for profit, white women's preference for enslaved women in an urban context demonstrated how "the marketing of black women's sexuality . . . [was] associated directly with the economic accumulation strategies of [Bridgetown's] white women."[102] In Barbadian slave society free(d) women of African descent also owned, sold, and passed slave property to their relatives.[103] The difference in these circumstances of slave ownership and the ideologies of racialized gender lay in the pervasive and oppositional ideological perceptions of white and black womanhood and the constituent factors of economic and sexual power that gave white women elevated status.

White Women and the Sexual Economy of Enslaved Women

Eighteenth-century probate records from Barbados point to these important linkages between white female economic power and enslaved women's sexual vulnerability. Recent scholarship has indicated that white women in slave societies occupied more powerful roles in the economy than previously imagined through their engagement with different markets, including the buying, selling, and hiring out of slaves.[104] Historians have used probate records to track white women's economic power but also to mark the ways white slave owners depended on enslaved women's reproduction and future fecundity to secure their family's economic prospects.[105] This situation produced a sexual power dynamic in which white women's commodification of enslaved women's reproduction and sexuality also created conditions in which white women could not be similarly commodified. In other words, because white women could buy, sell, and bequeath enslaved women's sexualized bodies, evidenced in probate records for example, their own sexual identity was protected through its links to white racial and gendered power.

However, this "security" was not infallible. White women's bodies were protected from assault only by men who were not their husbands, and then not all the time.[106] The concept of marital rape did not exist in the eighteenth-century British Empire and white women certainly suffered from their powerlessness in marriage.[107] But in legal and ideological terms they could essentially be protected from or defended against certain forms of assault and could not be sold or traded as slaves in Barbados, providing them with a type of sexual identity, power, and honor unavailable to women of African descent. Building on the case of Agatha Moore's sexual transgressions made public, an interrogation of the probate records of elite white women who inherited, bought, and sold enslaved women, illustrates the critical and crucial relationship between the economics of slavery and the sexual power created and enjoyed by white women and reproduced through enslaved women's bodies in Bridgetown.

Bridgetown's unique eighteenth-century demographics provided space for white women to practice and reproduce the system of slavery. This practice, shaped by majority black and white female populations, enabled white women to fully utilize domestic slaves who would be considered "surplus" in the plantation setting. Enslaved women's bodies supported the economic and heritable aspects of white women's lives by being expendable in perpetuity, passed among white relatives, and used to pay for proper church burials. More important, the wills and deeds of white slave-owning women evidenced strategic manipulation of coverture and property laws at play in this temporal and geographic location. As noted above, by the first decades of the eighteenth century, white women rose to be a small majority of the white Barbados population, unlike other British Caribbean colonies in the same period.[108] This population of white women was decidedly urban and predominantly slave owning, and the households held mostly black women in bondage.[109] The intimacy of women inside these homes suggests that sexual ideologies of black and white women formed in close proximity.

White women who occupied this slight demographic majority influenced the economic, social, and sexual power of eighteenth-century Bridgetown.[110] Hilary Beckles argues that "the linking of white womanhood to the reproduction of freedom meant that the entire ideological fabric of the slave-based civilization was conceived in terms of sex, gender, and race."[111] Many of the areas of power—racial, sexual, and economic—tethered white women's hierarchical and sexual position to that of enslaved black and free(d) women of color. Probate records and deeds reveal these multiple layers of power that certain white women (spinsters, single women, and widows) mobilized. The legal language and proposed fate of enslaved women in the wills and deeds of white women indexes several aspects of power wielded by white women to control their economic legacy and that of their daughters, nieces, and other female kin. These documents corroborate ongoing scholarship on the vital (economic and socio-sexual) roles and privileges white women inhabited in British Caribbean slave societies, just as they reduced enslaved women to their commodifiable futurity.[112]

Free(d) women of color also benefited from slave ownership, social ties to white individuals, and the right to distribute their slaves to family members through wills and deeds.[113] However, as in the unusual case of Rachael Pringle Polgreen, elite status was rare and existing legal restrictions on the lives of free(d)people of color created insecurities and tensions not experienced by white women.[114] Many free(d) people were not far removed from slavery and had relatives who were still enslaved. The social and familial relationships free(d) people maintained with enslaved people resulted in backlash from the white population in various forms including legal, social and economic obstacles. Manumissions remained cost prohibitive and required a fee for annuities so that, "the freeing of slaves [was] a privilege of a small, white, wealthy elite."[115] Moreover, as Joanna in Chapter 2 fought to prove her manumission, many others experienced challenges to their free status.[116] With the complicated constraints based on racial discrimination that forced free(d) people of color into precarious circumstances, it is difficult to argue that slave ownership and economic well-being marked a leveling between the races.[117] As discussed in previous chapters, economic prosperity was rare among free(d) people and those who owned slaves participated in the system that perpetuated white supremacy. Probate records in the British Caribbean make a focus on slave ownership and economic ventures inevitable. More important, many of the documents leave out a racial designation that creates specific challenges for marking economic and social distinctions between the races. There are, however, certain codes read by historians that reveal the race of the document's author.[118] The examples below of white women's wills and deeds were distinguished from those of free(d) women of color by their familial relations to elite white men, often through marriage, and their subversion of coverture laws to which white women were particularly subjected.[119] These facts help identify white women in the records as well as illustrating the specific ways white women benefited economically from slavery and enslaved women bodies.

Married women forfeited property on marriage but retained power over servants and slaves and largely controlled the domestic business of the household.[120] It is significant that, as mentioned above, unmarried white women, or *femmes soles*, wielded different powers from their married counterparts. The status of remaining unmarried, whether through the death of a husband or spinsterhood, allowed white women the freedom to buy or sell property including estates, pass on property to kin and friends, and give the same to whomever they chose.[121] For instance, in September 1792, Elvira Cox of St. Michael left a will instructing her executors, "to sell all houses and slaves except Flora for the most money that can be gotten."[122] Cox then bequeathed Flora to her "Brother in Law Benjamin Alleyne Cox & Anthony Barker Esquire." She stipulated that Alleyne Cox and Baker allow Flora to work and conduct business without interference from any heirs or anyone else purporting interest in Flora. Cox, by this document, granted Flora the ability to labor for her own purposes, freedom of movement, and choice of occupation. Presumably preferable to other arrangements, including being sold, Cox gave Flora the opportunity to experience more independent arrangements within slavery. Yet, as in some of the "generous" bequests to enslaved women in the probate records of white women, Flora was not given her freedom. Cox directed that if "Flora shall at any time hereafter be able from her labour and Industry . . . raise [a] Sufficient sum of money that shall or may be required by any Law of this Island," then Alleyene Cox and Baker must permit and enable Flora to pay for her own manumission.[123] What did it mean to Flora to work for her freedom after years of serving Cox without remuneration? Seemingly Flora gained her freedom; in 1793 she baptized an enslaved woman named Frances who was listed as her property.[124] In this case, unmarried or widowed white women retained control of the lives of their slaves even in death and though Flora fared differently, Mary Ann, Betty, Matty & Molly Thomas, and Sam remained property that consolidated the financial stability of their relatives.[125]

Other women mobilized their power in ways similar to Elvira Cox. In February 1794, Mary Sisnett, a Bridgetown widow, directed that Doll, Judy, and Margarett, "three Negro women slaves," be liquidated as property and the money arising from their sale used to pay for the Christian burial and any other of Sisnett's outstanding debts.[126] Any surplus money arising from the sale of the three women was for Sisnett's daughter Mary Ann Sisnett. The widow stipulated that the rest of her property in land, buildings, and "thirteen other slaves" go to the Honorable Joshua Gittens and Mr. Daniel Broadbent in "trust to and for the sole and only proper use and behoof of my said dear daughter Mary Ann Sisnett and her heirs."[127] The ongoing fate of the "thirteen other slaves" and the future wealth of Sisnett's daughter rested in the legal power Sisnett held as a widow. The ability to manipulate coverture laws on behalf of her daughter rested on complicated legal maneuvering. In order to protect white female economic power and control, Sisnett and many of her peers manipulated the legal barriers of coverture laws. White women deployed legal strategies both to retain property, human or otherwise, and to ensure that the property stayed in the control and for the benefit of themselves when remarrying or for their female relatives.[128] Anticipating the event of her daughter's marriage, Sisnett stated that the property in trust should be retained by Gittens and Broadbent so that the any profits pass into

> the proper hands of my said daughter and not to any husband she might hereafter intermarry with during the life of such husband . . . nor shall the same or any part thereof be subject charged or liable to the control debts engagements forfeitures contracts encumbrances or intermeddling of such husband and the receipts alone of my said daughter for the same or any part thereof . . . shall be good and sufficient discharges to my said trustees.[129]

Sisnett's forceful language and instructions to keep her daughter's property out of a husband's control reflect a widow's keen understanding of an economic and legal system in which white women were often left vulnerable to the whims of men. In the parish of St. Phillip on the south east coast of Barbados, widow Hannah Hayes (née Downes) was about to marry Edward Wiggins Scott in 1778. In anticipation of her own pending nuptials, Haynes arranged for her property to go to Bridgetown resident Samuel Drayton in trust. Carefully attending to the fine details of this entailment, Haynes secured her own property from coverture by giving Drayton "ownership" of her "Negro, Mulatto, and Indian Slaves . . . in consideration for the sum of ten shillings . . . [namely] Arrow and Walker [sic] men, Dolly, Prudence, Candace, Elvey, Olidah, Pallas, Fanny and Celinda (Women) Tobey, Sam, [Sammons] and William (boys) Lenora, Anna-Maria, Violet, Betty-Brown and Aggey (girls) with their increase of the females."[130] The deed specified that this arrangement was to hold her slaves and other property for the use of herself and her intended husband, "during the term of their joint natural lives" and then should pass on to any children they may produce.[131] Notwithstanding the unusual instance of indigenous slaves in late eighteenth-century Barbados, Haynes convinced her intended husband to forfeit his rights to ownership over her slaves, thereby directly subverting the coverture laws. Her trust arrangement, like Sisnett's, secured her continued profit from the labor of her slaves and any of their forthcoming children, while also ensuring that any children yet to be born could inherit directly from her. This power subverted laws intended to weaken white women's status in society and enabled them instead to wield a significant level of control over their affairs and those of their white female relatives. These trust arrangements with white men who were not relatives were agreed on by both the trustees and intended husbands and exemplifies the economic flexibility white men sometimes offered in marriage and future estate affairs.

Mary Kidney, a Bridgetown spinster, also made trust arrangements for her property, leaving "a dwelling house or Tenement in St. Michael's town" to her mother Ann Kidney. After Ann Kidney's death, the house transferred to "[Doctor] George Hastle & Thomas Hope, merchants In trust of [Mary's] sister Elizabeth Woodroffe, wife of Jonas Woodroffe during their joint lives." Mary Kidney specified the conditions under which the trust should function, namely,

> that the rents and profits of the said house be always paid to . . . Elizabeth during her coverture, and her receipt shall be allowed [as] sufficient discharge in as full & effectual manner as if she was sole and unmarried and the said Jonas Woodroffe is hereby debarred & closed from any claim or demand whatsoever in and to the aforesaid dwelling house or the rents issues or profits thereof.[132]

Kidney then passed this property in trust onto any children of Elizabeth if she should die. Whatever feelings Kidney may have harbored for Jonas Woodroffe, the main priority was to subvert her sister's loss of property through marriage coverture. These examples indicate how white women understood the law and their economic vulnerability in a patriarchal society. It also shows the avenues through which white women could secure property including slaves, for themselves and female relatives. Unlike free(d) women of color, white women could decide the futures of white and black children in starkly different ways, and the sexual futures of white *and* black women were similarly distinct in outcome—enslaved women's sexuality was linked to white women's power and profit.

As Jennifer Morgan has demonstrated, slave owners in the early modern Atlantic depended on the reproductive capabilities of enslaved women in the early moments of the colonial enterprise. Specifying the preference of Barbadian slave owners to purchase African women, Morgan states that "between 1651 and 1675, 46 percent of all enslaved persons arriving to [Barbados] were

female, and by the 1660s Barbadian slaveowners saw women as valuable laborers whom they easily integrated into their workforce."[133] White women,
then, wielded and mobilized both economic and sexual power that depended
on ideologically sexualized enslaved women, whose (re)production of labor
and futures were profoundly controlled.[134] For instance, in August 1766
widow Elizabeth Grant of St. Michael left a will instructing her executors to
distribute her property specifically among her relatives. Her distributions included leaving "Maria, a woman, Quomino and Robin, boys and Harriet a
girl with all issue and increase" to her granddaughter Elizabeth. But if Elizabeth should die, then the abovementioned enslaved would go to the widow's
daughter Winnefred Moore.[135] In typical probate records of the eighteenth
century, white widows and spinsters left wealth in the form of slaves and their
future children to consolidate the financial stability of their relatives.[136] The
sexual and reproductive objectification of the "two negroe girls" proved integral to the wealth and power of white Barbadian women and their futures
were often tied to the very young and yet-to-be-born white children. These
circumstances further consolidated white female power in Barbados society,
and in Bridgetown enslaved women's sexual and reproductive capacities were
used to further the wealth and status of these young white women.[137] Conse-
quent to this dynamic of profit, images of enslaved women as sexually available and white women as virtuous persisted throughout the eighteenth
century.

The oft-cited works of Richard Ligon, Edward Long, and Elizabeth Fen-
wick suggest that early in Barbados's settlement and well into the nineteenth
century, women of African descent were imagined by white society as sexually deviant, brutish, shiftless, and beastly.[138] These stereotyped images existed in contrast to constructions of the refinement of white women in the
Caribbean. Speaking of creole white women in Jamaica, Edward Long
claimed, "the women of [Jamaica] are lively, of good natural genius, frank,
affable, polite, generous, humane, and charitable; cleanly in their persons
even to excess . . . and fond, to a fault of their children."[139] Other writers varied in opinion on the virtuous and educated qualities of white women. J. B.
Moreton, and even Long, thought white creole women suffered indulgences
not allowed their metropolitan counterparts, including improper dress and
too close associations with the black women domestic slaves by whom they
were reared.[140] Moreton, a bookkeeper in eighteenth-century Jamaica, wrote
extensively on white creole women who were ill-mannered and "those who
receive their education amongst negroe wenches and imbibe great part of

their dialect, principles, manners and customs."[141] Despite varying depictions of creole white women's virtues or lack thereof from the metropole and English men alike, sexualized and degraded images of enslaved women remained consistent. Clearly stereotyped in multiple ways, elite white creole women in the British Caribbean maintained important aspects of identity and privilege (social and economic) under which enslaved women suffered. Long wrote extensively about Jamaica's population of enslaved women and specifically stated, "The women here, in general, are common prostitutes."[142] The implications of such thought directly affected the manner in which enslaved women were treated, sexually abused, and assigned work.[143] Ultimately, as movable property, enslaved women's bodies often secured both the economic and social wealth of white women and their female relatives. This relationship of owner and property inevitably created, reproduced, and sustained a gendered and racial hierarchy where even lower-class white women enjoyed the social benefits of white supremacy.[144]

Related to the gendered economics of slavery is the relationship of economics to sexuality. By virtue of their sexual commodification white society imagined enslaved women as promiscuous, immoral, and objectifiable.[145] Enslaved women's reproductive potential placed their bodies in a position to reproduce the future of slavery and the white wealth this created.[146] More than this, the probate records display the tenuous nature of life for domestic enslaved women, who were regularly passed among owners' relatives. Appearing to mark the altruistic nature of female slave ownership and manumission, white women's probate provisions often exhausted enslaved women past their strength to labor before they were freed. Bessey, an enslaved woman belonging to Mary Sisnett, exemplifies the contradictory nature of "benevolence." Sisnett asks that Bessey be treated kindly by her daughter because "Bessey has always behaved herself well to me it is therefore my request that said daughter will treat her with kindness and humanity."[147] Some enslaved women gained freedom, property, and even annuities on their white female owner's death. But many more remained vulnerable to resale and stipulated acts of freedom, and even passed to other free(d) slaves as property. The positions enslaved women inhabited as property and sexual commodities can be further analyzed by returning to the scene that opened this chapter—the enslaved boy moving through Bridgetown and the court case that brought the boy to our attention. Enslaved women made up the demographic majority of Bridgetown. Their presence in public spaces, in the domestic realm, and their status as slaves led white men and women to expect and demand the sexual and reproductive availability of black female bodies. Ideologies of white womanhood and white female slave ownership opened up possibilities for profit and power. Finally, expectations of enslaved women's bodies in public made it possible for an enslaved boy to conceal himself dressed as a black woman.

The Boy, the Dress, and the Dagger

A closer examination of the enslaved boy sent out by his master dressed in women's clothes maps the unique demographics of Bridgetown in the eighteenth century. The boy's movements in black women's guise suggest the prevalence and expectation of enslaved women in town as public and sexually available, allowing him a certain freedom of movement. There are only a few references to the boy in the *Crofts v. Harrison* case but they provide insight into the power dynamics in eighteenth-century Barbados and the specter of racialized gender. The first mention of the boy appears in Judge Harrison's rebuttal to Dudley Crofts's complaint of financial and personal injury. Harrison, explaining why he imposed such a large bond for security on Crofts, argued that he felt Crofts was a criminal threat to Daniel Moore. He states:

> The reason which induced [me] to demand such a recognizance was because [of] a complaint made to [me] by the sd Daniel Moore against a Negro of [Crofts]. The negro [sic] had taken his Masters Sword which [Crofts] acknowledged to [me] he had directed him to take and went the proceeding night therewith disguised in womens Cloaths to the house of Thomas Withers Esqr where Mr Moore lived and where the Criminal Correspondence between [Crofts] & the wife of the sd Mr Moore was carried on and as from the circumstances I had reason to believe some mischief was intended by [Crofts] against Mr Moore . . . I thought it my Duty to require proper security from [Crofts].[148]

At issue for Harrison and the slave court case was whether Crofts instructed his slave to attempt murder or merely permitted the boy who had allegedly been summoned to the Moore/Withers house by a nurse working therein to answer a request. The next few references to this incident relate to witnesses testifying whether they heard Dudley Crofts acknowledge he directed his enslaved boy to go to the Moore/Withers household in disguise and with a sword.[149] Most of the witnesses present in the initial confrontation between Judge Harrison and Crofts agreed that Crofts acknowledged in public that he allowed the boy to go. But no one could confirm whether it was Crofts' intent to murder Daniel Moore or if the boy was responding to a summons from the Moore household. Crofts, his lawyer Thomas Lake, and two other witnesses testified that the boy was summoned to the house by another male slave named John who carried a message from the nurse, beckoning him to come at night and meet her "under a tree." They argue that he took the sword, with Crofts's permission, to defend himself from possible attack by another enslaved male named Toney belonging to Mr. Withers or Mr. Moore.[150] We do not have testimony in the voice of the enslaved boy, only fleeting moments where white male deponents state what they heard him say. Samuel Webb, a witness called on behalf of Dudley Crofts, deposed that he did not hear Crofts say he instructed the boy to take a sword to Mr. Withers but he did hear the boy say that "a negro named John belonging to the said Withers having come to him & told him, that the nurse at Mr Withers desired he would come to her under a tree in the Garden." Webb contends that the boy took the sword by his own decision to "defend himself.[151] The boy was eventually acquitted of all charges against him, an unusual action given his deceptive disguise and possession of a lethal weapon.

According to further testimony by witness Richard Hall, "it did not appear upon the trial of the said negro that he had made any attempts upon the House or Doors of Mr. Withers or that he offered any violence whatever, upon which he was acquitted."[152] However, it is clear that Judge Harrison and the men who tried him did not believe he acted on his own accord. In this instance we might think about how "will" is both recognized and disregarded by the colonial authorities in reference to enslaved criminality. This case provides an example of how colonial slave law arbitrarily recognized the boy's humanity in order to try him for his purported criminal actions, while at the same time denying he could have enacted his own will apart from the desires of his master. That he was acquitted despite being caught armed and in disguise elucidates how the authorities' could ultimately decide when to consider enslaved people sentient beings and when to deny their humanity and will.

It is also plausible that Crofts's motive for sending the boy was murder, as Agatha Moore stated in her deposition, "for that if her said Husband died, she would perform the Promise or Oath she had made to him, that she would marry the said Dudley Crofts."[153] Did Agatha Moore, then, enable the enslaved boy's attempt at murder by suggesting to Crofts that if he would do something to get rid of her husband she would marry him? Is this statement, so easily dismissed by Governor Robinson in later proceedings, evidence that the boy was directed to commit violence against a white man and thus, risk death himself?[154] Since the enslaved could not deny the requests of their owners, we might consider how the boy's actions were an enactment of his owner's will. Through his actions the boy was caught as an accessary to Crofts's sexual desires, entangled in Crofts's sexual interactions with Agatha Moore and his desire to possess her. Since "the notion of will connotes more than simply the ability to act and to do; rather, it distinguishes the autonomous agent from the enslaved," the boy could not refuse or disobey directions and was forced to participate in his own possible demise by being caught in a white household under questionable circumstances.[155] In other words, sexual agency for the enslaved was exercised in this instance, by becoming a vehicle for white men and women to act on their sexual desires. This is the fungibility of the enslaved exemplified, as they could be forced to carry out their owner's crimes with no opportunity to refuse, and under threat of death for their actions by either their owner or the colony. He faced danger both in resisting his master's will and in attempting to murder or bring harm to any white person, which carried the sentence of death.[156]

Moreover, the absence of testimonial discussion as to why the enslaved boy donned women's clothes points to the fungible condition of enslaved people and how racialized gender functioned in this colonial slave society.[157] In one way, this lack of concern addressed the enslaved boy's nonthreatening gender behavior. In "womens cloaths" he did not elicit a (sexual) threat to white masculinity. But there is more at stake here. In addition to the slave boy's unremarkable attire, we might ask what social expectations allowed a disguised enslaved "woman" to approach a white household at night? Urban enslaved women served white people in various capacities. They were domestic servants, nursemaids, wet nurses, sex slaves for personal hire or service in a brothel, washerwomen, and market women. If the enslaved boy had been instructed to murder Daniel Moore (a likely possibility despite his acquittal), an enslaved woman who was a stranger to a household would have been more easily admitted than an enslaved man. Black women comprised the majority of household servants, and interactions between white men and black women occurred frequently. It would not have been odd for a female slave to arrive at a stranger's house to deliver washing or market goods. Furthermore, black women's access to public space marked a difference in gendered and sexual expectations for enslaved and white women.[158] Elite women were not allowed in public unaccompanied, especially at night. Their sexuality was hidden, protected, and defended in the name of honor and virtue, which were at the very heart of white female identity. The frequency with which black women traversed urban spaces suggests how they were perceived as sexual agents, lascivious, and "unwomanly." As objects of commerce for different types of (sexual) labor, enslaved women were not associated with virtue, nor were their sexual identities protected from harm. As Long discusses in reference to enslaved wet nurses and domestic slaves, "there is scarcely one of these nurses who is not a common prostitute, or at least who has not had commerce with more than one man."[159] In contrast, Long's observations about the roles white women occupied demonstrate varied perceptions of black and white womanhood and their implied sexualities. He states that, "the domestic life of [white] women, which prevents them from exercising abroad as much as the other sex, naturally inclines them to love those active amusements which may be followed within doors."[160]

Enslaved women's mobility outside the domestic realm evoked a certain type of freedom elite white women could not exercise. Yet, the enslaved boy's movements and performance in female dress, through town and at night, expose the ways enslaved and black women's seemingly unfettered mobility often made them more vulnerable in this slave society. White women were protected by law and domestic enclosure, while enslaved women were required to perform a particular type of public availability resulting in danger. Dudley Crofts, through his enslaved boy, exploited this understanding of black women's public exposure and position, sending him out to perform the normative embodiment of black womanhood as publicly visible, unchaste, lascivious, sexually wanton, and available to serve.

Another way to consider the circumstances and consequences of the boy's surreptitious movements is to understand the intimacy of whites and enslaved in the domestic sphere. As the court case makes clear, there was a dispute between two white households, which no doubt caused anxiety among the enslaved laboring in each house. White strife and the breakup of households had profound effects for those bound to their owners.[161] White unrest might lead to liquidation of assets and in turn to slave sales or labor reassignment. Many white families had relatives on country estates and were involved in sugar production. Slaves could be moved around from town to country if households were in flux. The enslaved people residing with Crofts

and the Moore/Withers household likely felt a palpable fear. Moreover, despite racial rules of conduct, particularly those that regulated the behavior of
enslaved and free(d) people, household slaves served their owners intimately,
and thus at least some would have been aware of Agatha Moore's sexual infi-
delities.[162] Perhaps, the stress of the situation led the enslaved of each household to threaten each other. The boy may have been caught in a trap set by the
"white" nurse, who in trying to protect her family charges in the Withers/
Moore home, sought to stop the affair between Crofts and Agatha Moore and
used the armed boy to bring the situation to public notice.[163]

The crucial point here is the ways enslaved subjectivity (subjugated and
criminalized), male and female, enabled particular types of social, racial, sexual, and gendered power for white men and women. Key to understanding
this, in the absence of a comparable archive for enslaved men and women, is
a discussion of the labor and sexual roles they performed in the context of a
colonial port city such as Bridgetown. In addition, establishing the singular-
ity and similarities of this site and court case to other Caribbean contexts
further illuminates the specific relations of power deployed through sexuality
in such slave societies.[164] Agatha Moore's, and other white women's sexual
agency and ability to deny their consensual participation in non-conjugal sex
was predicated on the sexual exploitation of enslaved women. Indeed, the
performance of black womanhood enabled the boy to walk around at night
based on assumptions about black women being out in public spaces. By interrogating the relations of power—economic, gendered, racial, and sexual—
we expose important nuances of white women's relationship to patriarchy in
slave societies. In this context, the movements of a boy dressed as a girl/
woman relates directly to white women's sexualities and social power. The
preceding court case makes clear that even in circumstances of intimate exposure, white women had avenues of physical and material, if not emotional,
escape and cultural capital with which their reputations could be at least
marginally repaired in instances of "fornication" and even in cases of rape.[165]

Conversely, within the context of urban slavery, many enslaved women
were hired out to itinerant sailors, military men, and single local men for
domestic roles that included sexual access to their bodies. In such circumstances, these domestic intimacies may have created impossible situations for
those abused by the men who "rented" them. These domestic intimacies and
spaces were constituent to the relations of production and violence that defined slavery and in town, were the sites where the dynamics of power were
enacted. The range of legal codes passed to control enslaved behavior made

resistance to domestic violence a life and death decision. Over the course of the eighteenth century many acts of enslaved defiance were punished by death by the noose, fire, or gibbet. For enslaved offenses considered "heinous," colonial authorities emphasized the criminality of the enslaved and created a public spectacle as a lesson to others who might be contemplating a challenge to abuse. As we will see in the next chapter, these urban public spectacles provided reminders of the extant power mobilized by colonial rulers in the lives and deaths of the enslaved.

CHAPTER 4

Molly: Enslaved Women, Condemnation, and Gendered Terror

The Cruelty exercised upon the Negroes is at once shocking
to Humanity and a disgrace to human nature. For the most
trifling faults sometimes for meer whims (of their Masters)
these poor negroes are ty'd up and whiped most
unmercifully. . . . If a person kills a Slave he only pays his
value as a Fine. It is not a Hanging matter.
—Nicolas Cresswell, Journal, 1774

These slave laws, what are they in general but emanations
from the selfish feelings of the planters, who always constitute
a great majority of West India Councils and Assemblies, and
of the freeholders by whom the latter are elected?
—James Stephen, *The Slavery of the British West
India Colonies Delineated*

Whereas the Body of a Negro Wench named Molly, the
property of Mr. Isaac Wray in Speights Town, who was
condemned & Executed a few days since for the Horrid
Crime of Attempting to take away the life of John Denny
Esqr. By Poison, was after the Execution interred with
unusual Pomp & Solemnity, & the Body attended to the
Grave by Numbers of Negroes expressly invited & Meeted
together for that purpose; which procedure cannot but be
considered as an open Violation of the Laws.
—Governor of Barbados William S. Perry,
Barbados Minutes of Council, 1768

Sometime around Saturday, 17 December 1768, an enslaved woman named Molly, living in Speightstown, was executed. She was most likely hanged by the neck for an hour on elevated wooden gallows built for the purpose or from a nearby tree, to ensure a public spectacle. She was accused and condemned for attempting to poison John Denny, Esqr., a member of the Council, who was not her owner. Andrew Edwards, a local constable, was paid for apprehending her in the days before this moment and another slave likely pressed into service to assist in the execution.[1] From the surviving archival fragments found in the Barbados Minutes of Council, we know that Molly would have looked down on a crowd of enslaved men and women, gathered not only to bear witness to colonial brutality but to take her body from the gallows and bury her in the ways of their community. Similar to the silences surrounding other archival traces of enslaved women in previous chapters, we do not know which familial connections Molly left behind. The archive only documents what was meaningful to the governor's council, to her owner, and to the alleged victim in the case. This information included her name, her monetary value, and the crime of which she was accused. Her owner, Isaac Wray, petitioned the council for compensation for the loss of his slave property, which was granted.[2] Slave owners were paid twenty-five pounds from the colony's treasury for executed slaves.[3] We cannot know the circumstances leading up to Molly's conviction. The nullity of slave law made it virtually impossible to defend oneself against such accusations.[4] The enslaved community had a final chance to give Molly a voice, violating the sensibilities of white Barbadians. Our knowledge of the community's acts, however, depended upon chance. This story enters the archive not for our knowledge of the enslaved community's practices of mourning. It comes to us through an assertion of colonial power.

*   *   *

On 20 December 1768, during a meeting of the Barbados Council, Governor William S. Perry expressed his disgust at the blatant display of honor shown by the enslaved community toward Molly as, "a most Outrageous Insult to the person of a Public Magistrate & Member of the Legislature, whose Life had been endangered by the horrid attempts of this Wretch."[5] The enslaved community's commemoration of Molly following her death suggests that they held distinctly different view of the condemned woman. Clearly she was revered among the enslaved population of Speightstown. But their efforts to memorialize Molly through burial rituals sparked a potent counter-reaction from colonial authorities. In response to the perceived disrespect shown by the enslaved, Governor Spry issued a proclamation directing new regulations for burials of all "officially" executed enslaved people:

> I do hereby require & direct all ... if after the Condemnation of a Negro they shall think it expedient to order immediate Execution without making any Report of the Case to me, to Charge the Constables attending Such Executions, to carry the Body immediately into the Sea, and [By] weights to sink it in deep water, so that it may be impossible for the Negroes to take it up again.[6]

This single fragment of Molly's execution, burial, and the ensuing legislation delineates the multiple means by which enslaved bodies in urban Barbados were (dis)figured and disposable in the context of life, law, and death. Molly's officially sanctioned death offers a multilayered introduction to these issues via the reverberating response that her burial provoked throughout the colony. The ending of her life underscores the violent dislocation of many enslaved women, in life and in death, and the impact on the wider enslaved community. Moreover, revisiting the Barbados Minutes of Council and the execution records contained therein, represents the hollowness of the laws governing the enslaved and the debilitating effects of domination on their lives.

Placing at the center of analysis the gendered ideologies and circumstances that might have led Molly and other enslaved women to the gallows or to their graves reminds us of the limits of resistance and again troubles notions of agency. Enslaved women were considered "genderless" in relation to ideologies of motherhood, female vulnerability, and femininity. At the same time the expectations of enslaved women's labor as serving the intimate needs of white men and women placed them predominantly in domestic work in the urban context. These intimate environments placed enslaved women in harm's way as well as provided them specific domestic tools to challenge white authority. Condemned for allegedly poisoning a white man who was not her owner, Molly's urban and likely domestic labor led her into circumstances that made her vulnerable to the threat of sexual and other forms of violence even as the law disavowed these situations. Slave laws and the universal methods of enslaved executions became another way enslaved women were denied gender and the bodily protections afforded to elite white women. To be sure, enslaved

men felt the brutal effects of slave laws and punishment on Caribbean plantations and in towns; their bodies were also spectacularly displayed and mutilated. But it was precisely due to laboring in urban domestic spaces and being
hired out for sex that many enslaved women faced, acutely, the domination of
enslavement. Forced into intimacy with white men, they lacked the legal recourse to save their own lives.

The ways the enslaved like Molly were criminalized, punished, confined, put to death, and perversely immortalized by the white community
symbolizes the conditions of enslaved people as both objects and criminal
subjects. The construction of such slave laws and systems of punishment
and the manner in which the authorities grafted a "criminal" identity upon
the enslaved—with no recourse for physical or testimonial self-defense—
destabilizes concepts of "guilt" and "innocence" in a system that offered no
avenue for the enslaved to defend themselves.[7] Molly's execution, burial,
and the response it evoked from Barbados authorities illuminates important aspects of how the enslaved challenged the official narrative of terror
explicit in public executions through communal mourning as well as the
limits to their actions. Executions that occurred *after* Molly's prevented the
enslaved, for a time, access to the body of the executed, making it difficult,
if not impossible, to commemorate members of their community. The value
they placed on their condemned comrades stemmed from a place of honor
unacknowledged by the authorities.[8] The extreme measures of terror and
punishment used by the Barbados authorities reinforced their power over
enslaved people and showed how the legal and punitive system they created
could be manipulated for their own benefit and profit.[9]

This fragment of an enslaved women's execution will be analyzed from
multiple angles. Refusing to surrender to its empirical limitations yields significant meaning surrounding the manner in which enslaved women were
criminalized, put to death, and immortalized by both the colonial authorities
and the enslaved communities. This method of archival interrogation, including close readings of incomplete and inconclusive sources, serves to provide a critical understanding of the laws that regulated enslaved lives and
bodies from the standpoint of the enslaved. Moreover, this approach deconstructs this "legal system" in order to expose the corruption, invalidity, and
devastation of a structure of governance in which the enslaved remained utterly voiceless and without power.

Enslaved Executions, Arbitrary Deaths

In 1737, three decades before Molly's execution, Governor James Dottin complained to the Barbados Council about the amount of money the colony paid out to owners of executed slaves. He observed, "that many of these unhappy wretches have been unjustly condemned on a pretended misconstruction of the Act by which they are tried which besides the cruelty to the poor slaves has been a considerable loss to their owners & a great injury to the Publick."[10] Dottin then explained that the rigidity of the existing slave laws forced the judges of "slave courts" to condemn men and women for a variety of crimes not otherwise considered "heinous" enough to warrant death. According to Barbados law, "heinous and grievous crimes," which included "Murder, Burglaries, Robbing in the High-ways, Rapes, [and] burning of Houses or Canes," even if only "attempted," were to be tried by three free holders and two justices of the peace—all white male property owners.[11] As stipulated in the 1688 "Act for the governing of negroes" the Barbados Council compensated slave owners twenty-five pounds out of the public treasury for the loss of property in executed slaves.[12] Slave owners were compensated for the execution of their enslaved who were implicated in a variety of events. For example, if an enslaved woman or man damaged the property on a neighboring plantation— by murdering another slave, stealing livestock, or otherwise causing monetary harm—and s/he was brought to trial in town, s/he was tried and executed by the authority of the state.[13] The injured parties, including the owner of the executed slave, recouped their losses by petitioning the colonial council. If the damage resulted in minor quantities, the injured party would be paid out of the twenty-five pounds and the difference reverted to the owner of the condemned slave. A slave owner could also claim compensation if one of his/her slaves damaged property within his/her own plantation or residence. Ultimately, receiving monetary compensation encouraged owners to report the crimes of their slaves for the sake of the colony's protection.[14] According to the law, owners forfeited their compensation if evidence surfaced of willful neglect of their enslaved from lack of food and starvation.[15] Although the compensation records indicate many instances of enslaved men and women executed for theft of livestock, fowls, and other foodstuffs, it was rare for an owner to be fined for this neglect. Regardless of the owner's implication in the slaves' theft of food, possibly resulting from owner neglect, the slave was still executed.[16]

Compensation to slave owners for the loss of enslaved lives represented the extraordinary injustice the enslaved experienced from their criminalization. As Elsa Goveia reminds us, "the slave was a 'thing' rather than a person, a 'property' rather than a subject . . . except when [she] was to be controlled or punished" and their humanity recognized, "almost solely as a potential criminal."[17] Forced to vacillate between object and "criminal subject" at the authority's pleasure, the enslaved were commodified and subjugated in the afterlife. The laws passed to control the enslaved in Barbados ensured only the profit and protection of slave owners and other whites.[18] Just before Governor Dottin mentioned the unjust condemnations of slaves, he discussed improving the militia, issuing new taxes, raising revenue, and decreasing public debt, all of which mitigated the concern he expressed for the "unhappy wretches" condemned to die.[19]

In 1739, two years after Dottin's speech, the Barbados Assembly did revise the Barbados Slave Code of 1688, to which he referred. For the first time, this 1739 law gave slaves the right to testify, although only against free black, mulatto and Indian people, not in their own defense. The provision stated, "[that] hereafter the evidence or testimony of any Slave, where the same is supported with very good and sufficient corroborating circumstances, against a free Negro, Indian or Mulatto, whether Baptized or not, shall be received."[20] Consequently, this change exemplifies the precarious status of free people of color like Rachael Pringle and Joanna Polgreen discussed in Chapter 2, who would still not be able to testify in court under this new act. The act did not reduce the variety of crimes for which a slave could be executed, but it did provide slave owners ten days to appeal before their enslaved were put to death.[21] After Molly's execution, there are a few instances of slave owners petitioning the council to have condemnations overturned or sentences changed to bodily punishment, as exemplified with the cases of Grigg, Bess, and Somers in Chapter 1.[22] Molly's white owner, Isaac Wray, however, did not contest her execution. On Tuesday 19 February 1769, over two months after her death, Wray was issued by the Barbados treasury "payment of the Sum of £25 [Current Money], being the Value of a Negro Woman Slave named Molly, who was Executed according to Law."[23] The governor's efforts in 1737 to institute new rules may well have been inspired by owners' complaints of property loss rather than humanitarian interventions by owners. Nevertheless, this provision did little to rectify the problem of the false accusations Dottin had exposed.

The Act of 1739 included the prevention of "injustice being done to [negroes], & any improper liberties & advantages granted or allowed them, whereby they are countenanced or encouraged in their disobedience to the white inhabitants."[24] Although this language might appear to exemplify an unusual moment of legal and ostensibly moral reflection of the colonial authorities in Barbados, whereas the enslaved may be influenced by agitators to commit crimes, it demonstrates instead the antithesis of such consciousness by ultimately holding the enslaved culpable for their alleged criminal actions. Moreover, the 1739 act also casts doubt on the alleged "criminal" activities of the condemned. It states that the immediate execution of slaves after their sentencing prevents owners from bringing a "write of error" to contest such decisions,

> which, in some instances, [the decisions] hath been thought errone-
> ous; and many times, by the malice or ill will of the prosecutor, as well
> as by the obstinacy of the owner or possessor of the slave complained
> against, the pains of death have, in pursuance of the letter or con-
> struction of the said act, been inflicted on such slaves."[25]

Based on the language of Dottin's 1737 speech on the loss of money from "unjustly condemned slaves" and the "erroneous" decisions of the slave trials alluded to in the 1739 act, executions of enslaved people could occur at the caprice of their owners, the judges of slave courts, and the colonial government. The degree to which this happened is impossible to glean from an archive produced by the colonial authorities who held the power to conceal these incidents. In fact, the archival traces materialize ultimately in the context of financial concern. Yet, from the evidence from the authorities' own admissions, enslaved executions occurred with little to no proof of a crime.

Two more examples illustrate that the circumstances of arbitrary executions persisted into the late eighteenth century across the British Caribbean. Abolitionist James Stephen, Esqr., observed a late eighteenth-century slave court trial in Bridgetown in which four enslaved men were accused of murdering a white plantation doctor. New to the island, Stephen overheard his hosts' whisperings that another white man had actually committed the murder and "who had not however been prosecuted, or publicly charged with the offence."[26] The only witness, a young enslaved girl of fifteen, was sternly warned by the five white men adjudicating the case that if she concealed anything about the guilt of the four men, she would be implicated in the crime and punished accordingly.[27] On her testimony alone the four men, one quite elderly, were initially convicted. Shortly thereafter, two of the four men were subsequently acquitted when their owner provided alibis for them. But, as related to Stephen days later, the elderly Nick and his fellow bondsman Sambo "were literally roasted to death,"[28] for the crime on 26 December at Fontebelle beach on the west side of Bridgetown.[29] Indiscriminate slave executions occurred in Jamaica as well. In 1739, Jamaican assemblymen uncovered instances of slave executions in which slave owners turned their slaves into authorities for very minor crimes or "crimes of no account," in order to collect the compensation for them.[30] Forty years later, in 1779, Captain Thomas Lloyd of the Royal Navy testified to the British Privy Council on the "treatment of negroes" in Jamaica. Lloyd related that he had heard of the "practice of a planter . . . to frame [pretenses] for the execution of his worn-out slaves, in order to obtain the island allowance; and it was supposed he had dealt largely in that way."[31]

This evidence of enslaved "crimes" and "resistance" is usually interpreted solely from the broad perspective of those who created this archive—the slave owners and their representatives. But the concepts of "guilt" and "innocence" are evacuated of meaning in these documents where the opportunity of the enslaved to contest their accusations was illegal, and they could be killed at the whim of slave owners and colonial governments. This is not to discount the possibility that these execution records reveal moments and acts of resistance by the enslaved. Given the instances of runaway slaves and the insurrections that occurred throughout the British Caribbean in this period, it is clear that alternative interpretations are possible.[32] Additionally, as in the case of the unnamed boy in Chapter 3, records show that some enslaved were actually acquitted of the "crimes" of which they were accused but, as in *Crofts v. Harrison*, this occurred only at the discretion of the white male justices and Barbados Council.[33] Certainly the enslaved resisted their brutalization, but focusing only on such moments tragically obscures our view of the inherent injustice of the system of slavery, crime, and punishment to which the enslaved were subjected. Therefore, it is possible to doubt the veracity of an archive produced by people who had "virtually unlimited power over their property."[34] Despite the "empirical" evidence from the colonial authorities themselves that their system of slave crime and punishment was fallible at best, understanding that the enslaved were subject to tyrannical control and random death is evident by simply assessing the nature and language of slave laws passed in these societies. If an enslaved person was not allowed to testify in their own defense, there is no way to determine their role in the events leading to their convictions. Such facts put into question the system of punishment and the concept of culpability. Similarly, the entire archive itself opens to a deeper and broader scrutiny. What are the limits of a legal regime premised on the fungibility of the slave body, a legal regime that acquires the force of law only by excluding the voices of the enslaved?[35] Historical scholarship usually assigns the burden of proof of such atrocities to the scholar attempting to expose the system from the enslaved perspective and from sources produced in a judicial complex that negated recognition of enslaved "innocence." For example, execution cases might illuminate the ease with which bodily diseases became crimes in the minds of anxious white Barbadians. Mortality from disease remained a significant factor in the low life expectancy for both the white and African descent populations throughout the eighteenth century. As Chapter 1 explained, high mortality from yellow fever, smallpox, and dysentery, for example, decimated both the enslaved and white populations and contributed to high infant mortality rates.[36] If, for instance, Molly's alleged victim John Denny became ill—he survived the purported attempt after all—due to spoiled food in a tropical climate or one of the many diseases afflicting the colony, the law worked to assuage colonists' fear by creating an avenue to punish by suspicion and conjecture. Interrogating the unjust structure of slave law and the records emanating from within a system sustained by violence against enslaved people reveals a perspective attentive to their powerlessness and vulnerability to the whims of the white population.

Molly's alleged acts and her criminalization rendered her historically negligible—her words or intentions unrecorded—and demonstrated the power of colonial domination to define and subordinate the entire enslaved population. Yet the contradiction between the slave as property and as a human being who could, through his/her punishment, exemplify a lesson to other humans also points to the nature of the laws governing slaves that gave the authorities power to create any law to serve their own interests. Slave law did not protect the slave from capricious violence. Molly lived in a context of social death—the condition of societal alienation and exclusion—and without the protection afforded to white citizens within the law.[37] This status of enslaved subjectivity also represented a form of what Giorgio Agamben calls the "homo sacer"—"a juridical term from archaic Roman law designating an individual who, in response to a grave trespass, is cast out of the city."[38] Once designated homo sacer, an individual could be "killed with impunity by anyone,"[39] much the like the laws in force in the British West Indies, where "If a person kills a Slave he only pays [his/her] value as a Fine."[40] The difference between the homo sacer in ancient Rome and the enslaved subject in the British West Indies was that the slave did not have to commit "a grave trespass" to be abused with impunity. The fundamental condition of social death and commodification, on which enslaved lives were predicated, took the place of any action on the part of the enslaved to alienate themselves and be cast out of society—indeed, they were already alienated based on racial slavery. Moreover, before the nineteenth century, slave owners in the British West Indies constructed the slave laws without much influence from the English metropole. Thus the character of slave laws directly responded to the local slave systems that related to the slave as property and "as a reasoning subject who possessed intent and rationality solely in the context of criminal liability."[41] The consequence of this construction resulted in the perception of the enslaved as always criminally culpable.

Ultimately, the 1739 law did not end payments to owners or institute protections for the accused slaves. Rather, it sought to reduce the financial burden on the colony, as its final sentences indicate. The Assembly noted that had more care been taken with slave trials pursued under the 1688 act, "the large sums of money that have been paid out of the treasury for such executed slave might and ought to have been saved, as well as the life of such slave preserved."[42] The behavior of colonial authorities in charge of creating, defending, and enforcing the laws governing slaves resulted in the execution of slaves in cases where the sentence "in some instances, hath been thought erroneous," and consequently, the revenue of the colony was unnecessarily depleted.[43] We cannot know the prevalence of false accusations against the enslaved. The balance of archival power was never in their favor. However, the very concept of "crime" as a category in eighteenth-century Barbados must be revisited to expose the ways slave laws collapsed on themselves when one considers the status of a slave in law as a commodity without will.[44] This of course does not mean that the enslaved did not act to challenge the laws and conditions imposed on them. Rather it shows that the power of the colonial authority in Caribbean slave societies was often formidable, arbitrary and deathly, and always at the discretion of the master class. This was the logic of colonial power and makes clear its tragic reach.

Paying attention to the dubious nature of "slave laws" passed in colonial Barbados reveals the extant power wielded by local officials and the susceptibility of the enslaved as potential "criminals" to despotic punishment. One may wonder whether such legal conditions extended to European or creole

Barbadian whites, and if these unjust laws were merely a universal aspect of the violent early modern European penal culture brought across the Atlantic.[45] The poor and dispossessed in England suffered the end of the lash, starvation in the gibbet, the hangman's noose, and the spectacular public displays of their bodily mutilation.[46] To be sure, this contention was raised often during the British abolition debates of the late eighteenth and early nineteenth centuries by pro-slavery advocates, planters, and merchants intending to prove that their slaves were better off than England's poor.[47] In contrast, the evidence suggests the subjection of the enslaved to particular practices of punishment was used beyond its time in England, and as Vincent Brown explains, "the frequency of mutilations and aggravated death sentences, [normally] reserved for traitors in eighteenth-century England, signaled the expansion and racialization of the very concept of treason in the British West Indies."[48] Other scholars concur that in Jamaica and other British West Indian colonies, the systems of laws made stark the distinction between "enslaved and free and valorized the slaveholder's private penal power."[49] That is, there was something particular about punishments on the bodies of the enslaved in the eighteenth-century Caribbean, particularities not diminished in any way by false accusations. These laws expose the vast differences between the edicts by which the enslaved were adjudicated and the laws to which white colonists were subjected.[50] If the violence on white and black bodies appeared similar across the eighteenth-century Atlantic, the manner in which the enslaved were accused, criminalized, and put to death produced vastly different meanings and extended into the afterlife in powerful ways. These included the enslaved being punished for crimes against society at large, committing petty crimes, and cultural practices deemed criminal, and being executed for attempting to commit a crime—none of which constituted the same illegality or resulted in capital punishment on white bodies.[51]

In addition, Molly's apprehension by [Andrew] Edwards, a constable who was paid for her capture, illuminates the regulation of slaves by the larger white society empowering lower-class whites' racial, physical, and judicial power over people of African descent. The records do not indicate that Molly fled the scene of the alleged crime; her "apprehension" (as the records describe it) meant only taking her into custody. She would have been held in Speightown's public gaol (or perhaps in Bridgetown) until her trial. Lacking a formal title such as "esquire," Edwards was likely not an owner of considerable property or a merchant. But most white Barbadians, even those without slaves or wealth, saw themselves as part of the regulatory apparatus. All

whites were invested in the return of runaway slaves, the prevention of gatherings leading to insurrection, and the capture of enslaved "criminals." The
laws obligated planters, overseers, and other white citizens to regulate black
bodies throughout the colony. The technologies of urban enslaved surveillance, for example, emanated from laws punishing enslaved fugitivity and
gatherings.[52] Specific offices of control and regulation (constables, magistrates, judges) established a system of confinement within the town parameters allowing white individuals to interrogate and detain suspected slaves.
Property ownership was not a prerequisite to duty as constable or night
watchman. Constables and night watchers in town were appointed and paid
to regulate and control the enslaved population. The white men of the lower
classes thus clearly benefited from the criminalization of the enslaved population.[53] And, rooted in their belief in the insignificance and disposability of
enslaved life, colonial authorities built into such structures and laws avenues
for abuse, manipulation, and brutality. Consequently, the violence of such a
system produced specific conditions for enslaved women laboring in the island's towns.

(Un)Gendering, Condemnation, and the Law

While Jamaican overseer William Fitzmaurice asserted in 1791 "that [en-
slaved] women have many protections [from violence] which the men have
not, such as being taken as wives by plantation negroes, or to make them
useful for domestic purposes,"[54] the gendered and intimate circumstances of
urban and rural enslavement also led to a particularly gendered path to the
condemnation, execution, and murder of enslaved women. A return to the
scene and archive of Molly's life and death contests the representation that
enslaved women's work in the domestic realm within urban households afforded them easier labor and respite from the violence of sugar production
on the plantations. Attention to the ways enslaved women were condemned
and murdered throughout the island challenges scholarship that invokes the
"possibilities" and "social mobilities" purported to be inherent in both an
urban and domestic female enslaved experience and the presumed opportunities available to enslaved women who lived in intimate spaces with white
men.[55] The fragmented and obfuscating compensation records eliminate our
access to the events and circumstances surrounding their convictions and
deaths. Equally important, urban slave owners hired out enslaved women for

various jobs, including sexual services, which placed them in perilous circumstances. Molly's alleged attempt at poisoning John Denny was a capital offense. We do not know how Molly and John Denny knew each other. The records indicate he was not her owner. Still, we can speak to a range of circumstances typical in urban slavery that may have placed Molly and many enslaved women in precarious domestic arrangements with white men. This is not to impose a sexually invasive reading of Molly's life and death. Rather, pointing out the sexual dangers of enslaved women's domestic work demarcates the possible avenues available for white men to implicate enslaved women in a range of crimes.

Though we cannot access the circumstances surrounding Denny's alleged poisoning, we can assume that Molly interacted with him in the space of the town. She may have been hired out to him either as a stranger or as someone familiar with her owner, Isaac Wray. From later newspaper advertisements it becomes clear that female enslavement in an urban space most likely involved domestic work. For example, in the *Barbados Mercury* on 22 February 1783, such an advertisement specifies: "WANTED to hire, by the month or year, a negro woman, who must be well [recommended], as a good washer, &c. Honest, and constant to her business."[56] Slave owners like Rachael Pringle Polgreen hired out enslaved women to visiting men sailors, seamen, and incoming soldiers, or anyone in need of a laundress, seamstress, cook, or nursemaid. Many enslaved women were listed as without a specific skill or occupation. This meant that many were kept by white men as "concubines" or to serve their sexual needs.[57] Though not usually explicit in the advertisements, the sexually exploitative nature of female enslavement, both rural and urban, made for a threatening and violent servitude.

Molly and other urban women inhabited inferior positions in relation to their owners and with males who hired them on a temporary basis. And though this position of subjugation exposed them to a range of exploitations and abuse, including sexual violence, enslaved women's criminalizations, executions, and posthumous representations forcibly invalidated the possible terror they experienced or how their reaction to such violence may have implicated them in crimes as designated by the existing laws. These crimes included refusing to comply with an owner's demand. The existing laws criminalized Molly's behavior toward John Denny, so her death signifies the power of slave owner's possible retribution for perceived insubordination. Colonial authorities recognized the female body only so far as she reproduced commodities and as an effective laborer. Sexual violations, rape, and molestations against enslaved women were not considered legal offenses, but the responses by black women to such violence were criminalized.[58] This discussion is not intended to reproduce discourses of resistance, but rather to highlight the gendered ideologies and circumstances that brought some enslaved women to their deaths and to account for the consequences of resisting bodily assaults.

Enslaved women experienced ideologies of racialized gender in the ways they were used and commodified by society. Valuing them for their reproductive and labor capabilities, slave owners recognized enslaved gender only as it pertained to the owner's pleasure and profit. Probate records demonstrate slave owners' keen appreciation of the future increase of their slave holdings through childbirth.[59] Yet planters made little distinction between enslaved men and women in their capacity for hard labor. Similarly, when criminalized, the law did not discern between enslaved female and male bodies in punishment or condemnation. Acts passed for the governing of slaves in 1661 were organized around "their status as property; their striking difference in culture; their large numbers; their rebellious behavior."[60] With one exception, slave laws between 1661 and 1762 only refer to gender distinctions when clauses in the laws refer to "her or him" committing a crime or receiving punishment.[61] The exception manifests itself in 1749 when issuing instructions on how to punish "any Negro or other Slave or Slaves . . . for any threatening, fighting or quarreling with one another . . . insolent language," or other acts of insubordination or public misbehavior.[62] Punishment for these "crimes" included being whipped by the jumper or constable up to thirty-nine lashes: "But the punishment of Women big with child may be respited."[63] Concern with harming a potential valued laborer, slave owners and authorities postponed but did not stop punishment of enslaved women.

Unlike the manner in which society afforded white women particular forms of gender recognition, enslaved women's "protection" again stemmed from the white authorities' desire to protect possible damage to enslaved property in the form of unborn slave children. Enforcement of these laws rested in the power of slave owners, making it difficult to discern whether they took pregnancy into consideration when inflicting punishment. In every other regard, enslaved women were punished in the same manner as enslaved men, including "whipping, having one's nose slit, and [burning] in some part of his Face with a hot Iron."[64] There is no evidence that enslaved women were spared from executions by hanging or burning because of pregnancy.[65] What the colonial authority remained most concerned with was punishing enslaved bodies for individual and community example. That gender distinctions were considered arbitrary by colonial legislatures is not surprising. The significance of this, however, concerns the disavowal of experiences mostly particular (but not exclusive) to enslaved females, such as sexual violations and manipulations of their reproductive capabilities.

Not until the Slave Consolidation Acts of the 1780s and 1790s were debated and passed in some British West Indian colonies does the gendering of the female captive appear clearly in the laws.[66] Examples include debates on whipping enslaved women and finding ways to "ease" their labor to conserve reproductive capabilities.[67] Merely articulating differences between black female and male bodies, however, did not necessarily suggest easing the violence against enslaved women. The passage of "ameliorative" laws was fueled primarily by a desire to maintain the reproductive capacities of enslaved laborers in response to the ending of the slave trade, rather than as a protection of enslaved women's bodies.[68] This is significant in understanding how race and gender were constructed in the records and in the status of slaves as "property." In any case, it is evident that punishments during most of the eighteenth century were meted out on male and female bodies without distinction.

Executions of enslaved women occurred throughout the eighteenth century. Many more enslaved men were officially executed in this period than women, about 515 men to approximately 25 women.[69] These numbers reflect executions reported to and adjudicated by the authorities where explicit mention of gender appears in the documents. Several other execution accounts simply state "negro executed" and make it impossible to verify an exact number. Accounts of enslaved people dying from their owner's punishment typically evade the archive. These above numbers then do not reveal a range of enslaved deaths that occurred outside of state authority. Despite this vast numerical difference, enslaved women were vulnerable to male power in specific ways, as well as implicated in violent acts like their male counterparts. Moreover, a desire for an accurate counting risks reproducing the modes of quantification enslaved women and men experienced in their lives and that are characteristic of their archival representations. Instead, an analysis of the gendered and racial violence to which enslaved women were subjected and the illumination of their mutilated historicity, exposes the difficulty of a complete historical account of condemned women.[70] In these compensation records, often only a sentence or two, we can at least attend to the violence against enslaved women and their specific criminalizations that otherwise remain unremarkable to empirically driven historical studies.

In Barbados between 1700 and 1776, at least eleven owners sought compensation for male slaves executed for allegedly murdering enslaved women, while four female slaves were accused of murdering enslaved men and boys. The range of other charges included attempted murder of whites and theft. For example, on 6 August 1700, two petitions seeking compensation for executed female slaves were read in council. Thomas Maycock, Esqr., petitioned the council for a "Negro Woman named Black [Moll] which was Executed by Order of the Justices and freeholders "for Poysoning the Said Maycock."[71] On the same day, "a Petition [was read] of William Martindale praying an Order on the Treasurer for the payment of one Negro Man Named Emperor & one Negro Woman Named Sarah who Attempted to poyson the Said Martindale and was by the Justices Sentenced to Dye & Vallued at Twenty Five pounds Currtt: Money Each."[72] Scholars have noted that for enslaved women who labored in the house as cooks, poisoning may have been readily available as a means of resistance. However, both Maycock and Martindale survived these alleged attempts on their lives. That they both proved healthy enough to submit petitions for compensation of lost property places some doubt as to the actual circumstances of the acts committed against them. In the former case, moreover, we should pay particular attention to the partnership of Emperor and Sarah, who joined together to allegedly poison Martindale. They may have been related or in a relationship with each other. However, there are no surviving trial transcripts of slave execution cases in Barbados or archival evidence explicating the defense arguments of the enslaved, and thus their perspectives and social relationships remain a mystery.

Evidence also exists showing enslaved women's susceptibility to fatal violence from both white and black men. A number of compensation documents indicate that the murder of enslaved women often incriminated enslaved men who were executed for this crime. Systemic patriarchal abuse and white supremacy inherent to slavery placed enslaved women in precarious situations with all men in the society. On 6 August 1700, Addoe was "Sentenced to Dye" for the murder of an unnamed enslaved woman.[73] Seven years later, on 20 February 1727, an enslaved man named Jack "belonging to James Bruce Esqr., was executed as the Law directs" for the murder of an enslaved woman named Tibby.[74] Between 1728 and 1743 the slave courts convicted enslaved men for the murders of Eve, Peggy, [Quamina], and an unnamed enslaved woman.[75] In an unusual instance of a white man accused of murdering a slave, Peter Bascom faced the Court of Exchequer and the Barbados Council for the murder of an unnamed enslaved woman in 1729.[76] On 18 November, "Peter Bascom who attended by a Summons from [the] Board was called in & Ordered to be bound Over to his good behaviour for Six Months by the next Justice of Peace for killing a negro Woman Slave belonging to Mrs. Ashby."[77] Enslaved men convicted of murder most often died for the crime, but Bascom, a white man, escaped such a fate. Court records show that Bascom faced indictment for "destroying property" rather than murder, further objectifying the enslaved woman he killed.[78] Not only did the decision to bind Bascom over for "good behavior" deny the violence against the unnamed woman, but the authors of the historical record make it impossible to account for the nature of her killing. The enslaved woman's trauma from living as a captive and the circumstances of her murder evade the archive, precisely due to the ways slavery denied to the enslaved individual feelings, perspectives, or the legal means to challenge injustice.[79] The enslaved body, first damaged by the system of slavery, in the archive again succumbs to historical power.

It was rare for whites to be convicted of killing enslaved people, and when they were found guilty they were likely to be fined rather than jailed or executed. There had to be sufficient proof that it was done with malicious intent to induce harsher penalties, and whites could not be prosecuted at all if the murder took place during a punishment. According to the 1688 Slave Act, the white murderer of an enslaved person was fined twice the value of the slave to be paid to the owner in addition to another fine bounded him over to court for "good behavior." Mrs. Ashby owned the unnamed woman murdered by Peter Bascom, and Bascom appears in the archive without a formal title. It was likely, then, that Bascom was a lower-class white man, possibly a manager or overseer on Ashby's plantation. Any sexual undertones of the murder remain hidden, as we can only speculate on the nature of the situation. She may also have been killed for not performing work. Nonetheless, the ways black women were brutalized in enslavement could result in their deaths, since perceived resistance could easily lead to violent retribution, especially by those who knew they faced little risk of severe punishment.

Terrifying Power, Productive Afterlives

Five years before Molly was condemned and hanged, Barbados authorities issued a directive against the families of condemned slaves who attended the deaths and seemingly celebrated the freedom of their deceased in the after-life. After the execution of a slave in 1763, Governor Pinfold proclaimed that, "none of the family of the criminal be permitted on any Account or pretense whatsoever, to make or have any plays, Dancings, or Cabells or Riotting at any place whatsoever, in honor to or memory of the said criminal."[80] Molly's death also provoked an intensive and brutal display of power by the white slave-owning elite. This time the authorities went further by mandating that condemned bodies be removed from the slave community.

The governor's order to dispose of executed bodies by weights, and in the sea, not only took away the right of the enslaved population to perform a burial but also removed from white sight all reminders of the violated hu-manity of the enslaved and the possibility of their resistance. Dumping bod-ies into the sea, moreover, served to remind the enslaved of their position by invoking the Middle Passage, which rendered enslaved lives disposable prop-erty. The act of a water interment also performed a second death. As Vincent Brown explains, "[such actions] served to graft sacred and social power onto the bodies of condemned criminals."[81] The "impossibility" for the "Negroes to take [the body] up again" extended the formidable power of colonial au-thority into the realm of death. In Barbados, like Jamaica and other West In-dian colonies, the British colonial authorities executed slaves to display their social and racial power and to suppress the ability of the enslaved to harness "spiritual power" and practices.[82] But this action of removing the body en-tirely revealed an unusual practice—one that took spiritual power away from the enslaved community but also weakened the authorities' own ability to continue to attach political meaning to a specific space and body.

The Governor's 1768 proclamation for burying condemned slaves further di-rected that if the sea were inaccessible, "then the Constables shall have orders to throw the Carcase into an Old, useless Well, without any Ceremony; & to set a proper Watch, & use all diligence to prevent Negroes from visiting the place where the Body is thrown, or paying any Honour or Respect to it."[83] The enslaved community thus lost access to the bodies of the condemned to honor them and to revive spiritual communion. The condemned enslaved person became a "carcasse"—an unrecognizable decomposing "thing." The "old-useless well" also

evoked the characteristics of the condemned body in its criminal, and now im-
minently unhonorable, and inaccessible state. Putting a body out of sight also
reflected the extant contradiction of slave laws and punishment. On the one
hand, it served as a threat to the enslaved and an example of what would happen
if one rebelled against authority. On the other, the white population's need for the
body to disappear exemplified the vulnerability and insecurity of the slave-
owning class. The possibility of being harmed by the enslaved—their alive and
feeling "property"—tugged at the white community's own mortality, and thus
fear was the essential motivation behind these continually revised laws.

Molly's alleged attempt at poisoning was met with the violent reach of the
law to assuage the fears of the white population. But those fears could not be
appeased by death alone. The governor's order for executions taking place
after Molly's community burial reflected white lawmakers' efforts to manipulate the cosmologies of the enslaved by prohibiting their ability to perform
sacred rituals of death on those deemed criminals.[84] Slave trials and executions primarily took place in urban spaces but executioners on the perime-
ters of towns could also comply with the mandate by throwing the body in a
"useless well" and manning the site to prevent the enslaved from accessing it.
The new laws exposed the extent to which authorities recognized black humanity when criminalized and in a submissive, laboring, and "useful" state.[85]
The response to Molly's execution by the enslaved community thwarted the
"lesson" offered, contesting their condition and the inequities of slave law
and forcing a revision of existing laws. Yet in the aftermath of Molly's execution a different aspect of this contestation came to the fore—one that ultimately left the enslaved without power to access their deceased, forcing them
to honor their dead by means other than burial and ritual.

In the end, however, the desire for the terrifying lesson in spectacular
deaths of the enslaved made the Governor change his previous directive. His
December 1768 proclamation apparently caused a flurry of executions done
privately, without ceremony and in a "hurried" manner. On 20 June 1769, a
mere six months after Molly was put to death, the governor issued another
order concerning slave executions. In reference to the condemnation of a
slave named Sam Clift, convicted of robbing a white man, Governor Spry
declares his "Disapprobation of the Sudden Manner in which Slaves Condemned to Death for Capital offences, have been hurried to Execution" and
required that future slave executions invoke more public performance "to
deter Negroes & other Slaves from Committing the [like] Crimes; & that Examples, one of the great Ends of Punishments, may have more Weight, &

become more Notorious."[86] This proclamation explicates the modes of power and performance at play in the corpor(e)al punishment of enslaved bodies. The purpose of public executions for British authorities is that they should, "according to a strict economy, teach a lesson . . . a legible lesson."[87] An eighteenth-century Barbadian, the Reverend H. E. Holder, also speaks to the significance of performance in slave punishment. In his 1785 essay, "The Subject of Negro Slavery,"[88] Holder marks the point at which colonial authority rationalized or constructed a difference between physical and mental punishment. "Not bodily pain, but mental shame," he argues was the most effective means to punish and set an example of behavior.[89] Holder further claims that, "effective punishment [could] reform a rational being." Yet, if the enslaved were legally constituted as "property" what means were appropriate to reform or "mentally shame" a being that had no right to exist beyond chattel? How did "badges of ignominy, or marks of neglect" serve to destroy the "humanity" of the enslaved?[90] What of the ways in which the legal system offered no opportunity for the enslaved to claim innocence?

As a result of the governor's 1768 proclamation, "Examples, one of the great Ends of Punishments," could not be made of crimes or criminals if executions were not announced and committed publicly.[91] The governor soon realized that, "[a] secret punishment is a punishment half wasted"[92] and revised his order, calling attention to the lack of oversight and meaning in recent slave executions. He ordered new execution directives to be announced by drumbeat at the busiest sites in Bridgetown. These included specific instructions for the death of Sam Clift, who was "to be hanged by the Neck until he shall be Dead," and required that another slave participate in the execution.[93] Public notice was also given where the most enslaved people would be gathered: the Milk market, the Cage, and the Great Market.[94] Although the governor wanted more public performance and formality in slave executions, he left unchanged the manner in which the body was to be disposed. After Sam Clift "has Continued Hanging one full hour," his body was to be discarded out of reach of his family and friends.[95] Those executed after Molly, like Clift, were still rowed out to sea, thrown in, and sunk by weights, there to remain untouchable and unrecognizable to the enslaved community. The entire spectacle of punishment thus reproduced white racial power while preventing enslaved communities from mourning.

After her execution, the governor of Barbados characterized Molly as a "wretch"—a despised and miserable person—symbolizing the dismemberment, dislocation, and degradation of those who were criminalized and condemned. This powerful discourse demonstrates the productive nature of her execution, her vexed subjectivity as an "enslaved criminal," and the ways colonial authority pervaded the archive. To be productive, Molly's execution had to extend beyond the act of her death into the empirical representation of her life. Even after Molly was buried, her body was posthumously symbolized in a multiplicity of ways by both the white and enslaved populations. While her execution was intended to set an example to the enslaved that threats against white power would be met with violent ends, her death invoked, for the governor, the danger of collective mourning that might turn against the white population in vengeance.

Descriptions of slave funerals efface the detailed mourning practices of the enslaved and only a few references to their burial practices exist from eighteenth-century Barbados. These records hail from planters' or travelers' observations of black funerals (and probably not of those executed), which are distorted by the white observer's superstitions, worldviews, and prejudices against people of African descent. Richard Ligon remarked on enslaved funeral practices, referring presumably to those on a plantation: "When any of them dye, they dig a grave, and at evening they bury him, clapping and wringing their hands, and making a doleful sound with their voices."[96] In Dr. Pinckard's well-mined travel narrative of the late eighteenth century he describes at length his observations of the "Negro funeral" of a washerwoman named Jenny in Barbados. He writes of the procession of mostly black women, the deceased's "sud-associates" (connoting a life connected to other women) and the manner in which Jenny's body was interred "without either prayer or ceremony."[97] At the closing of the solemnity, Pinckard explains,

> When the whole of the earth was replaced several of the women, who had staid to chant, in merry song, over poor Jenny's clay, took up a handful of the mould, and threw it down again upon the grave of their departed friend . . . crying aloud 'God bless you, Jenny! good-by! remember me to all friends t'other Side of the Sea, Jenny!'[98]

Pinckard's description alludes to linkages between creole (Barbadian born) and African cosmologies and the afterlife, such as the women's pleas to "remember me to all friends t'other Side of the Sea, Jenny!" while Ligon remarks on the "doleful sounds" of their voices. Another British traveler, Nicolas Cresswell, remarked on similar funeral "behavior," witnessing enslaved burial practices of celebration in anticipation of going to "a better place." He writes,

"If one may judge from their [behavior] at their funerals. Instead of weeping and wailing, They are [Danceing] and Singing and appear to be the happiest Mortals on earth."[99] White assumptions of "happiness," "joy," and "dolefulness" among the enslaved populations in burying their dead obscure the sentiments of the enslaved who have lost a loved one. Equally important, white representations of clandestine and sacred moments often impose Christian moralities onto enslaved cultural practices. One such account of black funerals comes from a pro-slavery rebuttal to James Stephen's writings. Stephen's favorable remarks on the impending abolition of slavery in the British West Indies encouraged a passionate response from Alexander Barclay, who resided in Jamaica for twenty-one years.[100] Barclay was a planter. His defense of slavery alludes to the benefits he derived from the institution. In his text *A Practical View of the Present State of Slavery in the West Indies* (1828) he dedicates several pages to the description of the funerary practices of the enslaved population he observed. Barclay's main concerns with such rituals involved introduction of Christian religion into the lives of the enslaved. He derided their "pernicious custom" of nighttime burials, arguing that "the extinction of this most barbarous custom is a very happy and important change."[101] He describes one such funeral where

> The whole night, or the greater part of it, was spent in drumming on the gumbay, singing, dancing, and drinking:—before committing the corpse to the earth the whole party issued forth in a state of intoxication, two of them bearing the coffin on their heads, and proceeded in a body, dancing and singing, to every house in the plantation village, into which the deceased was carried to take leave.[102]

Barclay continues his impassioned description of the ways the "overexcitement by drinking and carousing...incapacitated some of those thoughtless creatures from attending their duty, and consequently subjected them to punishment."[103] White male observations of eighteenth-century black funerary practices deny the enslaved their own cosmologies and solemnity in such experiences. In particular, Barclay pays no attention to the mandatory nature of nighttime funerals. Throughout the eighteenth century, night was the only available time the enslaved could gather together and participate in such rituals, since they were required to work during the day.[104] Moreover, the legal codes passed to prevent black people from congregating may underlie some of Barclay's apprehensions.[105]

Funerals for and by the enslaved may have represented an idea of freedom in death from the violent oppression of their lives. Then, too, they were
an opportunity for the enslaved to come together and socialize if they were
allowed to do so by their owners—the occurrence of which may have been
more common in a town. But simplified representations of these events must
not obfuscate the complexity of emotions experienced by enslaved witnesses.
The enslaved woman Molly, whom they perceived as sharing their plight, was
hanged to death. In mourning her passing, the fear of white authority and
anger must have also been felt. Scholarship on African cosmologies and funerary practices in Barbados and the West Indies do important work to fill in
such silences in the traditional archive.[106] Rather than reproduce that extensive material, this discussion instead illuminates the intensity of power mobilized by Barbados authorities and present in the archive that serve to
profoundly silence and misrepresent the enslaved sacred practices and
sentience.

The reach of white power into both the lives and deaths of the enslaved
population proved extensive and overwhelming. The enslaved had no voice
in the court of law, no right to challenge their conviction or to argue against
the brutality of their treatment, and little control over the manner in which
the condemned passed from life into death. It is tempting to ask how many
of the enslaved suffered oceanic disposals, and for how long these proclama-
tions were in force as a way to signify the impact of such decisions on executions and their aftermath. More important, however, is that the colonial
authority had such power, as well as the level of indifference they exhibited
to enslaved lives and sacred practices. Revisiting the violence against and
posthumous vilification of an enslaved woman condemned by colonial authorities exposes the unrelenting power they exerted, not only in Barbados
but in other British colonial slave societies. It also shows, through an interrogation of the arbitrary enforcement of slave laws, that concepts of "guilt" and
"innocence" held little meaning. As much as one could access and wield
modes of resistance to such inequity, colonial power often had the violent
final word. Molly's death, along with those of other women executed publicly
or privately by the colony, represents the gendered conditions by which enslaved women found themselves faced with various forms of punishment.
Urban enslaved women like Molly encountered many forms of danger in the
socio-sexual conditions of their labor.[107] Enslaved women throughout Barbados also suffered violence at the hands of men of all races. The majority of
such women did not elicit historical documentation beyond their

compensation records. Reading along the bias grain of traditional archival sources produced in a system of violence against racialized and gendered subjects creates space for imagining the experiences and perspectives of enslaved women in all their, and our, uncertainties. Such records require this work.

CHAPTER 5

"Venus": Abolition Discourse, Gendered Violence, and the Archive

When abolitionists wanted to convey a sense of slavery's horror, they told stories about women. They emphasized the violations of women's bodies that accompanied enslavement—the sexual brutality, the vicious flogging, the enforced nakedness.

—Diana Paton, *No Bond But the Law*

One instance in particular happened during my stay in Bridge Town, in Barbados, that appeared to us truly shocking—Returning home one evening with Major Fitch, of the 90th regiment, later than usual, we heard for a considerable distance the most dreadful cries that could come from a human being.

—Captain Cook of the 90th Regiment

In 1780 or 1781, a young unnamed enslaved woman "about nineteen years old," chained to the floor inside her owner's tippling house near the "square in [Bridge Town]," cried out so loudly she could be heard from "a considerable distance." Exhausted, bleeding, and near death, she struggled with consciousness after three separate beatings, each thirty-nine lashes, with the cowskin whip wielded by her owner. It was the sound of her straining voice— "the most dreadful cries that could come from a human being"—and the sharp noise of the whip hitting her body that brought Captain Cook and Major Fitch of the 90th Regiment inside the tavern to witness and attempt to stop her punishment. She heard them demand entrance. She felt the blows on her body grow stronger. The door broke open; the men entered with hands on their swords. Her owner jumped behind the counter and an argument ensued. She heard her owner defend himself with the law. Only thirty-nine lashes at a time. Thirty-nine more lashes are due before daybreak. It was within the law.[1]

Sometime between 1761 and 1782, another unnamed enslaved woman struggled to still her swinging body as she hung by her wrists from the branches of a tree in a yard in Savannah La Mar, a coastal town in Jamaica. Her toes "just [touched] the ground." She screamed loudly, echoing her torture through the streets though she was not being whipped as was a common punishment for the enslaved. Her screams intensified when she swung forward making contact with the fire at the end of the stick held by her owner. He was burning her "private parts" in the intervals of her pendular movement. As she "shrunk from" the burning stick, her momentum only "returned her to her former position, when she again met the fire, and so repeatedly swung to and fro." Drawn to the scene by "the sound of her cries" Mr. Ross, Esqr., yelled out to her master to desist in this activity, and she watched as the stranger threw rocks at him "over the fence . . . which he [believed] had the effect of stopping the punishment." Ross was mortified by the "horrid cruelty" and related the story around town. It was received with "universal detestation," as "the perpetrator was by no means a man of character or reputation."[2]

Henry Hew Dalrymple was among one hundred or more white men examined by the house committee "appointed for the examination of witnesses on the slave trade [and slavery in the West Indies]" between 1788 and 1792. Dalrymple, served as "a lieutenant in the 75th regiment, in garrison at Gorée [Island, Senegal]" during the American War for Independence.[3] He would be appointed then asked to resign as Governor of the initial Sierra Leone settlement, to which the British sent over eleven hundred free(d) blacks relocated from settlements in New Brunswick and Nova Scotia.[4] Some would consider him an abolitionist. He once owned and sold a plantation in Grenada.[5] The committee asked Dalrymple, "were Negro Slaves, during your residence in the West Indies, considered as being, and as having always been, under the protection of law?" He replied:

I do not believe that they were considered as under protection of the law . . . In June last [1789], in the town of Saint George, in Grenada, I saw a Negress who was brought there to have her fingers cut off: this girl had committed a fault, and run away to avoid punishment. After being absent two days, she was brought to her master, who suspended her by the hands, and in that situation she was flogged in so cruel a manner that her back, breast, belly, and thighs, were cut in many places; she was left suspended by the hands till her fingers mortified . . . this happened Several months after the new act for the Protection of Slaves was passed. I saw a Negress who had no teeth, though a young woman, and she informed me that her mistress had with her own hands pulled out her teeth, and besides given her a severe flogging, the marks of which she bore upon her body at the time, though she had been flogged three years before.[6]

These accounts of unnamed women being whipped, burned, and brutalized embody the conditions of (urban) slavery, of public visibility and vulnerability, sexual violation, alleged criminality, troubled agency, and death—all of which have been considered in the previous chapters. The specificity of urban space and slavery led to both domestic intimacy with white owners and a public spectacle of torture, using technologies of punishment distinct to port towns.[7] Everyday acts of violence on enslaved women also included sexualized punishments, though they are rarely archivally documented, and even more rarely through the voice of the victim.[8] The supposition that these women were guilty of a crime permeates the witnesses' accounts, however shocked they are by the "horrid cruelty."[9] It is possible that some of the women died from their wounds, but their fate remains impossible to document.[10] Instead, these four unnamable women become visible through violence, and this is the state in which they remain in history. How "does one recuperate lives entangled with and impossible to differentiate from the terrible utterances that condemned them to death?"[11] How do we write a history of the voiceless and violated?

There are questions that cannot be answered. Would the women have someone to attend to their wounds? Would they be attended to at all? How does a slave acquire special food to eat because she has no teeth? How was a woman treated by those expecting labor when she had no fingers? How did the women remember or carry the pain inflicted on them? Did the young woman chained to the floor die? Who would bury her? The woman terrorized with burning—how does one attend her wounds without further violation?[12] These brief glimpses of tortured enslaved women emerge only where authority is enacted, claimed, and life taken away—they come to us through encounters with power.[13] If any of these women survived such brutality, they would have had to continue living with the men and women who abused them—or be sold to strangers. They were property. There will always be an inadequacy in their recounting.

The above accounts originate in the *House of Commons Sessional Papers* commonly used in histories of Caribbean slavery. Generated by the Privy Council during the slave trade abolition debates of the late eighteenth century, these images represent the horror of white male witnesses, abolitionist presentations of the inhumanity of slavery, and the British government's exploration of making slavery less destructive on enslaved bodies and more financially productive.[14] These enslaved women's hypervisibility is distinct from Rachael Pringle Polgreen's only in their anonymity. They all emerge in the frame of capital. In several volumes of interviews, a diverse array of white men (ship surgeons, infantrymen, military officers, overseers, planters, clergymen, and abolitionists) related violent scenes of enslaved women's physical victimization from a shocked and horrified white male gaze. The opening scenes of this chapter rewrite some of these events from the standpoint of the violated enslaved women to challenge the power of archival discourse that privileges the self-interests of both the male witnesses and the Privy Council and effectively erases the subjectivity of the enslaved. Changing the structure of these archival records and switching the pronouns from "I" (witnessed) to "she" (saw) creates an epistemological reorientation. We witness the scene from the enslaved women's view as they might have seen the white men, both punishers and observers. As each scene is retold, the archival voice—the voice of power and authority— is increasingly present and invasive, demonstrating the process of archival erasure and the silencing of enslaved women in pain even as they seem to be the focal point of the narratives. Our empathy, like that of the white male witnesses, merely projects our feelings of horror onto the women, "at the expense of the slave's suffering."[15] Through this archival presentation they are again lost to historical analysis. These documents demand an ethical reconsideration.

Diana Paton posits that "the female slave flogged by her sadistic master was the most powerful image generated by the British abolition campaign."[16] She argues that historians' focus on the whipping of enslaved women, to the exclusion of other forms of violence, including the carceral, is due to the abundant archive of abolitionist "propaganda."[17] Concentrating attention on corporeal punishment, Paton contends, manufactures false dichotomies between free and enslaved, English people and Caribbean slaves, and effaces important aspects of slavery including the use of prisons, and the significance of state punishment.[18] While acknowledging this important historiographical shift toward the continuity of punishment in slavery and "freedom," the following discussion revisits the records of the British abolition debates to purposely dwell on the violence enacted on enslaved women's bodies. Attention to the infliction of pain on enslaved female bodies—to the "practice's real significance"—is an effort to find a way to methodologically and ethically engage with these violated and briefly glimpsed lives. These narratives unavoidably "[traffic] between fact, fantasy, desire, and violence,"[19] arouse white witnesses, and inevitably reproduce the originary violence.[20] Employing what Nicole Fleetwood terms "excess flesh"—that is, "the ways in which black female corporeality is rendered as an excessive overdetermination and as overdetermined excess"[21]—I focus on the "spectacular" and hypervisible reproduction of violated enslaved bodies in the previous and following analysis, to higlight both the consistent invisibility of enslaved female subjectivity as well as the ways the repetitive, "excessive" images of black female bodies generated by abolitionists can be deemed as excessive and therefore unreliable historical material. Similar to the exposition of the mutilated historicity of enslaved women like Jane and Molly analyzed in previous chapters, these similarly harrowing accounts require an analysis that at once acknowledges these acts of violence, highlighting how we consume these narratives, and gestures to another mode of historicization.[22] Offering an alternative way of witnessing these scenes produces a hermeneutic refraction that allows us to ethically account for these extinguished lives, although it cannot fully subvert the power of the archive to silence and commodify. This methodological labor is an attempt to carefully bring them into the historical record. Moving through such an archive of fleeting and "excessively" violated life requires attending to the historical impossibilities of representing and historicizing their pain while persisting in narrating enslaved women's stories.

This final chapter confronts the space between historiography, the archive, and theories of enslaved female subjection. It will show how enslaved women disappear by the violent circumstances of their lives, the shapes in which they materialize by the form and historical context of the archive, and the ways they are rendered unreachable by historiographical arguments and even critical questionings. In other words, I contend with the European representations of enslaved women's bodies, the historiography of abolition, and the difficult questions posed by scholars on the impossibility of recovering enslaved women without reproducing the violent circumstances from which they emerge in the archives. The first part of this work contextualizes the British parliamentary debates and the evidence gathered in response to petitions for and against abolishing the slave trade. Cognizant of the profit amassed through sugar production, parliamentarians sought information in order to save the enterprise of slavery while considering ending the slave trade. The questions asked by the Privy Council, the House of Commons, and the House of Lords directly addressed the treatment of slaves in the West Indies and consequently centralized the "deviant" character of enslaved women. Planters, merchants, and parliamentarians recognized enslaved women as a vital demographic in the colonies—an essential cog in the machine of profit. These abolition discourses both shape and construct the archive in which the violent accounts of the enslaved women noted above appear. Attention to the production, form, and content of these debates illustrates the ways this archive constructs these women only through the (white) male gaze and the record of the trauma inflicted on their bodies. It thus illuminates the vexed and violated subjectivities of enslaved women who were evoked by pro- and anti-abolitionist advocates through discussions of their fecundity, sexual excesses, and in scenes of subjugation.

Though constantly evoked in the Privy Council report, enslaved women (and men) are excluded from recounting their own violations except through the voices and interpretations of various classes of white men. This archival silence effectively mutes the very subjects of this inquiry and profoundly suppresses enslaved subjectivity, not only in the moment of its creation but also in its subsequent uses in histories of this abolition movement.[23] Elucidating the discourses of racialized gender in these debates, as well as the ubiquity and brutality of the violent images that dominate this archive, challenges us to grapple with the historicizing of enslaved female subjects. The final section of this study offers a close reading of this chapter's opening scenes to consider the enslaved women's "dreadful cries" as another genre of humanity and a historical opening evoked rhetorically in the throes of trauma and the threshold of death.

Abolition and the Reproduction of (Gendered) Slavery

Historical accounts of abolition offer limited discussions of the production of this archive, leaving in shadow precisely how the Privy Council generated questions and how those questions shaped the testimony of witnesses in particularly gendered ways. Recent exceptions include the work of Seymour Drescher, Diana Paton, and Sasha Turner. Drescher, not dealing specifically with the gendered aspects of the debates, engaged the issue of shifting British political perceptions in *Capitalism and Anti-Slavery* in 1987. He argues that the Council's inquiry constituted a shift in the way the British political system viewed Africa and the West Indies, and that the questions raised shamed Europeans who accepted the "immoral standards" of African practices of enslavement in West Africa. Essentially, Drescher claims that these inquiries and debates constituted a reprimand of Europeans who conducted business under "African" standards.[24] In 1996, Diana Paton, using records from the emancipation debates of the early nineteenth century, also traces the gendered discourse of parliamentarians and their consideration of banning the use of the whip on enslaved women.[25] The debates of Paton's study occurred immediately prior to emancipation in the British West Indies in 1838 and concerned the issue of controlling and integrating "free" laborers into British Jamaican society. It is crucial to pose similar questions of the late eighteenth-century period, when British parliamentarians and West Indian planters were not envisioning an immediate emancipation as they debated the abolition of the slave trade and to expose how these earlier debates framed those that followed. Finally, Sasha Turner's work documents how enslaved women experienced the discourse of the slave trade debates on plantations in Jamaica, as planters attempted to preserve their childbearing capabilities.[26] In this earlier period of debates, questions about West Indian slavery were gendered in ways that reflected planters' and parliamentarians' assurance that slavery could be made more "humane" even as production was increased.[27] These issues point to the reification of property relations and economic concerns that were coterminous with humanitarian issues, in turn marking the inherent flaws in humanitarian enterprises.[28] And, during this abolition movement, contemporaries were specifically inundated with accounts of whippings of both enslaved women and men. Moreover, these excessive representations of violence often came from ordinary people, allowing us to understand quotidian forms of violence against enslaved people prior to the nineteenth century in places like Barbados, where prisons did not proliferate as in Jamaica and "ameliorative" legislation was not adopted until after 1825.[29] My discussion does not seek to reproduce the important social histories of this moment completed by scholars such as those mentioned above. Instead, this exploration engages violence, the archive, and enslaved women's historical representation to explore another method of historical inquiry that at once acknowledges the discursive and physical violence simultaneously enacted on enslaved women, and the distortions of their historicity. In order to contextualize the violent images in the late eighteenth-century debates and point to the production of equally violent gendered discourses about enslaved women, a brief sketch of late eighteenth-century abolition activity is crucial.

The development of this early British abolition movement reached a critical momentum in the late 1780s, as did the evidence gathered by the Privy Council, leading abolitionists, and both houses of Parliament that are the substance of this archive. Abolitionist sentiment percolated early in the eighteenth century. Legal cases brought by Granville Sharpe in the 1770s defending the freedom of slaves brought to England by their (Caribbean) owners were important precursors to the critical moment of parliamentary action in 1788. In addition, the first petitions submitted by English Quakers (with support from Philadelphia abolitionists), though subsequently ignored by Parliament, found their way to the chambers in 1783. Thwarted by a strong West Indian planter lobby, the first efforts at gaining a governmental debate on abolition failed to take hold.[30] Disappointed but not daunted, the Quaker abolitionists continued to publish pamphlets and looked for opportune moments to press their issue in Parliament. Until 1787, abolitionist activists operated in relative isolation from each other across England, but in May that year Quakers and other activists formed the highly organized Society for Effecting the Abolition of the Slave Trade (London Committee), setting up a vital base from which to launch national campaigns.[31] Thomas Clarkson set out across the country to gather "evidence" and support for the movement.[32] By the end of the year, major campaigns in Manchester, London, and Birmingham delivered approximately 60,000 signatures in support of abolition, taking the government and pro-slavery business community by surprise.[33]

Once these sentiments were transformed into an abolition movement, the Society for Effecting the Abolition of the Slave Trade—comprised of Quaker abolitionists and social reformists like Clarkson—gathered petition signatures and "evidence" on the deplorable conditions of the African slave trade.[34] These were submitted to Parliament to pressure them into action. William Wilberforce, a minister of Parliament from Yorkshire, assisted the movement by bringing the debates into Parliament, and his personal friend William Pitt, the prime minister, opened several debates on the floor. This movement, with its origins earlier in the eighteenth century, has been superbly documented by a number of historians.[35]

This brief overview simply provides context to the beginning of the Privy Council inquiry.

In February 1788, William Pitt "launched an inquiry of the privy council committee for trade and plantations into the slave trade."[36] This Privy Council committee gathered witnesses to give evidence on the conditions of the slave trade and slavery in the British West Indies.[37] The first round of testimony was taken from men who directly benefited from the economics of slavery and who defended the trade and West Indian slavery in stark terms.[38] Informants included colonial agents, the governors, and councils for each island, who responded to formulaic questions in reference to the laws, treatment of slaves, conditions of sugar production, and practices of obtaining African captives. They even presented material relating to the success of the French Caribbean colonies such as Saint Domingue, which at the time far surpassed the sugar exportations of all the British West Indian islands combined.[39] This latter conversation illuminated particular anxieties about French prosperity and trade, ignorant of the dramatic events of the Haitian Revolution that would unfold just a year later. David Brion Davis remarks that the "slave-trade investigations embodied the spirit of the scientific Enlightenment;" a moment to accumulate "facts," and, "to reject unprovable claims, including those arising from humanitarian zeal."[40] Interestingly, Davis argues that "the investigations can be seen as a ritual of expiation that temporarily exorcised the slave trade's worst evils." For parliamentarians, bearing witness to the terrifying testimony "was morally preferable . . . than to pretend that the evils did not exist."[41] Yet, this kind of empathy transfers the inaccessible experience of enslaved pain and torture to the men's own moral status, vindication, and guilt. The enslaved again become, "a vessel for the uses, thoughts and feelings of others"—of abolitionists, parliamentarians, planters, and merchants.[42] What expiation did the subjects of the inquiry gain? Whatever ethical reprieve the testimony may have allowed the MPs, it also made clear that the British government and parliamentarians assumed that sugar production and slavery could be made more efficient even while considering the end of the slave trade.

Scholars agree that 1787–88 was a key moment and that the abolition movement was reinvigorated in 1792 after the defeat of an abolition bill initiated by Wilberforce in 1791.[43] Events across the Atlantic in the mid- to late eighteenth century, including the Seven Years' War, the Somerset case, the end of the American Revolution, the beginning of the revolution in Saint Domingue, the slave uprising in Dominica, and the British acquisition of former French Caribbean colonies (Treaty of Paris, 1763), all affected the agendas of pro- and anti-abolition lobbyists.[44] Although the slave trade was not to end for another fifteen years, the discussions in 1792 set the ground-work for future debates about the fate of slavery in the British Empire.

The various pieces of the Privy Council report comprise documentation about different aspects of the slave trade and slavery in each of the British West Indian islands. Over the four years between 1788 and 1791, the Privy Council also interviewed significant numbers of lower and middle-class white men who made their living on the sea or in the West Indies.[45] Thomas Clarkson helped to gather these witnesses, including soldiers, ship workers, and clergymen, in hopes they could provide first-hand accounts and obser-vations of both the slave trade from Africa to the West Indies and conditions of slavery in the British Caribbean colonies.[46] Evidence was also given by avowed abolitionists, including Clarkson himself, James Ramsey, Olaudah Equiano, and Ottobah Cugoano. Formerly enslaved themselves, Equiano and Cugoano published widely read narratives of their captivity.[47] Lists of ques-tions were also sent by the Privy Council to be filled out by governors, agents, and governing councils of the individual islands. The questions covered the laws protecting slaves, their clothing and provisioning, their working hours and conditions, and information on mortality among the enslaved popula-tion. In addition, the Council asked about agricultural innovations on the plantations, including use of the plow and oxen for improving sugar cultiva-tion. The testimonies of men on both sides of the debate fill multiple volumes with accounts of the violence of the slave trade and Middle Passage, public spectacles of punishment in West Indian towns, and the unrelenting labor of plantation slaves. Unsurprisingly, despite the significance of white women to the economic enterprises of British Caribbean colonies such as Barbados and Jamaica, no women appear in the interviews due to patriarchal perceptions that political spaces were inappropriate venues for white women.

Nonetheless, many of the interview questions were specifically gendered, such as those about the conditions in which enslaved women reared children. For example, John Orde, Esqr., a British Navy lieutenant who spent ten years in the West Indies, was asked by the committee if the practice of "rewarding the mother who has borne and brought up a certain number of children" would increase the enslaved population in lieu of the trade. Orde replied in the affirmative because, he claimed, "at present Negro women are certainly averse to bearing children, and careless in bringing them up . . . [as] having children interrupts their libidinous pursuits, and makes them less desirable to the men."[48] Denied the ability to "mother," allusions to enslaved women in these debates ungendered and sexualized their bodies simultaneously. Robert Hibbert, Esqr., representing West Indian proprietors and merchants, responded to a similar question. He was asked whether "Negroes increase or diminish generally," in Jamaica? Hibbert confidently argued their decrease on sugar estates was due to the fact that "the proportion of males on most sugar-estates exceeds that of females; the lock-jaw, to which infants are subject within a few days after their birth . . . and the indiscriminate intercourse with the other sex, which the women are too apt to accustom themselves to when young."[49] Thomas Norbury Kerby, Esqr., a native of Antigua, concurred that the high mortality rate or "decrease" of enslaved children was caused primarily by "the inattention of their mothers—as they are apt to consider young children an incumbrance and a great bar to their pleasures; and as it is a means of preventing their nocturnal meetings and dances."[50] Deflecting the responsibility for the debilitating conditions causing low birth rates and disavowing the dangers to enslaved women in refusing sexual predation of white men, these testimonies render enslaved women deviant and affectively deficient. And, this is how they remain in the archive.

Unsurprisingly, most of the planter and merchant interviewees insisted that "every possible kindness, care, and attention" was given to "negroes" by their masters."[51] In order to turn attention away from the violent modes of production under which enslaved women and men labored, the rampant sexual violence committed against enslaved women, and their desperate efforts to maintain their own wealth, elite residents of the West Indies depicted enslaved women as lascivious and therefore the cause of high infant mortality. Yet contradictions abound in these images. Given the cultural commentary on slave owners and their enslaved "concubines" and the reality of short life expectancies on sugar plantations, the representations of female slaves as hypersexualized cannot be reconciled with the known dangers to black lives on Caribbean sugar islands.[52] Repeated references to enslaved women's uncontrollable sexuality evoked a racialized and gendered image that harkened back to the seventeenth century.[53] The utility of these images for the anti-abolitionists provided an implicit acknowledgment of enslaved women's vital role in the reproduction of slavery and the obsessive attention to enslaved women's bodies by English men since the earliest contact with Africa.[54] Their ability to insert steadfast and denigrating images of enslaved women into the debate about the slave economy exemplifies an important aspect of white male power—their authority to commit devastating acts on the enslaved while blaming them for their condition. This discourse was not simply the language of the abolition debate; the images followed enslaved women into freedom.[55] Furthermore, the Privy Council did not challenge these representations. They merely asked how changes in law, religious instruction, and punishments might change enslaved women's behavior and result in economic gains through increased (re)production. Few islands actually adopted ameliorative slave laws except Jamaica, Grenada, and Dominica and some of the Leeward Islands. These "Consolidated Slave Acts" did little to change the conditions of enslaved lives.[56]

Other depictions of sexualized enslaved women emerge from men who were considered "neutral" on the issue of the slave trade or supported abolition. Doctor Jackson lived in Jamaica from 1774 to 1778. Testifying before the committee, he described various instances of excessive cruelty to the enslaved in the country around Savannah La Mar. His varied observations of plantation life, including the behaviors of white creole women, led him to "[perceive] that the condition of the Negroes was hard, and that their treatment was cruel."[57] Seemingly sympathetic to the enslaved people who endured such abuse, Jackson stated several times that their punishment "appeared to me extremely severe," and that "it was not generally understood that . . . the Negroes had such a power [as redress for cruel treatment]." He added that, "he could not perceive, after a good deal of knowledge and acquaintance with [slaves], that they were at all inferior to unlettered White men."[58] Yet when prompted, the doctor, like his anti-abolition counterparts, constructed a sexualized image of lascivious enslaved women. Implicitly acknowledging the exploitation of female slaves, he noted that "there was no restraint" in "intercourse between the White people and the plantation Slaves." He certainly recognized that brutal labor conditions and "the idea of raising children to be subject to cruel treatment, often renders enslaved women indifferent to [motherhood]."[59] In the end, however, Jackson reverted to the depiction of enslaved women as sexual aggressors. On being asked if cruel treatment motivated the women to procure abortions, Jackson answered, "It is reasonable to suppose it so—I will add another reason why Negro women of good form are unwilling to have children; that it diminishes their charms for the White men."[60] Even enslaved men did not escape this discursive sexualization of aggressiveness. Dr. Jackson remembered "Negroes having been castrated for trespass on the Black Mistress of the overseer."[61]

Similarly, Major General Tottenham provided evidence about the severe cruelty against enslaved men and women and the special vulnerability of women to sexual exploitation. Tottenham began his inquest stating that in Barbados the slaves were "treated with the greatest cruelty."[62] His sympathy for the plight of the enslaved compelled him to give evidence against the trade, "and look upon it as a duty incumbent on me."[63] A witness to devastating slave sales in which "refuse" slaves were abandoned "and left in the yard to die, for nobody gave them anything to eat or drink,"[64] Tottenham made clear his opinion of the desperate plight of those in bondage on the island. Yet he too reinforced the underlying belief that the enslaved embodied immorality, though through no fault of their own. When asked by the Privy Council if abolishing the slave trade would lead to significant "injury to West Indian Islands and Great Britain," Tottenham replied:

> I think a present abolition would be attended with very serious consequences; but if those unfortunate beings were put under proper regulations, not left to the tyranny of their cruel masters, and should be instructed to know the difference between virtue and vice, and the propagation of them was properly encouraged, and encouragement held out to them to behave well, I think that at a future period, that the Slave Trade would die away of itself.[65]

The subtext of both the questions raised by the Privy Council and the answers given concerned the dehumanization of enslaved women both as potential "breeders" to replenish the enslaved population and as hypersexual predators. Deindividuated and silenced, enslaved women performed a pivotal role in the debates on abolition. Planters blamed them for the decline in the enslaved population. Abolitionists evoked their "immorality" to illuminate the corruption of slavery. These images also ignored important aspects of enslaved women's reproductive lives. The above accounts, given by white male observers, focused solely on the role of enslaved women's "licentious behavior" and forced on them an agency to control their sexual lives that did not exist—it was impossible for them not to consent to the advances of sexually predatory planters or other white men. Similarly, these white men disregarded enslaved women's own refusal to bear children and to resist planter's efforts to "breed" them, whether through abortive measures or infanticide.[66] No doubt enslaved women sometimes chose sex partners, but the longue durée of these unions could not be guaranteed. Ultimately, the environmental and physical reality of sugar production damaged enslaved women's reproductive capabilities to such a degree that they were rendered infertile or gave birth to children who died young.[67]

These depictions of enslaved women—both seemingly sympathetic and hostile—deflect the violence of slavery onto enslaved women and enact a form of archival violence. This violence occurred in multiple forms—in the depictions of beaten and tortured female bodies from the titillated gaze of male witnesses, in the images of enslaved women's aggressive sexuality to which both black and white men fell victim, and in the disembodied and voiceless iterations of enslaved women who emerge in the archive only in distorted form. This embodiment—of beaten, bloody, brutalized, sexually predatory black women—produces an epistemological problem that the archive cannot resolve. Ultimately, this epistemic violence simultaneously led to and justified the objectification and violation of enslaved women. More than this, the violent images of enslaved women being beaten and tortured combined with the aggressive sexualized discourse consolidated white (colonial) patriarchal power.

Attention to the production of this massive quantity of evidence provides another way to understand the intention behind archival production and power. Simply citing these records as historical evidence only skims the surface of meaning. An analysis that centers on how gender shaped the production of this archive illuminates a strikingly different epistemology—one in which white men and women battered, abused, and disfigured enslaved African and Caribbean women physically, discursively, and archivally. This challenges our ability to historicize and account for their perspectives in the imperial debate. Moreover, this approach demonstrates how central enslaved women were to abolition debates, to the slave economy and to the planters, parliamentarians, and abolitionists who perpetuated their historical objectification. The task then is to expose how women gained this critical position while striving to create an accounting attentive to this historical disfigurement.

Screaming Through Silence

Lunae, 7° die Martii 1791
Captain Cook called in; and further examined.
May not the law abovementioned be evaded by splitting one crime into several and at short intervals giving the Slave the limited number of lashes for each?

One instance in particular happened during my stay in Bridge Town, in Barbados, that appeared to us truly shocking—Returning home one evening with Major Fitch, of the 90th regiment, later than usual, we heard for a considerable distance the most dreadful cries that could come from a human being; and as we approached the square in Bridge Town, we found that those cries came from the house of a man that sold liquor, and we heard repeated application of the whip to a creature whom we apprehended to be dying . . . a Negro girl of about nineteen, chained to the floor, and nearly expiring with agony and the loss of blood.[68]

Do any particular instances of wanton cruelty, as distinguished from ordinary punishments, occur to your recollection?

[Mr. Ross]
It is possible I may recollect some, though, never having it in contemplation of being examined on such a subject, I cannot say I have particularly recorded them in my mind. One instance of punishment out of the common line, of a very extraordinary nature, does now occur to my recollection, though it is a great number of years ago, at Savannah la Mar. I recollect my attention being attracted by the shrieks of some poor wretch suffering torture within a yard or [inclosure], and on looking through, I observed a young female suspended by the wrists to the branch of a tree, and her body exceedingly agitated, swinging backward and forward.[69]

How do we "exhume the [enslaved] lives buried under this prose? Is it possible to tell a story of degraded matter and dishonored life that doesn't delight and titillate, but instead ventures toward another mode of writing?"[70] This final section raises questions about archival and historical representation, subjection (becoming a subject and being subjugated), and violence as a political tool exchanged between the violator and violated.[71] The above transcripts are reproduced in order to remind us where we began this chapter and to bring the language of the archive back into critical view. Each scene reenacts what parliamentarians and the white male witnesses regard as extraordinary violence—outside the normative and acceptable modes of pain required to sustain slavery. The women's momentary mentions, thrust into the archive through brute force, remain historical ephemera. Telling a story of "dishonored life" requires a refusal to let our desires for empirical substantiation remand these fleeting violated lives back into oblivion.

As described above, enslaved women's experiences of violence are often alleged to be exaggerated by abolitionists, spectacular and sexualized by the male witnesses, in part because the violence exceeds our ability to reach the enslaved female subjects beyond their terror. While it is not possible to avoid reproducing the violence of slavery and the archive if one wants to account for violated lives, we can interrogate the meaning and consequences of such images.

In the above accounts, the enslaved women's embodied distress is located within a narrative of the heroic white male witnesses who attempted to stop the punishment, castigate the perpetrator of "bad character," and save the women from further torture or death. Each man describes his intervention, his view, her body, and his shock. The recounted scenes are less about understanding the enslaved female subjects or their agony and more about showing the moral outrage of the white male witness and the depravity of the abuser. Similar to the questions posed by the Privy Council, which was ultimately uninterested in the humanity of enslaved women and men, these brutalized enslaved women become further objectified in the descriptions of their bodies, hanging or chained, burned or whipped. Captain Cook's entire testimony about slavery in the West Indies, in which the first account was found, focused on five episodes of brutally violated black bodies in Bridgetown, most of them female. These retellings reflect his captivation with the sadistic and sexually suggestive punishment of slaves, even as he articulated sympathy with the women he described. This violence was perceived as exceptional by the parliamentarians, "as distinguished from ordinary punishments"—an aberration in its excess.[73] Its excessiveness—part of the agenda of abolitionist propaganda—makes it empirically unreliable. Enslaved women's denigrated position survives from their constrained archival presence into the historical narratives we attempt to write.

In other accounts this violence is routinized to such a degree as to render it unremarkable. The Council asked Mr. Coor, a Millwright and overseer in Jamaica, if "any instances [have] fallen within your notice, wherein, besides regular punishments, Negroes have been treated by the overseers with capricious cruelty?"[74] Mr. Coor, testified that over time he became desensitized to violence on enslaved bodies such that, "by degrees and custom it became so habitual, that I thought no more of seeing a Black man's head cut off than I should now think of a butcher cutting off the head of his calf."[75] Similarly, asked if he, "[grew] less sensible to the severity of [slave] treatment," Mr. John Terry, of Askrig, Yorkshire testified that in Grenada, "I did; and in time

became more inured to it."[76] The repetition of and white inurability to violence on black bodies constructed enslaved subjectivity through domination,
which enabled parliamentarians, abolitionists and planters alike to justify violence that was socially acceptable on black bodies.[77] The Privy Council
asked witnesses the same question many times in different configurations,
but the meaning was the same: there was a level of punishment on the enslaved that was understood as acceptable and necessary. It was the nature of
the punishment, its "wanton cruelty," rather than the fact of punishment that
motivated both the Privy Council's questions and the white male witnesses'
responses.[78] Even the use of the term "wanton" evoked "a sexually immodest
or promiscuous woman,"[79] which shaped the reception of such images of
brutality.

The sexual nature of enslaved punishment, rarely so obviously recounted,
exposed the enslaved women's bodies to their owners, to strangers, and to the
historical record. Another witness reported, "one Negro woman . . . had been
tied up all night by her hands, and had been abused with Cayenne pepper by
her mistress in a way too horrid and indecent to mention."[80] Slave owning
women also do not escape depraved representations. Nevertheless, buried
within the man's account of himself, his actions and his shame, and the
uniquely bad character of the violator, the women of these accounts remain
objects viewed, pitiable, and vulnerable to sexual characterizations. Focused
on what is perceived as exceptional violence allows the colonial authorities,
parliamentarians, or even self-proclaimed sympathetic witnesses to accept
certain forms of punishment as permissible. The violated women enter our
view in a tortured state, their genitals exposed to voyeurs, without a name, a
future, or a past. Suspended by their hands and in that moment in time, we
do not know how or whether they survived such an encounter.

Each scene also exemplifies the significance of urban spaces to sights and
sounds of slave punishment and illustrates how even in private spaces—a
tavern or backyard—the chance of public witnessing increased. The enslaved,
often forced by their owners to watch, could not escape viewing punishment
on plantations as they signified a lesson—a warning against resistance. Mr.
Coor answered the Privy Council's question on "unusual" punishments by
relating a story about Old Quasheba, who was sent to the hothouse (the plantation slave "hospital") for running away. She was tied by the hands and
hoisted upward by a rope thrown over a beam. Mr. Coor heard, "A most dis-
tressful cry," coming from the hothouse. Old Quasheba's cry echoed outside
the hothouse all afternoon, "and about five o'clock the noise ceased," and

Coor was informed "the old woman is dead."[81] In town, neighbors, strangers, and townspeople living in much closer proximity to each other might witness such brutality unintentionally. Aware of how sounds from torture traveled, some slave owners sent their slaves to the wharfs and the gaol, "for punishments by those who did not chuse to disturb their neighbours with the cries of the parties."[82]

In many of the scenes described in the Privy Council interviews, white men visited Caribbean towns bustling with the activities of sugar production and the labor of slaves. Many remembered the crowded harbors and the moments and spaces where suffering was particularly audible. Some told of unique technologies of punishment only available in town, such as "the crane" used to hoist enslaved people up by their arms to be whipped. Sometimes the whippings were regimented. Mr. William Fitzmaurice reported that the usual mode of punishing town slaves,

> was to send them down to the wharfs, tie them up and flog them . . .
> others were sent to the work houses, and put in chains and flogged
> every morning, or every Monday morning . . . the Slaves are Stript,
> tied up to the crane, with two or one fifty-six pounds weight tied to
> their feet, and what is called a commissioner, or handkerchief tied
> round them for the sake of decency, and flogged in that manner.[72]

What are the productive and resistive qualities of nonverbal sounds of pain that can "take the rich content of the object's/commodity's aurality outside the confines of meaning precisely by way of this material trace?"[83] In other words, what meaning can we glean through enslaved women's screams from violence that cannot be translated into a coherent narrative? How might terrifying sounds be an opening to represent the lives of the nameless and the forgotten, to reckon with loss, and "to respect the limits of what cannot be known?"[84] Sound from enslaved bodies might be another way of marking enslaved historicity through the violence they endured. By reckoning unflinchingly with our methods and ethical practices as historians, our responsibility to our sources and subjects long dead, we might historically represent what has typically been unrepresentable.

We know that archival sources direct the narratives we produce. Unlike the Inquisition records of the circum-Spanish Caribbean, where the Catholic Church influenced the production of a vast archive of representations of enslaved voices (though still mitigated by European voices), the British colonial authorities remained largely uninterested in first hand accounts of enslaved female experiences.[85] Execution records, compensation claims, runaway advertisements, and these testimonial scenes of punishment reproduce only the voices and economic concerns of slave-owning men and women. Significant scholarship on Atlantic slavery emanates from these sources. Other critical work interrogates the relationship between power and narratibility in historical practice and the quotidian effects of violence on enslaved women's bodies.[86] Taken together, this range of work helps us understand the stakes of survival and death in the colonial British Caribbean, and equally important, the stakes of historical representation. Such a concern is critical if we are to make plain the effects of such violence on our efforts to document this past and these subjects. This is a matter not only of reading along the bias grain, but also explicitly demonstrating how power works in making certain historical subjects invisible, brutally hypervisible, and silent. This is an effort to (re) construct another kind of history that does not reproduce colonial (and disciplinary) power. Incorporating concerns of power and the reproduction of quotidian and archival violence, moves us outside the paradigms of resistance into more complex accounts that offer a range of experiences, responses to domination, and articulations of humanity.

Within the Privy Council interviews, many of those being questioned spent time in different British Caribbean ports and remarked on the sights and sounds of punishment. Indeed, the above accounts reveal the moments when the witness first heard the sounds of "the most dreadful cries" or "the shrieks of some poor wretch" that called them into witnessing. It was the screams of the women, echoing through the town, that brought strangers into the scenes of the women's entrapment and torture, and dense urban architectures produced a specific aurality that was public and far reaching. With no method of escape from their violent confinement, enslaved women forced themselves into history with their screams—insisting that someone reckon with their battered bodies. Their pained and loud cries forced their torturers to confront their humanity, even as it was being degraded. They called out others to witness their violation and their owners' inhumanity. They can be heard in the archive even with the passage of time. Their final acts are not ultimately heroic, but simply human. What does it mean to listen to this moment of anguish and suffering as an act of historical defiance? Is there something in the despair of their screams that conjures a powerful subjectivity that permeates the fortress of the archive?

These questions push us to listen to and sit with the pain of slavery to understand how, in a moment of subjection produced through violence, a "counter-history of the human" emerges that critiques objection, commodification, and a liberal humanist guise.[87] The shrieks and cries are a rhetorical genre of the enslaved,[88] that (at once) demands our attention as it communicates an historical and human condition in response to routinized violence (the condition of the everyday in slavery). Rhetorical genre in this sense connotes a human vocal response born out of "recurring conditions . . . involving a social context."[89] The scream becomes a rhetorical expression to violence emanating from the repetitive violations of the social context of slavery. Connected to the way that the subjection of slavery (the simultaneity of becoming a subject and being subjected to domination) produces the enslaved object/subject, "this aurality [of violation] resists certain formations of identity and interpretation by challenging the reducibility of phonic matter to verbal meaning."[90] The enslaved women's screams become both an affective and inaccessible form of expression, impossible to cohere or translate into narrative form. The enslaved women's "most dreadful cries" are a momentary refusal to be historically silenced but remain inaccessible to historical articulation. Their screams do not subvert nor destroy relations of power. They demand historical attention but do not depend on our empirical corroboration or narrativization. This is the historical genre of the enslaved in the colonial archive.

In many ways, this book is about resistance even as it challenges the imposition of that paradigm on the study of slavery. It is about resistance to historical methodology that limits our ability to recognize or historicize sparsely and violently produced enslaved female subjects; resistance to our search for subversive agency as the dominant way to understand enslaved humanity; and resistance to what is disciplinarily or historically "impossible." It also refuses to settle for the unrepresentability of pain by looking for moments when the subjects do represent themselves—perhaps not in predictable forms—but "in the break"[91]—in the rupture within the moment of absolute terror. Something emerges from that violence even as humanity is being broken down or extinguished. This is a different form of agency—one that does not expect resolution or revolution in outcome. What can be heard from "the most dreadful cries?"—that "terrible beauty"?[92] Perhaps resistance to the violence of slavery is survival, the will to survive, the sound of someone wanting to be heard, wanting to live or wanting to die. But the struggle against dehumanization is in the *wanting*. And sometimes, we can hear it.

Epilogue

Slavery is not an indefinable mass of flesh. It is a particular,
specific enslaved woman, whose mind is active as your own,
whose range of feeling is as vast as your own; who prefers
the way the light falls in one particular spot in the woods . . .
For this woman, enslavement is not a parable. It is
damnation. It is the never-ending night. And the length of
that night is most of our history.
　　　　　　　　—Ta-Nehisi Coates, *Between the World and Me*

In writing this epilogue, I want to return to the beginning, to the roots of my
methodological and ethical concerns and underscore what it means to reckon
with the tragic permanency of historical silence and erasure. There will always be unanswerable questions from an archive that cannot fully redress the
loss of historical perspectives and insights from the enslaved. I went to Barbados searching for something I would never find. Emerging empty-handed
from these archives, the silence deafening, I was confronted head on with the
questions this book has attempted to answer. I had intended to write about
the ways enslaved women labored, built communities, and experienced the
confinements of urban life. I had talked extensively with historians who had
done archival work in the region and gathered their tips and advice on orga-
nizing my time as I went to search for my subjects in the historical records.
Yet nothing prepared me for the encounter with the paucity of material about
enslaved women, the complete absence of material by enslaved women, and
the intensity of archival and physical violence on enslaved women that I
would struggle with over the next decade.

There were none of the voices I sought to document; no whole figures
emerged that I could trace beyond a momentary mention. The women I did
find were battered, beaten, executed, and overtly sexualized. They were listed
on estate inventories only as Phoebe, Mimba, or "Broken Back Betty," and

sometimes only as "negroe"—stripped bare of all that was meaningful in their lives. Bequeathed in wills and deeds, or counted and dying on slave ships, they could not tell me about these conditions or what they thought, how they loved, or from where they came. The permanent loss of this knowledge was harrowing. Looking back now, I understand how both naïve and hopeful I was going into this project. I believed I would find "that one source" no one else had yet discovered. I would be able to tell a story from the standpoints and thoughts of the women about whom I wished to write. I would discover a document that revealed the inner everyday lives of the enslaved in plain language that I could simply translate. I encountered images of Rachael Pringle Polgreen across the island made into dolls, posters, and postcards— her caricature (re)commodified for twenty-first-century tourists. I scoured a century of execution compensation records and read about Molly and numbers of other women who had been executed, and I found the conditions of their lives buried with them. There was nothing about age, family life, or the circumstances leading to their convictions. I could not prove, at the time, what I felt to be true: the system of slavery assumed enslaved people were criminals when they were instead victims of an impossible legal structure. I discovered a court case where an enslaved boy dressed in women's clothes with a hidden dagger walked across town at night, dragged into the affairs of white Barbadians, yet silenced within the frame of law. Not even his name was mentioned. The few surviving newspapers contained brief advertisements of runaway slaves; one of them was Jane, conjured by the variety of scars on her body. Her owner mentioned no relatives or considered the life she left behind when she was captured and brought across the Atlantic.

I was drawn to each of these people by the loss of their histories and my unfulfillable desire to recuperate something about them. I found only their archival mention, fragment, or image, and knew something must be said. At the time of their discovery I did not yet know what they embodied, only that they represented a range of theoretical concerns I began to ponder because of their incomplete and violated nature. My questions shaped the way I would seek to bring these women into history, as well as a way to bring the discipline of history into a more transparent and reflexive frame. It was the context and the manner in which enslaved women were silenced that provoked my focus on addressing this process of erasure and the violence of their physical, historical, and archival condition.

After twenty-two months of archival research in Barbados, England, and South Carolina, I returned to the United States with a determination to address the issue and causes of archival silence. Through the life of this project I worked within a historical disciplinary structure that required more sources to make the project "viable" and within the logic of historical methodology, which purported that a history of silence could not be written when there was not enough material to fill an article, let alone a book. I resolutely thought about and challenged the process from which these disciplining rules and (desires) emanated. The women in the book—Jane, Agatha, Rachael, Joanna, Molly, and the many more whose names did not survive—required more than the limits a single discipline allowed, and I spent the next several years developing methodological pathways into their lives. These included explorations about their historical or historiographical representations, thinking through the theoretical significance of colonial power in the realm of law and punishment, and changing the archival language and gaze to reflect the gaze and perspective of the women in the fragments.

History is produced from what the archive offers. It is the historian's job to substantiate all the pieces with more archival evidence, context, and historiography and put them together into a coherent narrative form. The challenge this book has confronted is to write a history about what an archive does not offer. My theoretical questions guided me to move toward particular methodologies that would assist me in explicating the limits and possibilities of enslaved women's historical subjectivities. Molly, for example, symbolizes both the violence of slavery on bodies and the violence of the laws that prevent the enslaved from claims of humanity and innocence. Rachael Pringle Polgreen's metanarrative demonstrates the troubling and silencing nature of historical production—it shows the way her rehearsed narrative obscures her perpetuation of slavery's violence. Jane and the unnamed women in the final chapter illuminate the manner in which mutilation—physical and symbolic—conditioned their historicity leading to questions about the impossibility of recovery. The nature of the archive from which they emerge requires this effort. We cannot redeem or rescue them, but we can reconsider their pain.

This project has not been without risk for me, and perhaps for my readers as well. It has not hewn to those historical practices that require a vast empirical base from which to generalize. There is political risk in presenting seemingly "defeated" and disfigured subjects and of presenting "too much death" and violence. And, there is risk in the archival encounter. Confronting sources that show only terror and violence are a danger to the researcher who sees her own ancestors in these accounts. To sit with these sources requires the capacity to hold and inhabit deep wells of pain and horror. One must persist for years in this "mortuary" of records to bring otherwise invisible lives to historical representation in a way that challenges the reproduction of invisibility and commodification. This process of historicization demands strategies to manage the emotional response one has to such brutality in order to persist with these subjects—to be willing to take up and sit with this aspect of human degradation and to find meaning. When writing Chapter 5 I spent weeks reading hundreds of accounts of dismembered, burned, and whipped enslaved women and men. There were many times I had to put the documents down and walk away. But I knew I had to gather myself and return to them. I have by now spent years absorbing the brutalizations inflicted on people of African descent and witnessing the process by which—"humans [cease] to be."[1] To spend time in this temporal and geographical space is to risk emotional strength. It obliterates the possibility of objectivity. It is an exercise in endurance.

When I teach courses in early modern Caribbean history and slavery, I assign my students a final paper requiring them to analyze a primary source from the era and region we have covered over the semester. Several class days are spent practicing with different documents, some of which I used for this book. We read wills left by women of color, compare the Code Noir to the Barbados Slave Acts, and read the Haitian and American declarations of independence together to analyze language and the meanings of freedom. The students' enthusiasm turns into agony and anxiety when they have to choose their own source to analyze for their final assignment. They have many questions about where to look, what constitutes an appropriate source, and what is the required number of secondary sources they will need to contextualize their document. What is most striking however, is the repeated question that sometimes rises into complaint: how do I find a source written by an enslaved person or from their perspective? Aside from the few surviving slave narratives there are some students who wish to write about the gendered violence particular to the experience of enslaved women, or routine and everyday life of slavery but find the records at best empty of this concern; at worst there are documents in which slave owners blame the women for their "insatiable desires" or reduce enslaved people to their price or physical debility. At the heart of my students' question is the realization of how difficult it is to narrate from a place of silence. It then dawns on them that their assignment is as much about working with what is there as with what is not. This is the same concern I had struggled with when I began this project over a decade ago.

Dispossessed Lives insists that historical studies of the black Atlantic inform the ways in which race, gender, and sexuality continue to shape the lives
of African-descended people worldwide. It is a history of how people of African descent became disposable, when black lives were objectified and thus
vulnerable to the caprice, lusts, and economic desires of colonial authorities.
It documents the strategies and structures that made black Atlantic lives subject to violence of thought and action. It offers material to reflect on the
stakes of resistance in such systems and the reproduction of raced and gendered configurations of vulnerability. It begins to mark the way that the archive and history have erased black bodies and how the legacies of
slavery—the racialized sexism and the legal, socioeconomic, and physical
violence against people of African descent—manifest in the violence we continue to confront. It is a gesture toward a reckoning of our own time. It is a
history of our present.

NOTES

Introduction

1. The traditional archive refers to the majority of documents produced during the era of slavery in the British Caribbean by colonial administrators, planters, white men and women, and governing bodies in the metropole.

2. Hilary Beckles, *Natural Rebels: A Social History of Enslaved Women in Barbados* (Kingston: Ian Randle, 1989), 7.

3. Hilary Beckles, *Centering Woman: Gender Discourses in Caribbean Slave Society* (Kingston: Ian Randle, 1999), 63.

4. Here I am not arguing that antebellum slavery histories have a wealth of sources to draw on from the enslaved perspective. Instead, I want to point out that the records of colonial Caribbean slavery are even sparser and there are strikingly few narratives left by enslaved women. For more information on the Caribbean slave narratives that do exist, see Nicole N. Aljoe, "Caribbean Slave Narratives," in *The Oxford Handbook of African American Slave Narratives*, ed. John Ernest (New York: Oxford University Press, 2014), 362–70.

5. For scholarship on enslaved women in the U.S. and Caribbean, see Adele Logan Alexander, *Ambiguous Lives: Free Women of Color in Rural Georgia, 1789–1879* (Fayetteville: University of Arkansas Press, 1991); Henrice Altink, *Representations of Slave Women in Discourses on Slavery and Abolition, 1780–1838* (New York: Routledge, 2007); Edward Baptist, "'Cuffy,' 'Fancy Maids,' and 'One-Eyed Men': Rape, Commodification, and the Domestic Slave Trade in the United States," *American Historical Review* 106 (December 2001): 1619–50; Edward Baptist and Stephanie M. H. Camp, eds., *New Studies in American Slavery* (Athens: University of Georgia Press, 2006); Beckles, *Centering Woman* and *Natural Rebels*; Daina Berry, *Swing the Sickle for the Harvest Is Ripe: Gender and Slavery in Antebellum Georgia* (Urbana: University of Illinois Press, 2007); Kathleen Brown, *Good Wives, Nasty Wenches, and Anxious Patriarchs: Gender, Race, and Power in Colonial Virginia* (Chapel Hill: University of North Carolina Press, 1996); Steeve O. Buckridge, *The Language of Dress: Resistance and Accommodation in Jamaica, 1750–1890* (Kingston: University of the West Indies Press, 2004); Barbara Bush, *Slave Women in Caribbean Society, 1650–1838* (Bloomington: Indiana University Press, 1990); Judith Ann-Marie Byfield, LaRay Denzer, and Anthea Morrison, eds., *Gendering the African Diaspora: Women, Culture, and Historical Change in the Caribbean and Nigerian Hinterland* (Bloomington: Indiana University Press, 2010); Victoria Bynum, *Unruly Women: The Politics of Social*

and Sexual Control in the Old South (Chapel Hill: University of North Carolina Press, 1992); Stephanie Camp, *Closer to Freedom: Enslaved Women and Everyday Resistance in the Plantation South* (Chapel Hill: University of North Carolina Press, 2004); Gwyn Campbell, Suzanne Miers, and Joseph Calder Miller, eds., *Women and Slavery: The Modern Atlantic* (Athens: Ohio University Press, 2007); Humberto R. Campos, "Voices of Caribbean Women in the Slave Period Between 1780–1830: A Closer Look at the History of Mary Prince" (dissertation, University of Puerto Rico, 2002); Camillia Cowling, *Conceiving Freedom: Women of Color, Gender, and the Abolition of Slavery in Havana and Rio de Janeiro* (Chapel Hill: University of North Carolina Press, 2013); Juanita De Barros, *Reproducing the British Caribbean: Sex, Gender, and Population Politics* (Chapel Hill: University of North Carolina Press, 2014); Maureen G. Elgersman, *Unyielding Spirits: Black Women and Slavery in Early Canada and Jamaica* (London: Routledge, 1999); Aisha K. Finch, *Rethinking Slave Rebellion in Cuba: La Escalera and the Insurgencies of 1841–1844* (Chapel Hill: University of North Carolina Press, 2015); Sarah L. Franklin, *Women and Slavery in Nineteenth-Century Colonial Cuba* (Rochester, N.Y.: University of Rochester Press, 2012); Doris L. Garraway, *The Libertine Colony: Creolization in the Early French Caribbean* (Durham, N.C.: Duke University Press, 2005); David Barry Gaspar and Darlene Clark Hine, eds., *More Than Chattel: Black Women and Slavery in the Americas* (Bloomington: Indiana University Press, 1996); Thavolia Glymph, *Out of the House of Bondage: The Transformation of the Plantation Household* (Cambridge: Cambridge University Press, 2008); Annette Gordon-Reed, *The Hemingses of Monticello: An American Family* (New York: Norton, 2009); Annette Gordon-Reed, *Thomas Jefferson and Sally Hemings: An American Controversy* (Charlottesville: University of Virginia Press, 1997); Sandra Lauderdale Graham, *Caetana Says No: Women's Stories from a Brazilian Slave Society* (Cambridge: Cambridge University Press, 2002); Sandra Lauderdale Graham, *House and Street: The Domestic World of Servants and Masters in Nineteenth-Century Rio de Janeiro* (Austin: University of Texas Press, 1992); Saidiya Hartman, *Lose Your Mother: A Journey Along the Atlantic Slave Route* (New York: Farrar, Straus, and Giroux, 2008); Saidiya Hartman, *Scenes of Subjection: Terror, Slavery, and Self-Making in Nineteenth-Century America* (Oxford: Oxford University Press, 1997); Martha Hodes, ed., *Sex, Love, Race: Crossing Boundaries in North American History* (New York: New York University Press, 1999); Sharon Ann Holt, "Symbol, Memory, and Service: Resistance and Family in Nineteenth-Century African America," in *Working Toward Freedom: Slave Society and Domestic Economy in the American South*, ed. Larry E. Hudson, Jr. (Rochester, N.Y.: University of Rochester Press, 1994), 192–210; Patricia Hunt, "The Struggle to Achieve Individual Expression Through Clothing and Adornment: African-American Women Under and After Slavery," in *Discovering the Women in Slavery: Emancipating Perspectives on the American Past*, ed. Patricia Morton (Athens: University of Georgia Press, 1996), 227–40; Marlon James, *The Book of Night Women* (New York: Penguin, 2009); Thelma Jennings, " 'Us Colored Women Had to Go Through a Plenty': Sexual Exploitation of African-American Women," *Journal of Women's History* 1, 3 (Winter 1990): 45–74; Jacqueline Jones, *Labor of Love, Labor of Sorrow: Black Women, Work, and the Family from Slavery to the Present* (New York: Vintage, 1985); Doris Y. Kadish, *Fathers, Daughters, and Slaves: Women Writers and French Colonial Slavery* (Liverpool: Liverpool University Press, 2014); Wilma King, " 'Raise Your Children Up Rite': Parental Guidance and Child Rearing Practices Among Slaves in the Nineteenth-Century South," in *Working Toward Freedom*, ed. Hudson, 143–62; Wilma King, "The Mistress and Her Maids: White and Black Women in a Louisiana Household, 1858–1868," in *Discovering the Women in Slavery*, ed. Morton, 82–106; Suzanne Lebsock, *Free Women of Petersburg: Status and Culture in a Southern Town, 1784–1860* (New York: Norton, 1984); Lucille Mathurin Mair, *A Historical Study of Women in Jamaica*, ed. Hilary Beckles and Verene Shepherd (Kingston: University of the West Indies Press, 2006); Lucille Mathurin Mair and Dennis Ranston, *The Rebel Woman in the British West Indies During Slavery* (Kingston: Institute of Jamaica Publications, 1995); Ann Paton Malone, *Sweet Chariot: Slave Family and Household Structure in Nineteenth-Century Louisiana* (Chapel Hill: University of North Carolina Press, 1996); Stephanie McCurry, *Masters of Small Worlds: Yeoman Households, Gender Relations, and the Political Culture of the Antebellum South Carolina Low Country* (New York: Oxford University Press, 1995); Melton McLaurin, *Celia, a Slave: A True Story of Violence and Retribution in Ante-Bellum America* (Athens: University of Georgia Press, 1991); Bernard Moitt, *Women and Slavery in the French Antilles, 1635–1838* (Bloomington: Indiana University Press, 2001); Janet Henshall Momsen, *Women and Change in the Caribbean: A Pan-Caribbean Perspective* (Kingston: Ian Randle, 1993); Brian L. Moore, Barry W. Higman, and Carl Campbell, eds., *Slavery, Freedom and Gender: The Dynamics of Caribbean Society* (Mona: University of the West Indies Press, 2001); Jennifer Morgan, *Laboring Women: Gender and Reproduction in New World Slavery* (Philadelphia: University of Pennsylvania Press, 2004); Patricia Morton, *Disfigured Images: The Historical Assault on Afro-American Women* (New York: Greenwood, 1991); Nell Irvin Painter, "Representing Truth: Sojourner Truth's Knowing and Becoming Known," *Journal of American History* 81 (September 1994): 461–92; Nell Irvin Painter, *Sojourner Truth: A Life, a Symbol* (New York: Norton, 1996); Leslie Schwalm, *A Hard Fight for We: Women's Transition from Slavery to Freedom in South Carolina* (Urbana: University of Illinois Press, 1997); Marie Jenkins Schwartz, *Born in Bondage: Growing Up Enslaved in the Antebellum South* (Cambridge, Mass.: Harvard University Press, 2000); Pamela Scully and Diana Paton, eds., *Gender and Slave Emancipation in the Atlantic World* (Durham, N.C.: Duke University Press, 2005); Stephanie Shaw, "Mothering Under Slavery in the Antebellum South," in *Mothering: Ideology, Experience, and Agency*, ed. Evelyn Nakano Glenn, Grace Chang, and Linda Renine Forcey (New York: Routledge, 1994), 237–58; Mimi Sheller, *Citizenship from Below: Erotic Agency and Caribbean Freedom* (Durham, N.C.: Duke University Press, 2012); Christine Stansell, *City of Women: Sex and Class in New York, 1789–1860* (Urbana: University of Illinois Press, 1987); Brenda E. Stevenson, *Life in Black and White: Family and Community in the Slave South* (New York: Oxford University Press, 1996); Andrea Stuart, *Sugar in the Blood: A Family's Story of Slavery and Empire* (New York: Knopf, 2012); Emily West, *Enslaved Women in America: From Colonial Times to Emancipation* (Lanham, Md.: Rowman and Littlefield, 2015); Deborah Gray White,

Ar'n't I a Woman?: Female Slaves in the Plantation South (New York: Norton, 1985); Shane White and Graham White, "Slave Clothing and African-American Culture in the Eighteenth and Nineteenth Centuries," *Past and Present* 148 (August 1995): 149–86; Shane White and Graham White, "Slave Hair and African-American Culture in the Eighteenth and Nineteenth Centuries," *Journal of Southern History* 61, 1 (February 1995): 45–76; Betty Wood, "Some Aspects of Female Resistance to Chattel Slavery in Low Country Georgia, 1763–1815," *Historical Journal* 30, 3 (1987): 603–22; and Betty Wood, *Women's Work, Men's Work: The Informal Slave Economies of Lowcountry Georgia* (Athens: University of Georgia Press, 1995). For innovative historical scholarship on women who did not leave an archive, see Camilla Townsend, *Malintzin's Choices: An Indian Woman in the Conquest of Mexico* (Albuquerque: University of New Mexico Press, 2006) and Natalie Zemon Davis, *Women on the Margins: Three Seventeenth-Century Lives* (Cambridge, Mass.: Harvard University Press, 1997). For a range of theoretical work on the archive, see Antoinette Burton, *Archive Stories: Facts, Fictions, and the Writing of History* (Durham, N.C.: Duke University Press, 2005); Dipesh Chakrabarty, *Provincializing Europe: Postcolonial Thought and Historical Difference* (Princeton, N.J.: Princeton University Press, 2000); Natalie Zemon Davis, *Fiction in the Archives: Pardon Tales and Their Tellers in Sixteenth-Century France* (Stanford, Calif.: Stanford University Press, 1987); Jacques Derrida and Eric Prenowitz, *Archive Fever: A Freudian Impression* (Chicago: University of Chicago Press, 1996); Gayatri Chakravorty Spivak, "Can the Subaltern Speak?" in *Marxism and the Interpretation of Culture*, ed. Lawrence Grossberg and Carl Nelson (Urbana: University of Illinois Press, 1988), 271–315; Carolyn Steedman, *Dust: The Archive and Cultural History* (New Brunswick, N.J.: Rutgers University Press, 2002); Ann Laura Stoler, *Along the Archival Grain: Epistemic Anxieties and Colonial Common Sense* (Princeton, N.J.: Princeton University Press, 2010); Diane Taylor, *The Archive and the Repertoire: Performing Cultural Memory in the Americas* (Durham, N.C.: Duke University Press, 2003); Michel-Rolph Trouillot, *Silencing the Past: Power and the Production of History* (Boston: Beacon, 1995); and David Zeitlyn, "Anthropology in and of the Archives: Possible Futures and Contingent Pasts, Archives as Anthropological Surrogates," *Annual Review of Anthropology* 41 (2012): 461–80.

6. For a critique of narratives of resistance in slavery studies, see the work of literary scholar Jenny Sharpe in *The Ghosts of Slavery: A Literary Archaeology of Black Women's Lives* (Minneapolis: University of Minnesota Press, 2003), xiv–vi. Sharpe draws on a range of scholars interested in complicating notions of agency including Michel-Rolph Trouillot, who states, "Everything can become resistance to the point that we are not sure whether or not the word stands for an empirical generalization, an analytical category, or a vague yet fashionable label for unrelated situations." Trouillot, "In the Shadow of the West: Power, Resistance and Creolization in the Making of the Caribbean Region," in *Born Out of Resistance: On Caribbean Cultural Creativity*, ed. Wim Hoogbergen (Utrecht: ISOR, 1995), 9.

7. Recent or forthcoming scholarship continues a scholarly interest in the plantation societies of the Caribbean with a focus on Barbados. Trevor Burnard's forthcoming

book, *Planters, Merchants, and Slaves: Plantation Societies in British America, 1650–1870* (Chicago: University of Chicago Press, 2015) renews attention to the strivings and aspirations of British colonists in their attempts to profit from developing plantation systems. Justin Roberts, *Slavery and the Enlightenment in the British Atlantic, 1750–1807* (New York: Cambridge University Press, 2013) conducts a study of plantation regimes in early modern Virginia, Barbados, and Jamaica, and Simon Newman, *A New World of Labor: The Development of Plantation Slavery in the British Atlantic* (Philadelphia: University of Pennsylvania Press, 2013) returns to seventeenth-century Barbados to examine the system of indentured servitude and its foundational impact on the development of racial slavery.

8. Townsend, *Malintzin's Choices*, 7.

9. For a discussion of "power and historical production," see Trouillot, *Silencing the Past*.

10. I am indebted to the generosity of Barbadian historians including Dr. Pedro Welch and Dr. Karl Watson, who shared their vast knowledge and personal archival research with me over the last decade. Many of the sources they shared are used in this book. I have reinterpreted these sources using analyses interrogating archival power.

11. Avery F. Gordon, *Ghostly Matters: Haunting and the Sociological Imagination* (Minneapolis: University of Minnesota Press, 2008), xviii. For an important discussion of the relationship between "evidence and history," see Burton, *Archive Stories*, 1.

12. Gordon, *Ghostly Matters*, 8.

13. Many thanks to Melanie J. Newton for helping me with this formulation. Personal Communication, October 2014.

14. Newton, Personal Communication.

15. Hartman, *Scenes of Subjection*, 11.

16. This method is explained more fully in Chapter 2. It is the way I describe a methodology by which the archival record is stretched to accentuate the figures of enslaved women whose presence influences ontological conditions of others but who are not mentioned in particular archives. This analysis is achieved without destroying the integrity (historical veracity) of the original archival documents. It is a different approach to colonial records than in Ann Laura Stoler's important work, *Along the Archival Grain*, where she skillfully reveals the weaknesses in colonial power through an affective reading of nineteenth-century Dutch colonial documents. In my approach I am specifically interested in what can be gleaned from the imbalances in which enslaved women are either invisible or distorted in their representations in the traditional archive.

17. Barry Higman's study on the British Caribbean provides an important discussion of urban slave life in the early nineteenth century. See Higman, *Slave Populations in the British Caribbean, 1807–1834* (Mona: University of the West Indies Press, 1997), 226–59. For other studies on urban slavery around the Atlantic world, see Herman Bennett, *Blacks in Colonial Mexico: Absolutism, Christianity, and Afro-Creole Consciousness, 1570–1640* (Bloomington: Indiana University Press, 2003); Herman Bennett, *Colonial Blackness: A History of Afro-Mexico* (Bloomington: Indiana University Press, 2009);

Jorge Cañizares-Esguerra, Matt D. Childs, and James Sidbury, eds., *The Black Urban Atlantic in the Age of the Slave Trade* (Philadelphia: University of Pennsylvania Press, 2013); Patrick Carroll, *Blacks in Colonial Veracruz: Race, Ethnicity, and Regional Development* (Austin: University of Texas Press, 1991); Mariana L. R. Dantas, *Black Townsmen: Urban Slavery and Freedom in the Eighteenth-Century Americas* (London: Palgrave Macmillan, 2008); Claudia Dale Goldin, *Urban Slavery in the American South, 1820–1860* (Chicago: University of Chicago Press, 1976); Graham, *House and Street*; Philip J. Havik, "Gendering the Black Atlantic: Women's Agency in Coastal Trade Settlements in the Guinea Bissau Region"; Dominique Rogers and Stewart King, "Housekeepers, Merchants, Rentières: Free Women of Color in the Port Cities of Colonial Saint-Domingue, 1750–1790," in *Women in Port: Gendering Communities, Economies, and Social Networks in Atlantic Port Cities, 1500–1800*, ed. Douglas Catterall and Jodi Campbell (Leiden: Brill, 2012), 315–56, 357–98; Graham Russell Hodges, *Root and Branch: African Americans in New York and East Jersey, 1613–1863* (Chapel Hill: University of North Carolina Press, 1999); Thomas N. Ingersoll, *Mammon and Manon in Early New Orleans: The First Slave Society in the Deep South* (Knoxville: University of Tennessee Press, 1999); Mary C. Karasch, *Slave Life in Rio de Janeiro, 1808–1850* (Princeton, N.J.: Princeton University Press, 1987); Franklin W. Knight and Peggy K. Liss, *Atlantic Port Cities: Economy, Culture, and Society* (Knoxville: University of Tennessee Press, 1991); Philip Morgan, "Black Life in Eighteenth-Century Charleston," *Perspectives in American History* n.s. 1 (1984): 187–232; Philip D. Morgan, "British Encounters with Africans and African-Americans, Circa 1600–1780," in *Strangers Within the Realm: Cultural Margins of the First British Empire*, ed. Bernard Bailyn and Philip D. Morgan (Chapel Hill: University of North Carolina Press, 1991), 157–219; Gary Nash, *Forging Freedom: The Formation of Philadelphia's Black Community, 1720–1810* (Cambridge, Mass.: Harvard University Press, 1988); Mieko Nishida, *Slavery and Identity: Ethnicity, Gender, and Race in Salvador, Brazil, 1808–1888* (Bloomington: Indiana University Press, 2003); Colin Palmer, *Slaves of the White God: Blacks in Mexico, 1570–1650* (Cambridge, Mass.: Harvard University Press,1976); João José Reis, *Slave Rebellion in Brazil: The Muslim Uprising of 1835 in Bahia,* trans. Arthur Brakel (Baltimore: Johns Hopkins University Press, 1993); John Robertson, *Gone is the Ancient Glory: Spanish Town, Jamaica, 1534–2000* (Kingston: Ian Randle, 2005); Seth Rockman, *Scraping By: Wage Labor, Slavery, and Survival in Early Republican Baltimore* (Baltimore: Johns Hopkins University Press, 2008); Richard C. Wade, *Slavery in the Cities: The South, 1820–1860* (New York: Oxford University Press); Pedro Welch, *Slave Society in the City, Bridgetown, Barbados, 1680–1834* (Kingston: Ian Randle, 2003); Shane White, *Somewhat More Independent: The End of Slavery in New York City, 1770–1810* (Athens: University of Georgia Press, 1991); and T. Stephen Whitman, *The Price of Freedom: Slavery and Freedom in Baltimore and Early National Maryland* (Lexington: University Press of Kentucky, 1997).

18. The scholarship I am referring to here includes but is not limited to Herbert Gutman, *The Black Family in Slavery and Freedom, 1750–1925* (New York: Vintage, 1976); John Blassingame, *The Slave Community: Plantation Life in the Antebellum South*, rev.

ed. (Oxford: Oxford University Press, 1979); and Lawrence Levine, *Black Culture and Black Consciousness: Afro-American Folk Thought from Slavery to Freedom* (New York: Oxford University Press, 1978). This work was also in response to Stanley Elkins, *Slavery: A Problem in American Institutional and Intellectual Life* (Chicago: University of Chicago Press, 1959), in which he argued that U.S. slavery was a total system that reduced the enslaved to "Sambos" who were totally dominated, defeated, and did not resist. In Caribbean historiography some works also engage agency/resistance, such as Beckles, *Natural Rebels* and Bush, *Slave Women in Caribbean Society*. To be clear, this book argues that the resistance thesis in slavery studies has obscured other complex modes of action and agency that do not always resemble subversion or community building. This is not to argue that the enslaved did not actively resist their conditions within systems of domination.

19. Trouillot, "In the Shadow of the West," 9. I take the definition of "liberal humanism" from Catherine Belsey, *The Subject of Tragedy: Identity and Difference in Renaissance Drama* (London: Routledge, 2013), 8, who writes, "Liberal humanism proposes that the subject is the free, unconstrained author of meaning and action, the origin of history. Unified, knowing and autonomous, the human being seeks a political system which guarantees freedom of choice."

20. For a broad range of historical texts on British Caribbean slavery, see Robin Blackburn, *The Overthrow of Colonial Slavery, 1776–1848* (New York: Verso, 1988); Richard Dunn, *Sugar and Slaves: The Rise of the Planter Class in the English West Indies, 1624–1713* (Chapel Hill: University of North Carolina Press, 1972); Elsa Goveia, *Slave Society in the British Leeward Islands at the End of the Eighteenth Century* (New Haven, Conn.: Yale University Press, 1965); Gad Heuman, *Between Black and White: Race, Politics and the Free Coloreds in Jamaica, 1792–1865* (Westport, Conn.: Greenwood, 1981); and Higman, *Slave Populations in the British Caribbean*.

21. Hartman, *Scenes of Subjection*, esp. 52–56.

22. Walter Johnson, "On Agency," *Journal of Social History* 37 (2003): 120.

23. Hartman, *Scenes of Subjection*, 6. Johnson has recently reprised this conversation in *Slavery's Ghost: The Problem of Freedom in the Age of Emancipation* (Baltimore: Johns Hopkins University Press, 2011), 8–30. This book revisits the limits of freedom for African Americans in the post-emancipation era as Hartman discussed in *Scenes of Subjection*.

24. Hartman, "Venus in Two Acts," *Small Axe* 12, 2 (2008): 10.

25. Justin Roberts lodges a similar and important critique against the paradigm of agency as resistance in histories of slavery in *Slavery and the Enlightenment in the British Atlantic, 1750–1807* (Cambridge: Cambridge University Press, 2013), see esp. "Introduction," 1–25. Roberts points to the traditional and classic texts in British Atlantic history over the last several years to argue that the power dynamics and violence of early modern plantations were more complex than the historiography and framework of agency reveals. However, this critique originates much farther back in the scholarship on "subaltern" histories, and we have benefited from critical interdisciplinary engagement from

a wide variety of scholars in anthropology and feminist, African diaspora and cultural studies, many of whose publications date to the early 1990s. Moreover, a gendered reading of resistance/agency narratives further complicates this paradigm, challenging the notion of agency as a gender neutral phenomenon. At stake then, is how agency is deployed in the scholarship on slavery and how enslaved women are represented in this narrative as "sexual agents."

26. Camp, *Closer to Freedom*, 2.

27. Ibid.

28. For a longer discussion of how agency is gendered in feminist scholarship, see Saba Mahmood, *Politics of Piety: The Islamic Revival and the Feminist Subject* (Princeton, N.J.: Princeton University Press, 2005).

29. See also Marisa J. Fuentes, "Power and Historical Figuring: Rachael Pringle Polgreen's Troubled Archive," *Gender and History* 22 (November 2010): 3.

30. Vincent Brown, "Social Death and Political Life in the Study of Slavery," *American Historical Review* 114, 5 (December 2009): 1248; my emphasis.

31. Stephanie Camp deploys this term in *Closer to Freedom*, xxix. Its original incantation is credited to Edward Said, who used it to describe "resistance to colonial domination" (18). Camp applied the term to the antebellum South. She was aware that alternate spaces were never autonomous from slave holders' power or trespass, but she explains that "rival geography did, however, provide space for private and public creative expression, rest and recreation, alternative communication, and importantly, resistance to planters' domination of slaves' every move" (19).

32. Taking the phrase from tailoring, in which fabric is cut at an angle to produce elasticity: reading along the bias grain stretches the archive to accentuate the presence of enslaved women when not explicitly mentioned in certain documents. See Chapter 3 for the application of this method.

33. Gordon, *Ghostly Matters*, 4–5.

34. There is a vast and substantial canon of black feminist scholarship on issues of representation and epistemology. The texts that influenced and are cited in this study include Jean Besson, "Reputation and Respectability Reconsidered: A New Perspective on Afro-Caribbean Peasant Women," in *Women and Change in the Caribbean: A Pan-Caribbean Perspective*, ed. Janet Momsen (London: James Currey, 1993), 15; Jennifer De-Vere Brody, *Impossible Purities: Blackness, Femininity, and Victorian Culture* (Durham, N.C.: Duke University Press, 1998); Sabine Broeck, "Enslavement as Regime of Western Modernity: Re-Reading Gender Studies Epistemology Through Black Feminist Critique," *Gender Forum: An Internet Journal of Gender Studies* 22 (2008), accessed July 3, 2015; Elsa Barkley Brown, "'What Has Happened Here': The Politics of Difference in Women's History and Feminist Politics," *Feminist Studies* 18, 2 (1992): 295–312; Katherine E. Browne, *Creole Economics: Caribbean Cunning Under the French Flag* (Austin: University of Texas Press, 2004); Hazel V. Carby, "Policing the Black Woman's Body in an Urban Context," in *Identities*, ed. Kwame Appiah and Henry Louis Gates, Jr. (Chicago: University of Chicago Press, 1995), 735–55; Patricia Hill Collins, "Who's Going On?:

Black Feminist Thought and the Politics of Postmodernism," in *Working the Ruins: Feminist Poststructural Theory and Methods in Education*, ed. Elizabeth A. St. Pierre and Wanda S. Pillow (New York: Routledge, 2000), 41; Angela Y. Davis, "Reflections on the Black Woman's Role in the Community of Slaves," in *Words of Fire: An Anthology of African American Feminist Thought*, ed. Beverly Guy-Sheftall (New York: New Press, 1995); Paula Giddings, *When and Where I Enter: The Impact of Black Women on Race and Sex in America* (New York: William Morrow, 1984); Sander Gilman, "Black Bodies, White Bodies: Toward an Iconography of Female Sexuality in Late Nineteenth-Century Art, Medicine, and Literature," in *"Race," Writing, and Difference*, ed. Henry Louis Gates, Jr. (Chicago: University of Chicago Press, 1985); Farah Jasmine Griffin, "Black Feminists and Du Bois: Respectability, Protections, and Beyond," in *The Study of African American Problems: W. E. B. Du Bois's Agenda, Then and Now* (Thousand Oaks, Calif.: Sage, 2000); Beverly Guy-Sheftall, "African American Women: The Legacy of Black Feminism," in *Sisterhood Is Forever: The Women's Anthology for a New Millennium*, ed. Robin Morgan (New York: Washington Square Press, 2003), 176; Jacquelyn Dowd Hall, "'The Mind That Burns in Each Body': Women, Rape, and Racial Violence," in *Powers of Desire: The Politics of Sexuality*, ed. Ann Snitnow, Christine Stansell, and Sharon Thompson (New York: Monthly Review Press, 1983); Evelyn Hammonds, "Toward a Black Feminist Aesthetic," *Sojourner* 7 (January 1982); Evelyn Brooks Higginbotham, "African-American Women's History and the Metalanguage of Race," *Signs: Journal of Women Culture and Society* 12, 2 (1992): 251–74; Evelyn Brooks Higginbotham, "Beyond the Sound of Silence: Afro-American Women in History," *Gender and History* 1, 1 (1989): 50–67; Darlene Clark Hine, "Female Slave Resistance: The Economics of Sex," *Western Journal of Black Studies* 3 (Summer 1979): 123–27; Janell Hobson, *Venus in the Dark: Blackness and Beauty in Popular Culture* (New York: Routledge, 2005); Sharon Patricia Holland, *Raising the Dead: Readings of Death and (Black) Subjectivity* (Durham, N.C.: Duke University Press, 2000); bell hooks, *Outlaw Culture: Resisting Representations* (New York: Routledge, 1994); bell hooks, "Seduced by Violence No More," in *Transforming a Rape Culture*, ed. Emilie Buchwald, Pamela R. Fletcher, and Martha Roth (Minneapolis: Milkweed, 2005); Joy James, "Foreword: 'Tragedy Fatigue' and 'Aesthetic Agency,'" in *Unmaking Race, Remaking Soul: Transformative Aesthetics and the Practice of Freedom*, ed. Christa Davis Acampora and Angela L. Cotton (Albany: State University of New York Press., 2007); Toni Morrison, *Playing in the Dark: Whiteness and the Literary Imagination* (Cambridge, Mass.: Harvard University Press, 1992); Carina Ray, *Crossing the Color Line: Race, Sex, and the Contested Politics of Colonialism in Ghana* (Columbus: Ohio University Press, 2015); Dorothy Roberts, "Crime, Race and Reproduction," *Tulane Law Review* 67, 6 (June 1993): 1945–77; Joan W. Scott, "Gender: A Useful Category of Historical Analysis," *American Historical Review* 91, 5 (December 1986): 1053–75; Joan W. Scott, "The Evidence of Experience," *Critical Inquiry* 17, 4 (July 1991): 773–97; Valerie Smith, "Split Affinities: The Case of Interracial Rape," in *Theorizing Feminism: Parallel Trends in the Humanities and Social Sciences*, ed. Anne C. Hermann and Abigail J. Stewart (Boulder, Colo.: Westview, 1994); Hortense J. Spillers, "Mama's Baby, Papa's Maybe:

An American Grammar Book," *Diacritics* 17, 2 (July 1987): 65–81; Filomina Chioma Steady, "The Black Woman Cross-Culturally: An Overview," in Steady, *The Black Woman Cross-Culturally* (Cambridge: Schenkman, 1981); Ula Y. Taylor, "Black Feminisms and Human Agency," in *No Permanent Waves: Recasting Histories of U.S. Feminisms*, ed. Nancy A. Hewitt (New Brunswick, N.J.: Rutgers University Press, 2010); Ula Y. Taylor, "The Historical Evolution of Black Feminist Theory and Praxis," *Journal of Black Studies* 29, 2 (November 1998): 234–53; Rosalyn Terborg-Penn, "African Feminism: A Theoretical Approach to the History of Women in the African Diaspora," in *Women in Africa and the African Diaspora: A Reader*, ed. Rosalyn Terborg-Penn and Andrea Benton Rushing (Cambridge, Mass.: Harvard University Press, 1996); Alice Walker, *In Search of Our Mothers' Gardens: Womanist Prose* (1983; Orlando: Mariner Books, 2003); Michele Wallace, "Invisibility Blues," in *The Graywolf Annual Five: Multicultural Literacy*, ed. Rick Simonson and Scott Walker (St. Paul: Graywolf, 1988); Alexander Weheliye, *Habeas Vicus: Racializing Asssemblages, Biopolitics, and Black Feminist Theories of the Human* (Durham, N.C.: Duke University Press, 2014); Patricia J. Williams, *Alchemy of Race and Rights: Diary of a Law Professor* (Cambridge, Mass.: Harvard University Press, 1992); Deborah Willis, ed., *Black Venus 2010: They Called Her "Hottentot"* (Philadelphia: Temple University Press, 2010). For a more comprehensive list organized by field, see Sherri L. Barnes, *Black American Feminisms: A Multidisciplinary Bibliography*, University of California, Santa Barbara Libraries, http://blackfeminism.library.ucsb.edu/, accessed 7 June 2015.

Chapter 1. Jane: Fugitivity, Space, and Structures of Control in Bridgetown

Epigraphs: Katherine McKittrick, *Demonic Grounds: Black Women and the Cartographies of Struggle* (Minneapolis: University of Minnesota Press), xvi; M. NourbeSe Philip, *A Genealogy of Resistance and Other Essays* (Toronto: Mercury Press, 1997), 95; "Runaway: Jane," 13 January 1789, *Barbados Mercury*, Bridgetown Public Library (hereafter BPL).

1. "Country marks" refer to scars from West African ethnic scarification practices. For a study on ethnic identity and country marks, see Michael Gomez, *Exchanging Our Country Marks: The Transformation of African Identities in the Colonial and Antebellum South* (Chapel Hill: University of North Carolina Press, 1998).

2. African captives were often branded by slave ship crews to identify them for the particular merchant company and ship to which they were to belong. Stephanie Smallwood speaks of this as part of the commodification process in *Saltwater Slavery: A Middle Passage from Africa to American Diaspora* (Cambridge, Mass.: Harvard University Press, 2008).

3. For work on the assignation of ethnic identity to West Africans see James Sweet, *Recreating Africa: Culture and Kinship in the African Portuguese World, 1441–1770* (Chapel Hill: University of North Carolina Press, 2003).

4. Veena Das, "Language and Body: Transactions in the Construction of Pain," in

Social Suffering, ed. Arthur Kleinman, Veena Das, and Margaret Lock (Berkeley: University of California Press, 1997), 69.

5. Katherine McKittrick, *Demonic Grounds: Black Women and the Cartographies of Struggle* (Minneapolis: University of Minnesota Press), xii, 44.

6. McKittrick, *"Demonic Grounds,* xi.

7. The built environment refers to manmade structures including buildings, streets, parks, and sites of punishment. For further discussion of urban environments, see Kevin A. Lynch, *The Image of the City* (Cambridge, Mass.: Harvard-MIT Joint Center for Urban Studies, MIT Press, 1960).

8. NourbeSe Philip, *A Genealogy of Resistance* and McKittrick, *Demonic Grounds*, 49.

9. Hortense Spillers, "Mama's Baby, Papa's Maybe: An American Grammar Book," in Spillers, *Black, White, and in Color: Essays on American Literature and Culture* (Chicago: University of Chicago Press, 2003), 67.

10. Ibid., 206.

11. Stephanie Smallwood also identifies the processes by which African captives were made into commodities, including branding, regulation of sustenance, and the mathematical equation slave traders applied to prevent death during the Middle Passage. See Smallwood, *Saltwater Slavery*.

12. Philip, *A Genealogy of Resistance*, 99–100.

13. Allen Feldman, *Formations of Violence: The Narrative of the Body and Political Terror in Northern Ireland* (Chicago: University of Chicago Press, 1991), 8 and Spillers, "Mama's Baby, Papa's Maybe," 67.

14. James Ford, "Editor's Notes," *Black Camera* 5, 2 (Spring 2014): 3–4. See also Saidiya Hartman's discussion of "stealing away" and of the enslaved appropriating spaces for clandestine activities in *Scenes of Subjection*, esp. 68–70. See also John Hope Franklin and Loren Schweninger, *Runaway Slaves: Rebels on the Plantation* (Oxford: Oxford University Press, 1999).

15. Stephanie Camp, *Closer to Freedom*, xxix. In this chapter I am asking if this rival geography allowed for all of those possibilities if we consider how the scars on enslaved bodies carried memories of violence into all these actions and the how the persistent threat of white interrogation and surveillance remained a present force in these spaces.

16. Gomez, *Exchanging Our Country Marks*, 139.

17. Diana Paton, *No Bond But the Law: Punishment, Race, and Gender in Jamaican State Formation, 1780–1870* (Durham, N.C.: Duke University Press, 2004), 11. Paton also makes the important corrective to understanding the practice of corporal body punishment as a characteristic of pre-modern society and incarceration as a modern phenomenon by discussing the confluence of these practices in slave and post-emancipation British Caribbean societies.

18. This particular law passed in 1688 was passed to make provisions for newly arrived Africans to acclimate to slavery in Barbados. Running away was a common occurrence with newly arrived captives introduced to the terror of their new lives. The law

was briefly repealed and then reenacted in 1692. It stated that if, "any Negroe or Negroes, or other Slave or Slaves, after he, she or they have lived in this Island one whole
year, that is are, or shall run-away or absent him, her or themselves . . . and shall continue absent for an during the space of thirty days, shall suffer death for the same."
Richard Hall, *Acts, passed in the island of Barbados. From 1643, to 1762, inclusive; Carefully revised, innumerable Errors corrected; and the Whole compared and examined, with
the original acts, In the Secretary's Office. By the late Richard Hall, Esquire: One of the
Representatives in the General-Assembly, for the Parish of St. Michael; and one of His
Majesty's Justices of the Peace, for the said Island, near Thirty Years; And since his Death,
continued by his son, Richard Hall. To which is added, An index; and abridgment: With
many useful Notes, References and Observations, never before published. And also A List
of all the Laws, passed from the Settlement of the Island; which are now become Obsolete,
Expired, or have had their Effect* (London: printed for Richard Hall, 1764), 131.

19. Jerome S. Handler, "Slave Revolts and Conspiracies in Seventeenth-Century
Barbados," *New West Indian Guide* 56, 1/2 (1982): 9–10.

20. For a longer discussion of the concepts of fugitivity and precarity there are substantial works in cultural studies and literary theory including Hartman, *Scenes of Sub-
jection*; Nathaniel Mackey, *Paracritical Hinge: Essays, Talks, Notes, Interviews* (Madison:
University of Wisconsin Press, 2005); Daphne Brooks, *Bodies in Dissent: Spectacular
Performances of Race and Freedom, 1850–1910* (Durham, N.C.: Duke University Press,
2006); Judith Butler, *Frames of War: When Is Life Grievable?* (London: Verso, 2009); and
Stefano Harney and Fred Moten, eds., *The Undercommons: Fugitive Planning & Black
Study* (Wivenhoe: Minor Compositions, 2013).

21. We do not know whether Jane ran to Bridgetown, but she represents the many
enslaved men and women who ran to town to better conceal themselves in a more dense
population. There were also a few ads from the jailor describing the marks on a captured
slave so that owners could be located to come and claim their property. This practice
was characteristic of most slave societies in the Americas. Diana Paton discusses this in
some detail in *No Bond But the Law*, 11.

22. "Runaway: Sarah Clarke," 5 April 1783, *Barbados Mercury*, BPL. "Bandy," describes bowed legs "Curved laterally with the concavity inward," Online Oxford English
Dictionary.

23. I examined all runaway advertisements available in surviving Barbados newspapers in the Bridgetown Public Library from 1783, 1784, and 1787–1789 for the *Barbados
Mercury* and *Barbados Gazette* newspapers. The advertisements in these papers were
sometimes repeated in subsequent weeks but on average there were about twelve runaway advertisements for every year. This small sample revealed a range of information
for individual enslaved women (and men) that is useful when discussing the condition
in which they emerge in the archive and how the fleeting moments of viewing absconding fugitive slaves challenges our ability to fully account for and narrate the entirety of
enslaved lives.

24. "Runaway: Affey," 1 September 1787, *Barbados Mercury*, BPL.

25. "Runaway: Daphney," 6–9 April 1788, *Barbados Gazette*, BPL.

26. "Runaway: Joney," 9–22 November 1788, *Barbados Mercury*, BPL.

27. "Runaway: Potenah," 25 August 1787, *Barbados Mercury*, BPL.

28. "Runaway: Mary," 22–26 September 1787, *Barbados Mercury*, BPL.

29. Roger Norman Buckley, *The British Army in the West Indies: Society and the Military in the Revolutionary Age* (Gainesville: University Press of Florida, 1998), 160.

30. Dunn, *Sugar and Slaves*, 106 and Pedro Welch, *Slave Society in the City: Bridgetown Barbados, 1680–1807* (Kingston: Ian Randle, 2003), xiv.

31. For the seminal text on the development of an Atlantic sugar economy see Sidney Mintz, *Sweetness and Power: The Place of Sugar in Modern History* (New York: Viking, 1985).

32. "Commissioner's Books of 58 Acts," Lucas Manuscripts, *Journal of the Barbados Museum and Historical Society* (hereafter *JBMHS*) 11, 2 (February 1954): 62. The journal editor states this act is listed with no date. It is placed in the original *Commissioner's Book Containing 58 Acts* between the dates 1650 and 1682 on page 339, BDA. But Martyn Bowden cites the Act as being established in 1657 based on the Lucas Manuscripts as well, in Bowden, "Three Centuries of Bridgetown: An Historical Geography," *JBMHS* 49 (2003): 4.

33. Higman, *Slave Populations of the British Caribbean* and Welch, *Slave Society in the City*. Each acknowledges this reality but this chapter dwells specifically on the meaning of such symbols to the urban enslaved from their perspective.

34. The term "plantation complex" is taken from the definition of Philip Curtain, *The Rise and Fall of the Plantation Complex: Essays in Atlantic History* (Cambridge: Cambridge University Press, 1990), xi.

35. Paton, *No Bond But the Law*, 6.

36. Ibid., 7.

37. Diana Paton demarcates this transition in practices of punishment in post-emancipation British Caribbean contexts but here I am pointing to the specificities of urban slavery. For the details of Paton's argument, see *No Bond But the Law*, 7, 144. Paton argues that there were similarities in punishment between the pre and post-emancipation periods but states there was a difference in the legal parameters and format of flogging in post-emancipation British Caribbean colonies. However, evidence of the practices of punishment in urban slavery throughout the eighteenth century in Barbados and Bridgetown specifically suggest there were laws regarding the number and intervals of whipping enslaved bodies.

38. Handler, "Slave Revolts and Conspiracies," 10. Opportunities for escape to another island were very rare from Barbados, although there is evidence some enslaved people were stolen by colonists and taken off the island. In addition, it was possible for male slaves employed on ships to escape to other islands. But freedom remained tenuous on other island slave societies. On islands geographically closer to each other, the chance to row to another island increased. For a discussion of escape by canoe within the French islands, see Franklin W. Knight, *General History of the Caribbean* (London: UNESCO and Macmillan Education, 1997), 3: 330.

39. Letter from Governor Hay to Board of Trade (No. 8), 31 August 1774, Board of Trade Correspondence, CO28/55: 82, National Archives London (hereafter NAL).

40. Ibid.

41. Bowden, "Three Centuries of Bridgetown," 33. For a first hand account of the hurricane refer to Mr. Fowler, *A General Account of the Calamities occasioned by the Late Tremendous Hurricanes and Earthquakes in the West-India Islands, Foreign as well as Domestic: with The Petitions to, and Resolutions of, the House of Commons, in Behalf of the Sufferers at Jamaica and Barbados: Also A List of the Committee appointed to manage the Subscriptions of the benevolent Public, towards their further Relief, Carefully collated from Authentic Papers* (London: J. Stockdale and W. Richardson, 1781).

42. Richard Ligon, *The True and Exact History of the Island of Barbadoes 1657*, ed. and ann. J. Edward Hutson (Wildey, St. Michael: Barbados National Trust, 2000), 37.

43. Letter of Mr. Crawford, 4 August 1788, Parish of Saint Michael Vestry Minutes, Barbados Department of Archives (hereafter BDA).

44. Higman, *Slave Populations of the British Caribbean*, 232.

45. Letter from Mr. Crawford, St. Michael Vestry Minutes, 4 August 1788, BDA.

46. Pierre Baptiste Labat, *The Memoirs of Pere Labat, 1693–1705: First English Translation*, ed. Jean Baptiste (London: Frank Cass, 1931), quoted in Frederick Smith and Karl Watson, "Urbanity, Sociability, and Commercial Exchange in the Barbados Sugar Trade: A Comparative Colonial Archaeological Perspective on Bridgetown, Barbados in the Seventeenth Century," *International Journal of Historical Archaeology* 13 (2009): 72.

47. Hartman, *Lose Your Mother*, 114–15.

48. Bowden, "Three Centuries of Bridgetown," 33.

49. Ibid.

50. George Pinckard, *Notes on the West Indies: Written during the expedition under the command of the late General Sir Ralph Abercromby: including observations on the island of Barbadoes, and the settlements captured by the British troops, upon the coast of Guiana; likewise remarks relating to the Creoles and slaves of the western colonies, and the Indians of South America: with occasional hints, regarding the seasoning, or yellow fever of hot climates*, vol. 2 (London: Printed for Longman, Hurst, Rees, and Orme, 1806), 443–44.

51. Barbados Minutes of Council, 23 November 1757, CO31/30: 100, NAL.

52. Karl Watson, "Capital Sentences Against Slaves in Barbados in the Eighteenth Century: An Analysis," in *In the Shadow of the Plantation: Caribbean History and Legacy*, ed. Alvin O. Thompson (Kingston: Ian Randle, 2002), 207.

53. Barbados Minutes of Council, 20 June 1769, Lucas MSS: 227, BPL.

54. Bowden, "Three Centuries of Bridgetown," 72.

55. For a discussion of Molly's execution, see Chapter 4 of this book.

56. See James Stephen, Esq., *The Slavery of the British West India Colonies Delineated, as it Exists Both in Law and Practice, and Compared with The Slavery of Other Countries, Antient and Modern* (London: Saunders and Benning, 1830), 2: xvii–xxxiii. See also Barbados Minutes of Council, 16 March 1784, CO28/60: 141, "A Certificate of

the Justices of the Peace who tried & found guilty two Negro Slaves named Sambo & Nick, burned alive for the murder of John Horsham Apothecary for Payment to Benjamin Alleyne Cox Esqr. For the Sum of Five Pounds Seventeen Shillings and one half penny: (exclusive of the Secretarys fee for the order being disbursed by him for the Expences of the said Execution)."

57. Stephen, *The Slavery of the British West India Colonies Delineated*, 2: xvii–xxxiii and Barbados Minutes of Council, 16 March 1784, CO28/60: 141, NAL.

58. Barbados Minutes of Council, 14 March 1758, CO31/30: 127, NAL.

59. Bowden, "Three Centuries of Bridgetown," 48. Before the completion of the fort government legislators, who were primarily planters, met at various taverns throughout the town. The Minutes of Council records for the eighteenth century often refer to James Fort as the site of executions.

60. "Special Call, on Account of the Great May Fire in Bridgetown–Proceedings thereof," 20 May 1766, Barbados Minutes of Council, Lucas MSS: 113–14, BPL.

61. "Governor Charles Pinfold's Speech," 14 March 1758, Barbados Minutes of Council, CO31/30: 140–41, NAL.

62. Letter from Governor William Spry, 29 November 1771, Board of Trade Correspondence, CO28/55: 154, NAL.

63. Letter from Governor Charles Pinfold, 25 May 1766, Board of Trade Correspondence, CO28/50: 114, NAL. Apprentice refers to a lower-class white person, in this case a boy, bound in a contract to someone usually to learn a trade or indentured as a servant.

64. At least three rebellions were discovered and put down in the mid to late seventeenth-century resulting in mass executions of people primarily enslaved on plantations throughout the colony. For a discussion of Barbados slave revolts, see Dunn, *Sugar and Slaves*, 255–62. See also Hilary Beckles, *A History of Barbados: From Amerindian Settlement to Nation-State* (Cambridge: Cambridge University Press, 1990), 35–40.

65. For a full discussion of the revolts and conspiracies in seventeenth-century Barbados, see Handler, "Slave Revolts and Conspiracies," 13–30. For literature on Tacky's Revolt, refer to Trevor Burnard, *Mastery, Tyranny and Desire: Thomas Thistlewood and His Slaves in the Anglo-Jamaican World* (Chapel Hill: University of North Carolina Press, 2004), 170–72, and Vincent Brown, *Slave Revolt in Jamaica, 1760–1761: A Cartographic Narrative*, Axis Maps, http://revolt.axismaps.com/project.html and Vincent Brown, *The Reaper's Garden: Death and Power in the World of Atlantic Slavery* (Cambridge, Mass.: Harvard University Press), 50, 148.

66. The term "seasoned" refers to the process between one and three years during which newly arrived Africans were acclimated by planters and other slaves to the new environment. They were exposed to diseases, and other life threats as they adjusted to a life of slavery, as discussed in Brown, *The Reaper's Garden*, 50. The "Mole Head" refers to the land at the end of a wharf. In the eighteenth century this same land was referred to as the Mole Head or Molehead.

67. Slave Sale Advertisement, August 2, 1783, *Barbados Mercury*, BPL.

68. Bowden, "Three Centuries of Bridgetown," 50.

69. Slave Sale Advertisement, 1787, *Barbados Gazette*, BPL.

70. See Smallwood, *Saltwater Slavery* and McKittrick, *Demonic Grounds*, 44, who uses the term "black dispossession."

71. Smallwood, *Saltwater Slavery*, 201.

72. For a discussion of the British parliamentary debates on slave trade abolition, see Chapter 5 of this book.

73. Letter from Governor Hay, 24 August 1773, Board of Trade Correspondence, CO28/55: 21, NAL.

74. Erik Seeman, "Jews in the Early Modern Atlantic: Crossing Boundaries, Keeping Faith," in *The Atlantic in Global History: 1500–2000*, ed. Cañizares-Esguerra and Seeman (Upper Saddle River, N.J: Pearson Prentice Hall, 2006), 39; Bowden, "Three Centuries of Bridgetown," 40–47 and Natalie Zacek, " 'A People So Subtle': Sephardic Jewish Pioneers of the English West Indies," in *Bridging the Early Modern Atlantic: People, Products, and Practices on the Move*, ed. Caroline A. Williams (Surrey: Ashgate, 2009), 97–112.

75. Bowden, "Three Centuries of Bridgetown," 47–48. For a longer discussion of Quakers in Barbados, see Kristen Block, *Ordinary Lives in the Early Caribbean: Religion, Colonial Competition, and the Politics of Profit* (Athens: University of Georgia Press, 2012).

76. Bowden, "Three Centuries of Bridgetown," 51.

77. Beckles, *Natural Rebels*, 76.

78. Hall, *Acts, passed in the island of Barbados, From 1643, to 1762*, 185.

79. Welch, *Slave Society in the City*, 83–84.

80. See Christopher Crain, Kevin Farmer, Frederick Smith, and Karl Watson, "Human Skeletal Remains from an Unmarked African Burial Ground in the Pierhead Section of Bridgetown, Barbados," *JBMHS* 50 (2004): 66–83.

81. See Chapter 2 of this book for a discussion of prostitution in eighteenth-century Bridgetown.

82. For a complete listing of laws regulating enslaved bodies refer to Hall, *Acts, passed in the Island of Barbados, From 1643, to 1762* and Samuel Moore, ed., *The Public Acts in Force; Passed by the Legislature of Barbados, From May 11th 1762 to April 1800* (Barbados: Published for the Legislature of Barbados, 1801).

83. For a discussion of the case in which this enslaved boy was implicated, see Chapter 3.

84. Hartman, *Lose Your Mother*, 115.

85. For a brief discussion of West Indian laws pertaining to runaways, see Elsa Goveia, *The West Indian Slave Laws of the 18th Century*, with C. J. Bartlett, *A New Balance of Power: The 19th Century* (Barbados: Caribbean Universities Press, 1970), 22–25.

86. Handler, "Slave Revolts and Conspiracies," 17–18.

87. Dunn, *Sugar and Slaves*, 67.

88. Bowden, "Three Centuries of Bridgetown," 23.

89. Dunn, *Sugar and Slaves*, 26.

90. Ibid., 60–62.

91. See Welch, *Slave Society in the City*; Higman, *Slave Populations of the British Caribbean*; and Beckles, *Natural Rebels* for a discussion of Barbados' significance to the initial growth of the sugar trade.

92. Frederick Smith and Karl Watson, "Urbanity, Sociability, and Commercial Exchange in the Barbados Sugar Trade: A Comparative Colonial Archaeological Perspective on Bridgetown, Barbados in the Seventeenth Century," *International Journal of Historical Archaeology* 13 (2009): 72, and Bowden, "Three Centuries of Bridgetown," 5.

93. Smith and Watson, "Urbanity, Sociability, and Commercial Exchange," 71.

94. Jerome S. Handler, *The Unappropriated People: Freedom in the Slave Society of Barbados*, with an introduction by Melanie Newton (Kingston: University of the West Indies Press, 2009).

95. Smith and Watson, "Urbanity, Sociability, and Commercial Exchange," 71. See also Welch, *Slave Society in the City*.

96. "Commissioner's Books of 58 Acts, 1657," 62 and Smith and Watson, "Urbanity, Sociability, and Commercial Exchange," 72.

97. Smith and Watson, "Urbanity, Sociability, and Commercial Exchange," 73.

98. Bowden, "Three Centuries of Bridgetown," 55–61. See also Welch, *Slave Society in the City* for American town population statistics for the eighteenth and nineteenth centuries.

99. Pedro Welch, "The Urban Context of the Life of the Enslaved: Views from Bridgetown, Barbados, in the Eighteenth and Nineteenth Centuries," in *Slavery Without Sugar: Diversity in Caribbean Economy and Society Since the 17th Century*, ed. Verene Shepard (Gainesville: University Press of Florida, 2002), 183.

100. Brown, *The Reaper's Garden*, 13.

101. Board of Trade Correspondence, CO28/18: 321–25, NAL.

102. Welch, *Slave Society in the City*, 63.

103. Testimony of Mr. Fitzmaurice, in *House of Commons Sessional Papers of the Eighteenth Century*, ed. Sheila Lambert (Wilmington: Scholarly Resources, 1975), 82: 232.

104. Dunn, *Sugar and Slaves*, 328. See also Ligon, *The True and Exact History of the Island of Barbadoes*.

105. Dunn, *Sugar and Slaves*, 328.

106. Letter from Governor Hay to the Lords of Trade and Plantations, 13 April 1776, Board of Trade Correspondence, CO28/56: 40 (front and back), NAL.

107. Barbados Minutes of Council, 19 February 1782, CO28/59: 216, NAL.

108. Minutes of the Saint Michael's Vestry, Monday, 4 August 1788, BDA.

109. Dunn, *Sugar and Slaves*, 334.

110. Barbados Minutes of the Assembly, Friday, 21 December 1739, HA3.7: 97–98, BDA.

111. Jenny Shaw, *Everyday Life in the Early English Caribbean: Irish, Africans, and the Construction of Difference* (Athens: University of Georgia Press, 2013), 58.

112. Peter Campbell, "St. Ann's Fort and the Garrison," *JBMHS* 35, 1 (1975): 3–16.

113. Campbell, "St. Ann's Fort and the Garrison," 3–16; Warren Alleyne, *Historic Bridgetown* (St. Michael: Barbados Government Information Service, 1003), 72, 84.

114. Barbados Minutes of the Assembly, Tuesday, 9 December 1740, HA3.7: 201, BDA.

115. Jerome Handler, "Freedmen and Slaves in the Barbados Militia," *Journal of Caribbean History* 19, 1 (1984), 6–7. See also Buckley, *The British Army in the West Indies* 128–69.

116. Handler, "Freedmen and Slaves in the Barbados Militia," 8–9.

117. Buckley, *The British Army in the West Indies,* 128–30.

118. Karl Watson, *The Civilised Island Barbados: A Social History, 1750–1816* (Ellerton, St. George: Caribbean Graphic Production, 1979), 19.

119. Ibid., 20.

120. Ibid.

121. Andrew Jackson O'Shaughnessy, *An Empire Divided: The American Revolution and the British Caribbean* (Philadelphia: University of Pennsylvania Press, 200), 98–99.

122. Letter from Governor Hay, 24 March 1776, Board of Trade Correspondence, CO28/56: 70, NAL.

123. Address of the Assembly to the Lords of Trade and Plantations, CO28/56: 70, NAL.

124. To see examples of such interventions in keeping their slaves from suffering death from judicial rulings refer to Chapter 4, where slave executions are discussed at length.

125. See for example, Goveia, *The West Indian Slave Laws.*

126. William Dickson, *Letters on Slavery by William Dickson, formerly private secretary to the late Hon. Edward Hay, Governor of Barbadoes. To which are added, Addresses to the Whites, and to the Free Negroes of Barbados; and Accounts of some Negroes Eminent for their Virtues and Abilities* (London: J. Phillips and J. Johnson and Elliot and Kay, 1789), 34.

127. See "An Act to prevent distempered, maimed, and worn-out Negroes from infesting the Towns, Streets and Highways of this Island, passed 18 January 1785" in *Parliamentary Papers: 1780–1849, Volume 25,* Great Britain, Parliament, House of Commons (London: H.M Stationery Office, 1827), 263–64.

128. Fowler, *A General Account of the Calamities,* 33. Matthew Mulcahy conducts an extensive study of the hurricane's impact on the greater West Indies in *Hurricanes and Society in the British Caribbean, 1624–1783* (Baltimore: Johns Hopkins University Press, 2006).

129. Fowler, *A General Account of the Calamities,* 33–34.

130. Ibid., 30.

131. Letter from Governor Cunningham, October 1780, Board of Trade Correspondence, CO28/57: 231, NAL.

132. Fowler, *A General Account of the Calamities*, 38.

133. Ibid., 32.

134. Ibid., 42.

135. Mulcahy, *Hurricanes*, 109.

136. Fowler, *A General Account of the Calamities*, 40.

137. Mulcahy, *Hurricanes*, 190.

138. Ibid.

139. Brown, *The Reaper's Garden*, 137. For a study of the production of social identities and space see Henri Lefebvre, *The Production of Space*, trans. Donald Nicholson-Smith (Oxford: Blackwell, 1991) and Katherine McKittrick, *Demonic Grounds: Black Women and the Cartographies of Struggle* (Minneapolis: University of Minnesota Press, 2006).

140. See Welch, *Slave Society in the City* for a discussion of the differences in slave punishment from country to town, esp. 17. A "jumper," also referred to as the "Common Whipper," was a man employed specifically in towns to whip slaves for their owners.

141. Higman, *Slave Populations of the British Caribbean*, 244.

142. Hall, *Acts, passed in the Island of Barbados, From 1643, to 1762*, 185.

143. Welch, *Slave Society in the City*, 164–65. See also Barbados Minutes of Council for the eighteenth century, wherein hundreds of petitions were submitted for the payment of constables and magistrates who worked the streets and jails controlling slave behavior and maintaining structures of confinement.

144. Higman, *Slave Populations in the British Caribbean*, 242.

145. Barbados Minutes of Council, 17 February 1742/3, CO31/21: 159, NAL.

146. Welch, *Slave Society in the* City, 178 and Bowden, "Three Centuries of Bridgetown," 97.

147. Bowden, "Three Centuries of Bridgetown," 23.

148. Copy and sketch of the Deed Poll of Cage Land, 3 January 1818 & 58th [Year] of His Majesty's Reign, 31. Courtesy of Professor Martyn Bowden.

149. Ibid.

150. Bowden, "Three Centuries of Bridgetown," 23.

151. Careenage refers to an open waterway separating the two sides of town.

152. Moore, *The Public Acts in Force*, 121.

153. Hall, *Acts, passed in the Island of Barbados, From 1643, to 1762*, 436.

154. Ibid., 437.

155. Ibid.

156. Welch, *Slave Society in the City*, 164.

157. In a report to the Council and Assembly the Magistrates of Bridgetown remarked, "that it has never been Optional with Proprietors [slave owners] whether they would or would not confine their Negroes in the Cage or the Gaol as the repository for such that commit capital offences." Barbados Minutes of Council 18 December 1810, Lucas MSS: 18, BPL.

158. Barbados Minutes of Council, 27 October 1702, CO31/6: 295, NAL.

159. Barbados Minutes of Council, 11 November 1759, Lucas MSS, 58, BPL. There are

other execution records later in the eighteenth century that do not provide a reason for execution of a slave including those executed "according to law." For example, "a petition of Thomas Alleyne, Esqr. For payment of the sum of L25 [current money], being the value of a negro woman Slave named Frankey (the Property of the abovesaid Petitioner) who was executed according to law," does not indicate Frankey's "crime," Barbados Minutes of Council, 1 October 1776, Lucas MSS, 17, BPL. This obscurity in the records leaves us with no way to account for how many enslaved people were executed for running away or how long authorities enforced this law. More importantly, the authorities' perception of the enslaved as objects took away the necessity of recording the circumstances or conditions of their deaths, especially when criminally convicted.

160. Karl Watson, *Capital Sentences Against Slaves in Barbados in the Eighteenth Century: An Analysis,*" in *In the Shadow of the Plantation: Caribbean History and Legacy,* ed. Alvin O. Thompson (Kingston: Ian Randle Publishers, 2002), 207.

161. Barbados Minutes of Council, 18 December 1810, Lucas MSS, 17, 19, BPL.

162. Welch, *Slave Society in the City,* 165.

163. Ibid.

164. Barbados Minutes of Council, 18 December 1810, Lucas MSS, 17, BPL.

165. Ibid., 15

166. Ibid., 20, emphasis in original document.

167. Copy of the Deed Poll, 31.

168. Alleyne, *Historic Bridgetown,* 63.

169. "Molly and Bessey," 13–17 October, 1787, *Barbados Gazette,* BPL.

170. "Ambah," 20 December 1788, *Barbados Mercury,* BPL.

171. Ibid.

172. "Fourteen . . . Negroes," 25 October 1788, *Barbados Mercury,* BPL.

173. See "Barbados Slave Act 1688" where the punishment for running away for thirty days or more was death (Hall, *Acts Passed in the Island of Barbados*).

174. Barbados Minutes of Council, 16 February 1747/8, Lucas MSS, 418, BPL.

175. Testimony of Captain Cook, 89th Regiment of Foot, Royal Navy, in Lambert, *House of Commons Sessional Papers,* 82: 204–5. "Infantry of Foot" refers to a company of soldiers who fought on foot with weapons.

176. Ibid.

177. Ibid.

178. Lefebvre, *The Production of Space,* 26. See also Higman, *Slave Populations of the British Caribbean,* 258. Higman argues that the "freedom" urban slaves had in town from owners renting their slaves to other people, which sometimes allowed the enslaved to work more independently, was offset by structures and symbols of punishment and colonial power.

179. Welch, *Slave Society in the City,* 164.

Chapter 2. Rachael and Joanna: Power, Historical Figuring, and Troubling Freedom

Epigraphs: Hartman, "Venus in Two Acts, 5; Troullot, *Silencing the Past*, 25; Will of Rachael Pringle Polgreen, 25 July 1791, RB6/19: 435–36, BDA.

1. Captain Henry Carter, Mariner, and William Willoughby, Gentleman, Deposition, 20 July 1793, Barbados Recopied Deeds, RB3/40: 442, BDA. Although in Pringle Polgreen's will Joanna's name was spelled "Joannah," I have chosen to privilege Joanna's apprentice documents and deed in which she initiates her own archival appearance and spells her name without the "h," even though this is an arbitrary spelling by the town clerk.

2. Joanna Polgreen to Richard Braithwaite, Deed of Manumission, RB3/40: 443, BDA.

3. See Fuentes, "Power and Historical Figuring."

4. I take this quote from Hartman, "Venus in Two Acts," 2, where she describes how the invisibility of enslaved women in the archive is sometimes disrupted by "an act of chance or disaster," 2.

5. J. W. Orderson, *Creoleana: Or, Social and Domestic Scenes and Incidents in Barbados in the Days or Yore and The Fair Barbadian and Faithful Black*, ed. John Gilmore (Oxford: Macmillan, 2002). See also Newton, *The Children of Africa in the Colonies*, 258–62. I employ the term "free(d)" here and throughout the chapter to refer to the status of people of color, like Polgreen who became free through manumission, in an effort to encompass the varied possibilities of "status" in Bridgetown's slave society.

6. For accounts of this narrative, see Orderson, *Creoleana*. See also Handler, *The Unappropriated People*; Buckley, *The British Army in the West Indies*; Beckles, *Centering Woman*; Welch and Goodridge, *"Red" and Black over White*; Newton, *The Children of Africa in the Colonies*; and Welch, *Slave Society in the City*.

7. These include Handler, *The Unappropriated People*; Buckley, *The British Army in the West Indies*; Beckles, *Centering Woman*; Pedro L.V. Welch and Richard A. Goodridge, *"Red" and Black over White: Free Coloured Women in Pre-Emancipation Barbados* (Bridgetown, Barbados: Carib Research & Publications Inc., 2000); and Welch, *Slave Society in the City*.

8. Newton, *The Children of Africa in the Colonies*, 61.

9. Free(d) and enslaved women's predominant participation in the produce and commodity informal markets in town as "hucksters" exemplified the alternative to prostitution. See Newton, *The Children of Africa in the Colonies*, 61.

10. See Hilary McD. Beckles, "White Women and Slavery in the Caribbean," *History Workshop Journal* 36 (1993): 66–82.

11. Beckles, *Natural Rebels*, 143–44.

12. Gayatri Spivak, "Can the Subaltern Speak?" in *Marxism and the Interpretation of Culture*, ed. Lawrence Grossberg and Carl Nelson (Urbana: University of Illinois Press, 1988), 271–315.

13. Buckley, *The British Army in the West Indies*, 165.

14. Handler, *The Unappropriated People*, 15–28 and Newton, *The Children of Africa in the Colonies*, 27–28.

15. For the original iteration of this narrative, see Orderson, *Creoleana*, 76.

16. Beckles, *Centering Woman*.

17. Handler, *The Unappropriated People* and Handler, "Joseph Rachell and Rachael Pringle-Polgreen: Petty Entrepreneurs," in *Struggle and Survival in Colonial America*, ed. David Sweet and Gary Nash (Berkeley: University of California Press, 1981), 376–92.

18. See Beckles, *Natural Rebels* and Bush, *Slave Women in Caribbean Slave Society*. Gray White's text *Ar'n't I a Woman?* pioneered in the effort to document the experiences of enslaved women in the antebellum United States in 1985, and Jennifer Morgan made an important link between reproduction and slavery in *Laboring Women*.

19. See Orderson, *Creoleana*; Sir Algernon Aspinall, "Rachel Pringle of Barbados," *JBMHS* 9, 3 (May 1942): 112–19; Joel Augustus Rogers, *Sex and Race: Negro-Caucasian Mixing in All Ages and All Lands* (New York: J.A. Rogers, 1944); Neville Connell, "Prince William Henry's Visits To Barbados in 1786 & 1787," *JBMHS* 25 (August 1958): 157–64; Handler, *The Unappropriated People*; Watson, *The Civilised Island*; F. A. Hoyos, *Barbados: A History from the Amerindians to Independence* (London: Macmillan, 1978); Handler, "Joseph Rachel and Rachel Pringle Polgreen"; Beckles, *Black Rebellion in Barbados* and *Natural Rebels*; Alleyne, *Historic Bridgetown*; Welch, *Slave Society in the City*; Stuart Hahn, "Rachel Pringle, the Notorious Barbados Madame," posted 2 February 2006 at Richard Bolai, *Timeless–TheBookmann–Feinin*, http://thebookmann.blogspot.com/; Cecily Jones, *Engendering Whiteness: White Women and Colonialism in Barbados and North Carolina, 1627–1865* (Manchester: University of Manchester Press, 2007) and Newton, *The Children of Africa in the Colonies*.

20. Welch, *Slave Society in the City*, 48.

21. Hartman, *Scenes of Subjection*, 85–86.

22. Trouillot, *Silencing the Past*, 29.

23. Hartman, *Scenes of Subjection*, 10.

24. Handler, "Joseph Rachell and Rachael Pringle-Polgreen," 383.

25. Records of Baptisms and Burials, St. Michael Parish Church, 23 July 1791, RL1/5: 538, BDA. William Lauder was her owner and her last name was presumably given by him.

26. Estate inventory of Rachael Pringle Polgreen, 13 August 1791, BDA. For a discussion of the monetary accumulation of free women of color in Bridgetown, see Welch, *Slave Society in the City*, 166–81.

27. This calculation is based solely on Polgreen's estate inventory. Jerome Handler wrote in *The Unappropriated People* that Polgreen owned nineteen slaves from his reading of Polgreen's will. In order to address this inconsistency I used the inventory list as opposed to the more general language of Polgreen's will, wherein she refers to her

unnamed enslaved people (those not explicitly freed) as "All the Rest, Residue and Remainder of my Estate, real and personal, here or elsewhere." See the Will of Rachael
Pringle Polgreen, 21 July 1791, RB6/19: 435–36, BDA.

28. Will of Rachael Pringle Polgreen. In an attempt to track the manumissions of
the women Polgreen requested be freed by her will, I traced manumission payments in
the St. Michael Parish Vestry Minutes in 1780–1788 and 1789–1805. Any slave holder
wishing to manumit an enslaved person was to pay fifty pounds to the Church Vestry in
the Parish in which she/he resided (this fee was raised to three hundred pounds in 1800
to discourage manumissions). I found no evidence that such manumission fees were
paid for those Polgreen wished to free during the years abovementioned. As Orderson
explains, "White men, who in general (it being often a stipulation with their favourite)
purchase [enslaved women] of their owners, in many instances their own parent,—and
subsequently giving a certificate on the back of the deed of sale, annulling their right of
property in the person of their favourite, in like manner give them a freedom not recognized by the laws." J. W. Orderson, *Cursory Remarks and Plain Facts Connected with the
Question Produced by the Proposed Slave Registry Bill* (London: Hatchard, Piccadilly;
Hamilton, Paternoster Row, and J. M. Richardson, 1816), 16, New York Public Library
(hereafter NYPL).

29. See Gilmore, "Introduction," in *Creoleana*, viii and Handler, *The Unappropriated
People*, 135.

30. Gilmore, "Introduction," in *Creoleana*, 1–18.

31. Aspinall, "Rachel Pringle of Barbados," 114.

32. Editorial, "Polgreen of Barbados," *JBMHS* 9, 3 (May 1942): 109. Thomas Rowlandson (1757–1827) was a half-French, half-British portrait, landscape, social satirist
painter of eighteenth- and nineteenth-century Britain. He was a contemporary of William Hogarth, who was known for depicting people of African descent, including prostitutes in eighteenth-century London, and whose work influenced many of Rowlandson's
scenes of Georgian British life. For an extensive discussion of Thomas Rowlandson's life
and art and Hogarth's influence on his art, see Marisa J. Fuentes, "Buried Landscapes:
Enslaved Black Women, Sex, Confinement and Death in Colonial Bridgetown, Barbados and Charleston, South Carolina" (Ph.D. dissertation, University of California at
Berkeley, 2007), esp. 31–32. For biographical studies on Hogarth and Rowlandson, see
Osbert Sitwell, *Famous Water-Colour Painters VI: Thomas Rowlandson* (London: Studio
Limited, 1929); Gert Schiff, *The Amorous Illustrations of Thomas Rowlandson* (New
York: Cythera, 1969); and David Dabydeen, *Hogarth's Blacks: Images of Blacks in Eigh-
teenth-Century English Art* (Athens: University of Georgia Press, 1987).

33. We know very little of how she acquired this name. In the historical works that
write of Rachael Pringle Polgreen, none have ventured to find out Mr. Polgreen's identity. For a summary sketch and unverifiable speculation of his life, see John Gilmore's
"Notes" to *Creoleana*, 235–39. Additionally, a James Polgreen appears in the Bridgetown
levy records in 1780 as the owner of several properties, but no clear linkage between him

and Rachael Pringle Polgreen has been established. It is possible, however, that Rachael Polgreen forged a relationship with a Mr. Polgreen similar to her "relationship" with Captain Thomas Pringle.

34. See Beckles, *Natural Rebels*, 72–89 and Newton, *The Children of Africa in the Colonies*, 34–35 and 105–6. Similar to the experiences of free women of color in the United States during slavery, free(d) Afro-Barbadian women faced stigmatism for their "public" visibility. Due to racial and gendered stereotypes of their immorality stemming from their public roles as market women and tavern keepers, some Afro-Barbadian women sought to distance themselves from these images through philanthropic and religious work.

35. Editorial, "Polgreen of Barbados," 109.

36. Trouillot, *Silencing the Past*, 28–29.

37. Polgreen signed her will with an "X," indicating that she was probably illiterate.

38. Gilmore, "Introduction," in *Creoleana*, 3.

39. Though Polgreen lacked literacy she clearly understood the power of the written word. Over the course of three years she placed at least three advertisements in the *Barbados Gazette, or the General Intellegencer*. The first appears in the 26–30 January edition advertising a lost gold ring, the next for a raffle of "paintings in oil" as well as her hosting a portrait taker named T. G. who offered accurate portraits to customers "nothing required," 4–7 February 1788, and finally the advertisement of lost silverware, 31 January–4 February 1789, *Barbados Gazette, or the General Intellegencer*, BPL.

40. Newton, *The Children of Africa in the Colonies*, 259.

41. See Orderson, *Creoleana*, 91–92, describing the tale of a young African boy named Prince who in the service of a ship is given the chance to return to his kinsmen in "Dahome." Instead of accepting freedom Prince returns to Barbados and enslavement proclaiming, "he liked the white people's ways, and their victuals and dress, and all that something in backara country, which he no have in he own." See also Orderson, *Cursory Remarks*, 9–10, wherein he contends that West Indian slavery exposed Africans to civilization and skills with which they are better off than their counterparts who remained in Africa.

42. Newton, *The Children of Africa in the Colonies*, 259 and 259–62, wherein Newton critically engages the gendered and racial context and content of Orderson's *Creoleana*.

43. See also Gilmore, "Introduction," in *Creoleana*, 13.

44. Orderson, *Cursory Remarks*, 22.

45. Ibid.

46. Ibid.

47. Orderson, *Creoleana*, 76.

48. Ibid., 76.

49. Hortense Spillers, "The Permanent Obliquity of an In(Pha)llibly Straight: In the Time of the Daughters and the Fathers," in *Black, White, and in Color: Essays on American Literature and Culture*, ed. Hortense Spillers (Chicago: University of Chicago Press, 2003), 249.

50. For a recent and important scholarly study on incest and the American family in nineteenth-century United States, see Brian Connolly, *Domestic Intimacies: Incest and the Liberal Subject in Nineteenth-Century America* (Philadelphia: University of Pennsylvania Press, 2014).

51. Spillers, "The Permanent Obliquity," 249.

52. See also Doris Garraway's discussion of incest and miscegenation in the eighteenth-century French Caribbean in *The Libertine Colony: Creolization in the Early French Caribbean* (Durham, N.C.: Duke University Press, 2005), 34, 278–81.

53. Orderson, *Creoleana,* 76–77.

54. Ibid., 76–78.

55. Ibid., 78. See also Connell, "Prince William Henry," 157–64.

56. Orderson, *Creoleana,* 79.

57. Ibid.

58. Ibid.

59. See, for example, Handler, *The Unappropriated People* and Welch, *Slave Society in the City.*

60. Abel Clinckett was a white Barbadian who expressed anxiety about the post-emancipation changes in Barbados society, including the inter-racial intimacy between white men and women of color and the threat of black political organizations to white political power. See Newton, *The Children of Africa in the Colonies,* 170, 214–15.

61. "Editorial," *Barbadian,* 21 May 1842, BPL. A West Indian sugar hogshead was a measurement for sugar in a wooden barrel between "1456–1792 pounds avoirdupois" according to Niklas Thorde Jensen in *For the Health of the Enslaved: Slaves, Medicine and Power in the Danish West Indies, 1803–1848* (Copenhagen: Museum Tusculanum Press, 2012), 295.

62. Gilmore, "Introduction," in *Creoleana,* 16.

63. "Advertisement by Rachael-Pringle Polgreen for a Lost Gold Ring," *The Barbados Gazette, or the General Intellegencer,* 31 January–4 February 1789, BPL. This advertisement was also found with information from Connell's article.

64. Orderson, *Creoleana,* 78 and Connell, "Prince William Henry," 164.

65. This is testimony gathered by the Privy Council of the British Parliament on the slave trade and slavery in the colonies, Sheila Lambert, ed., *House of Common Sessional Papers of the Eighteenth Century* (Wilmington: Scholarly Resources, 1975), 82: 203. Throughout Polgreen's archive she is referred to as Rachael Pringle, Rachael Pringle Polgreen, Mrs. Pringle Polgreen (in one newspaper advertisement referring to her hotel), and Rachael Lauder. The fact of her multiple namings in various sources reflects perfectly the archival power to which Polgreen had little access.

66. Newton, *The Children of Africa in the Colonies,* 169. See also Chapter 5 of this book for a full study on representations of violence against enslaved women in the Privy Council reports generated for the abolition debates.

67. John Baskett, *Acts of Assembly, Passed in the Island of Barbados: From 1648, to*

1712 (John Baskett, Printer to the King's most excellent majesty, and by the assigns of Thomas Newcomb, and Henry Hills deceas'd, 1721), 47.

68. Newton, *The Children of Africa in the Colonies,* 59.

69. Ibid.

70. See the Estate Inventory of Rachael Pringle Polgreen, 1791, BDA. On her death she also owned three boats.

71. For a discussion on venereal disease on plantations, see Burnard, *Mastery, Tyranny, and Desire.*

72. Lefebvre, *The Production of Space,* 106; emphasis original.

73. Long, *The History of Jamaica* and Ligon, *The True and Exact History of the Island of Barbadoes.*

74. Hartman, *Scenes of Subjection,* 85.

75. See for example, Handler, *The Unappropriated People*; Buckley, *The British Army in the West Indies*; Douglass Hall, *In Miserable Slavery: Thomas Thistlewood in Jamaica, 1750–86* (Kingston: University of the West Indies Press, 1999); and Burnard, *Mastery, Tyranny, and Desire.*

76. Refer to Tony Henderson, *Disorderly Women in Eighteenth-Century London: Prostitution and Control in the Metropolis,* 1730–1830 (New York: Pearson, 1999) for a study on prostitution in England during this era.

77. Julia O'Connell Davidson, "The Rights and Wrongs of Prostitution," *Hypatia* 17, 2 (2002): 86. Recent scholarship urges the study of sexuality and enslavement to shift our gaze toward the "erotic life of slavery," to understand how enslaved women experienced "desire and intimacy"—difficult, if not impossible, aspects of subjectivity to excavate from the archives of slavery. Akin to previous work concerned with the dichotomies of victim/agent and consent/coercion through which enslaved female sexuality has been studied, Jessica M. Johnson and Treva Lindsey argue that "sex could function as a tool of resistance as well as a vehicle for affirming humanity." Treva B. Lindsey and Jessica M. Johnson, "Searching for Climax: Black Erotic Lives in Slavery and Freedom," *Meridians: Feminism, Race, Transnationalism* 12, 2 (2014): 169–195, 175. However, the difficulty with this project is the reproduction of the liberal humanist discourse of agency as resistance and autonomous action that has permeated U.S. slavery historiography since the late 1970s.

78. Captain Henry Carter (Mariner) and William Willoughby (Gentleman), Recopied Deed Record Books, RB3/40: 442, BDA.

79. Captain Henry Carter (Mariner) and William Willoughby (Gentleman) Recopied Deed Record Books, RB3/40: 442, BDA.

80. Welch, *Slave Society in the City,* 89.

81. Roger Norman Buckley, *The British Army in the West Indies,* 159–169.

82. Joanna Polgreen to Rachael Pringle Polgreen, Deed of Indenture, Recopied Deed Record Books, RB3/40: 441, BDA.

83. Handler, "Joseph Rachell and Rachael Pringle-Polgreen," 387, my emphasis.

84. Will of Rachael Pringle Polgreen, 21 July 1791, RB6/19: 435–36, BDA.

85. Jackie Hill, "Case Studies in Indentured Servitude in Colonial America," *Constructing the Past* 9, 1 (2008): 56.

86. Joanna Polgreen to Robert Braithwaite, Deed of Manumission, RB3/40: 445, BDA.

87. For important discussions of "agency" in slavery scholarship, see Hartman, *Scenes of Subjection*; Walter Johnson, "On Agency," *Journal of Social History* 37, 1 (2003): 113–24; Paton, *No Bond But the Law*; and Johnson, *Slavery's Ghost*.

88. Mahmood, *Politics of Piety*, 17.

89. Ibid., 20. Mahmood's work in this context centers on the "women's piety movement" in Egypt circa the early 2000s. In *Politics of Piety*, 2, she sought a way to elucidate the actions of women who participate in Islamist movements when, from a normative, Western feminist perspective, they seemed to be "inimical to their 'own interests and agendas?'" Her theoretical work in this text offers a way to describe the actions of women of color in Barbados slave society who participated in and perpetuated the violence of slave-owning.

90. Ibid., 17. For another critique of "the romance of resistance" see Lila Abu-Lughod, "The Romance of Resistance: Tracing Transformations of Power Through Bedouin Women," *American Ethnologist* 17, 1 (February 1990): 41–55.

91. Mahmood, *Politics of Piety*, 17.

Chapter 3. Agatha: White Women Slave Owners and the Dialectic of Racialized "Gender"

Epigraphs: Edward Long, *The History of Jamaica, or General Survey of the Antient and Modern State of that Island: With Reflections on its Situation, Settlements, Inhabitants, Climate, Products, Commerce, Laws, and Government* (London: T. Lowndes, 1774), 2: 286; Barbados Council Minutes of Council, 4 October 1743, CO31/21/D1: 65, NAL; 6 October 1743, CO31/21/D1: 51, NAL.

1. Karl Watson, "Obsession, Betrayal and Sex in Eighteenth-Century Bridgetown," *JBMHS* 51 (2005): 250. I am indebted to Dr. Watson for bringing this case to my attention while I was conducting research in Barbados in 2005. Through sheer luck, as sometimes happens with archival research, I stumbled upon the original documents in the National Archives in Kew (London), shortly thereafter. Dr. Watson has since published a detailed and important analysis of the many facts of this case including a thorough genealogy of the Withers/Moore, Crofts, and Harrison families.

2. Barbados Minutes of Council, 4 October 1743, CO31/21/D1: 76–90, NAL.

3. There were two other enslaved people involved in the case both of whom were also acquitted of any criminal acts. Samuel Webb, a witness on behalf of Dudley Crofts, stated that a slave named John brought the boy a message from a nurse to come to the Withers/Moore house in the evening. Toney, another slave, was said to have threatened the boy with harm. For this reason, the deponent argued, the boy took the sword to protect himself. Barbados Minutes of Council, 4 October 1743, CO31/21/D1: 68, NAL

4. The law related to punishment for these crimes reads: "If any Negro or Slave whatsoever shall offer any Violence to any Christian, by Striking, or the like, such Negro or other Slave shall, for his or her first Offence, by Information given up on Oath . . . shall be severely whipped by the Constable . . . for his second Offence of that nature, he shall be severely whipped, his Nose slit, and be burned in some part of his Face with a hot Iron," John Baskett, ed., *Acts of Assembly Passed in the Island of Barbados: From 1648, to 1718* (London: by Order of the Lords Commissioners of Trade and Plantations, 1732), 118–26.

5. Bowden, "Three Centuries of Bridgetown," 23.

6. Act of 1739, No. 180, Sect. 1, in Richard Hall, *Acts Passed in the Island of Barbados*, 325.

7. Barbados Minutes of Council, 4 October 1743, CO31/21/D1: 43–90, NAL.

8. Ibid., 66, NAL.

9. Watson, "Obsession, Betrayal and Sex," 347.

10. Barbados Minutes of Council, 4 October 1743, CO31/21/D1: 76–90, NAL.

11. Ibid.: 43–90, NAL.

12. Welch, *Slave Society in the* City, 13–14; Beckles, "White Women and Slavery in the Caribbean," 7; Bush, *Slave Women in Caribbean Society*, 120–24; Morgan, *Laboring Women*, 74–76.

13. Handler, *The Unappropriated People*, 18–19.

14. Welch, *Slave Society in the City*, 94–96. For population statistics for the British Caribbean into the nineteenth century, see Higman, *Slave Populations in the British Caribbean*, esp. chaps. 4, 5.

15. Welch, *Slave Society in the City*, 94–96.

16. Beckles, "White Women and Slavery," 69–70.

17. Beckles, *Centering Woman*, 64. For a comparison of populations between the British Caribbean Islands, see Dunn, *Sugar and Slaves*, 311–13. On Jamaica refer to Burnard, *Mastery, Tyranny and Desire*, 22–24 and Mair, *A Historical Study of Women in Jamaica*, 23–28. For the Leeward Islands, refer to Natalie Zacek, *Settler Society in the English Leeward Islands, 1670–1776* (New York: Cambridge University Press, 2010), n 69. For population statistics in the nineteenth century, see Higman, *Slave Populations in the British Caribbean*, esp. chaps. 4 and 5.

18. Beckles, "White Women and Slavery," 69–70.

19. Ibid.

20. See Trevor Burnard, "'A Matron in Rank, a Prostitute in Manners': The Manning Divorce of 1741 and Class, Gender Race and the Law in Eighteenth-Century Jamaica," in *Working Slavery, Pricing Freedom: Perspectives from the Caribbean, Africa and the African Diaspora*, ed. Verene Shepard (New York: Palgrave, 2001), 133–52 and Natalie Zacek, "Sex, Sexuality, and Social Control in the Eighteenth-Century Leeward Islands," in *Sex and Sexuality in Early America*, ed. Merril D. Smith (New York: New York University Press, 1998). Burnard has written several articles and book chapters on the plight of white women in the British Caribbean but particularly in Jamaica. These works include

Trevor Burnard and Ann M. Little, "Where the Girls Aren't: Women as Reluctant Migrants But Rational Actors in Early America," in *The Practice of U.S. Women's History: Narratives, Intersections, and Dialogues*, ed. S. J. Kleinberg, Eileen Boris, and Vicki Ruiz (New Brunswick, N.J.: Rutgers University Press, 2007); "'Rioting in Goatish Embraces': Marriage and Improvement in Early British Jamaica," *History of the Family* 11 (2006): 185–97; "Evaluating Gender in Early Jamaica, 1674–1784," *History of the Family* 12, 2 (2007): 81–91; and "'Gay and Agreeable Ladies': White Women in Mid-Eighteenth-Century Kingston, Jamaica," *Wadabagei: A Journal of the Caribbean and Its Diasporas* 9, 3 (2006): 27–49.

21. For an excellent study of white women in colonial Barbados and North Carolina, see Jones, *Engendering Whiteness*. Jones conducts a comprehensive study of white women in various classes in these two sites. See also Beckles, *Centering Woman*, esp. chaps, 2 and 4, and Welch, *Slave Society in the City*. For other studies on gender and urban slavery in the wider Atlantic world, see Kristen Block, *Ordinary Lives in the Early Caribbean: Religion, Colonial Competition, and the Politics of Profit* (Athens: University of Georgia Press, 2012), esp. chaps. 1, 10; Rosemary Brana-Shute and Randy J. Sparks, eds., *Paths to Freedom: Manumission in the Atlantic World* (Columbia: University of South Carolina Press, 2009); Douglass Catterall and Jodi Campbell, eds., *Women in Port: Gendering Communities, Economies, and Social Networks in Atlantic Port Cities, 1500–1800* (Leiden: Brill, 2012); Amrita Chakrabarti Myers, *Forging Freedom: Black Women and the Pursuit of Liberty in Antebellum Charleston* (Chapel Hill: University of North Carolina Press, 2011); Emily Clark, *Masterless Mistresses: The New Orleans Ursulines and the Development of a New World Society, 1727–1834* (Chapel Hill: University of North Carolina Press, 2007); Camillia Cowling, *Women of Color, Gender, and the Abolition of Slavery in Havana and Rio de Janeiro* (Chapel Hill: University of North Carolina Press, 2013); David Barry Gaspar and Darlene Clark Hine, eds., *More than Chattel: Black Women and Slavery in the Americas* (Bloomington: University of Indiana Press, 1996), esp. chaps. 5, 15; Cynthia M. Kennedy, *Braided Relations, Entwined Lives: The Women of Charleston's Urban Slave Society* (Bloomington: Indiana University Press, 2005); Jane Landers, *Black Society in Spanish Florida* (Urbana: University of Illinois Press, 1999), esp. chaps. 6, 9; Mieko Nishida, *Slavery and Identity: Ethnicity, Gender, and Race in Salvador, Brazil, 1808–1888* (Bloomington: Indiana University Press, 2003); Pamela Scully and Diana Paton, eds., *Gender and Slave Emancipation in the Atlantic World* (Durham, N.C.: Duke University Press, 2005); and Jennifer Spear, *Race, Sex, and Social Order in Early New Orleans* (Baltimore: Johns Hopkins University Press, 2009).

22. For a range of scholarship that includes white women, gender, and slavery, see Henrice Altink, *Representations of Slave Women in Discourses on Slavery and Abolition, 1780–1838* (London: Routledge, 2007); Kathleen M. Brown, *Good Wives, Nasty Wenches, and Anxious Patriarchs: Gender, Race, and Power in Colonial Virginia* (Chapel Hill: University of North Carolina Press, 1996); Lois Green Carr and Lorena S. Walsh, "The Planter's Wife: The Experience of White Women in Seventeenth-Century Maryland,"

William and Mary Quarterly 3rd ser. 34 (1977): 542–71; Cornelia Hughes Dayton, *Women Before the Bar: Gender, Law, and Society in Connecticut, 1639–1789* (Chapel Hill: University of North Carolina Press, 1995); Kirsten Fischer, *Suspect Relations: Sex, Race, and Resistance in Colonial North Carolina* (Ithaca, N.Y.: Cornell University Press, 2002); Martha Hodes, *White Women, Black Men: Illicit Sex in the Nineteenth-Century South* (New Haven, Conn.: Yale University Press, 1997); Ann M. Little, *Abraham in Arms: War and Gender on the New England Frontier, 1620–1763* (Philadelphia: University of Pennsylvania Press, 2006); and M. B. Norton, "The Evolution of White Women's Experience in Early America," *American Historical Review* 89 (1984): 593.

23. For scholarship on white women in the Caribbean, refer to Carol Barash, "The Character of Difference: The Creole Woman as Cultural Mediator in Narratives About Jamaica," *Eighteenth-Century Studies* 23 (1990): 406–24; Trevor Burnard, "A Failed Settler Society: Marriage and Demographic Failure in Early Jamaica," *Journal of Social History* 28 (1994): 63–82; Burnard, '"A Matron in Rank, a Prostitute in Manners"'; Burnard, "Inheritance and Independence: Women's Status in Early Colonial Jamaica," *William and Mary Quarterly* 3rd ser. 48 (1991): 91–113; Burnard, '"Rioting in Goatish Embraces"'; Barbara Bush, "White 'Ladies,' Coloured 'Favourites' and Black 'Wenches': Some Considerations on Sex, Race, and Class Factors in Social Relations in White Creole Society in the British Caribbean," *Slavery and Abolition* 2 (1981): 245–62; Cecily Forde-Jones, "Mapping Racial Boundaries: Gender, Race, and Poor Relief in Barbadian Plantation Society," *Journal of Women's History* 10 (1998): 9–31; Jones, *Engendering Whiteness*; Erin Skye Mackie, "Cultural Cross-Dressing: The Colorful Case of the Caribbean Creole," in *The Clothes That Wear Us: Essays on Dressing and Transgressing in the Eighteenth Century*, ed. Jessica Munns and Penny Richards (Newark: University of Delaware Press, 1999), 250–70; Erin Skye Mackie, "Jamaican Ladies and Tropical Charms," *ARIEL: A Review of Literature* 37 (2006): 189–220; Sarah M. S. Pearsall, "'The Late Flagrant Instance of Depravity in My Family': The Story of an Anglo-Jamaican Cuckold," *William and Mary Quarterly* 3rd ser. 60 (2003): 549–82; Linda Sturtz, "The 'Dimduke' and the Duchess of Chandos: Gender and Power in Jamaican Plantation Management," *Revista Interamericana* 29 (1999): 1–11; Kathleen M. Wilson, "The Black Widow: Gender, Race, and Performance in England and Jamaica," in *The Island Race: Englishness, Empire, and Gender in the Eighteenth Century* (London: Routledge, 2002), 129–68; Natalie Zacek, "Between Lady and Slave: White Working Women of the Eighteenth-Century Leeward Islands," in *Women in Port*, ed. Catterall and Campbell, 125–50; Natalie Zacek, "Class Struggle in a West Indian Plantation Society," in *Class Matters: Early North America and the Atlantic World*, ed. Simon Middleton and Billy G. Smith (Philadelphia: University of Pennsylvania Press, 2008), 62–75; Natalie Zacek, "Searching for the Invisible Woman: The Evolution of White Women's Experience in Britain's West Indian Colonies," *History Compass* 7, 1 (2008): 329–41; Zacek, *Settler Society*; and Natalie Zacek, "Sex, Sexuality, and Social Control in the Eighteenth-Century Leeward Islands," in *Sex and Sexuality in Early America*, ed. M. D. Smith (New York: New York University Press, 1998), 190–213.

24. Thavolia Glymph provides an excellent critique of older historiographical analyses of white women as marginalized in plantation societies using sources from the perspective of enslaved women. See her chapter on "The Gender of Violence," in Glymph, *Out of the House of Bondage: The Transformation of the Plantation Household* (Cambridge: Cambridge University Press, 2008), 18–31, and nn 22, 55 (for reference to white women in plantation societies). For a broader discussion on gender and empire in the eighteenth century, Kathleen Wilson has written a vital chapter entitled, "Empire, Gender and Modernity in the Eighteenth Century," in *Gender and Empire*, ed. Philippa Levine (Oxford: Oxford University Press, 2004), 14–45. See also Kathleen Wilson, *The Island Race*, wherein she explores a range of gender configurations across the British empire. To learn about white women involved in transatlantic economic pursuits in eighteenth-century Jamaica, see Christine Walker, "Pursuing Her Profits: Women in Jamaica, Atlantic Slavery and a Globalising Market, 1700–1760," *Gender and History* 26, 3, Special Issue: "Gender, Imperialism and Global Exchanges" (November 2014): 478–501.

25. Jones, *Engendering Whiteness*, 167, and see also 161–62, 165–68.

26. Ibid. See also Zacek, "'Between Lady and Slave.'"

27. Morgan, *Laboring Women*, 74, and Brown, *Good Wives, Nasty Wenches, and Anxious Patriarchs*, 116–21. See also Beckles, *Natural Rebels*, and *White Servitude and Black Slavery in Barbados, 1627–1715* (Knoxville: University of Tennessee Press, 1989); Berry, *Swing the Sickle*; Bush, *Slave Women in Caribbean Society*; Judith Carney, *Black Rice: The African Origins of Rice Cultivation in the Americas* (Cambridge, Mass.: Harvard University Press, 2001); Judith Carney and Richard Nicholas Rosomoff, *In the Shadow of Slavery: Africa's Botanical Legacy in the Atlantic World* (Berkeley: University of California Press, 2009); Glymph, *Out of the House of Bondage*; Higman, *Slave Populations in the British Caribbean*; Larry Hudson, *To Have and to Hold: Slave Work and Family Life in Antebellum South Carolina* (Athens: University of Georgia Press, 1997); Jacqueline Jones, *Labor of Love, Labor of Sorrow: Black Women, Work, and the Family from Slavery to the Present* (New York: Vintage, 1995); Bernard Moitt, *Women and Slavery in the French Antilles, 1635–1848* (Bloomington: University of Indiana Press, 2001); Leslie A. Schwalm, *A Hard Fight for We: Women's Transition from Slavery to Freedom in South Carolina* (Urbana: University of Illinois Press, 1997); Brenda E. Stevenson, *Life in Black and White: Family and Community in the Slave South* (New York: Oxford University Press, 1996); Rosalyn Terborg-Penn, Sharon Harley, and Andrea Benton Rushing, eds., *Women in Africa and the African Diaspora* (Washington, D.C.: Howard University Press, 1987); and White, *Ar'n't I a Woman?*.

28. Morgan, *Laboring Women*, esp. chap. 1, "'Some Could Suckle over Their Shoulder': Male Travelers, Female Bodies, and the Gendering of Racial Ideology," 12–49.

29. Jones, *Engendering Whiteness*, 172.

30. Ibid.

31. See Hortense Spillers, "Mama's Baby, Papa's Maybe," where she acknowledges how enslaved men and women were allotted different metrics of space in the cargo hold, but the "rules of accounting" were the same whether for male or female captives, 72.

Whether they occupied different size compartments, they were ultimately commodified in the same manner.

32. Spillers, "Mama's Baby, Papa's Maybe," 67.

33. Ibid. Kathleen Brown, in her study of colonial Virginia also argues that race overshadowed gender in distinction from early modern English conceptions of difference, *Good Wives, Nasty Wenches, and Anxious Patriarchs*, 1. There are important debates around the issue of denigration based on human difference including class, race and gender. See for example, Cynthia Kierner, *Beyond the Household: Women's Place in the Early South, 1700–1835* (Ithaca, N.Y.: Cornell University Press, 1998). See also Fischer, *Suspect Relations*, esp. "Introduction," 5–8 and n12. I am interested in how enslaved women experienced gender or the lack thereof in the context of Barbados slave society.

34. The scholarship on African ethnicity, cultural practices, and retentions include important work in a variety of fields including history, anthropology, and musicology. Space prohibits listing all the important work in these varied fields, but the most cited include Herman L. Bennett, *Africans in Colonial Mexico: Absolutism, Christianity, and Afro-Creole Consciousness, 1570–1640* (Bloomington: University of Indiana Press, 2003); Paul Gilroy, *The Black Atlantic: Modernity and Double Consciousness* (Cambridge, Mass.: Harvard University Press, 1993); Gomez, *Exchanging our Country Marks*; Gwendolyn Midlo Hall, *Africans in Colonial Louisiana: The Development of Afro-Creole Culture in the Eighteenth Century* (Baton Rouge: Louisiana State University Press, 1992); Jocelyn Guilbault, *Zouk: World Music in the West Indies* (Chicago: University of Chicago Press, 1993); Jerome Handler and Frederick W. Lange, *Plantation Slavery in Barbados: An Archaeological and Historical Investigation* (Baltimore: Johns Hopkins University Press, 1974); Melville Herskovits, *The Myth of the Negro Past* (New York: Harper, 1941); Sidney Mintz and Richard Price, *The Birth of African American Culture: An Anthropological Perspective* (Boston: Beacon, 1992); Philip D. Morgan, *Slave Counterpoint: Black Culture in the Eighteenth-Century Chesapeake and Lowcountry* (Chapel Hill: University of North Carolina Press, 1998); James Sweet, *Recreating Africa: Culture, Kinship, and Religion in the African-Portuguese World, 1441–1770* (Chapel Hill: University of North Carolina Press, 2003); James Sweet, *Domingo Alvarez, African Healing and the Intellectual History of the Atlantic World* (Chapel Hill: University of North Carolina Press, 2011); Robert Farris Thompson, *Flash of the Spirit: African & Afro-American Art & Philosophy* (New York: Vintage, 1983); John Thornton, *Africa and Africans in the Making of the Atlantic World, 1400–1800* (Cambridge: Cambridge University Press, 1992); Margaret Washington, *A Peculiar People: Slave Religion and Community-Culture Among the Gullahs* (New York: New York University Press, 1988); and Jason Young, *Rituals of Resistance: African Atlantic Religion in Kongo and the Low Country South in the Era of Slavery* (Baton Rouge: Louisiana State University Press, 2007).

35. Spillers, "Mama's Baby, Papa's Maybe," 67.

36. Ibid.

37. Ibid., 73; emphasis original.

38. For a discussion of transgressive sexual relations in the British Caribbean, see

Burnard, "'A Matron in Rank, a Prostitute in Manners'"; Wilson, "The Black Widow"; Zacek, "Sex, Sexuality, and Social Control."

39. For an analysis of how this law affected whites and the enslaved see Stephen, *The Slavery of the British West India Colonies Delineated*, 23. This law held sway throughout the Atlantic world. In the South American context, the law lasted until the "free womb" laws reversed it in the 1870s. For other works that contextualize this law see for example, Camila Cowling, *Conceiving Freedom: Women of Color, Gender and the Abolition of Slavery in Havana and Rio de Janeiro* (Chapel Hill: University of North Carolina Press, 2013), 54–56. See also Jennifer Morgan, *Laboring Women*, for an important discussion of how reproduction affected the ways in which slave owners bequeathed, objectified, and worked enslaved women. To understand how this law operated in the North American context, see Annette Gordon-Reed, *The Hemingses of Monticello: An American Family* (New York: Norton, 2008), 46; V. Lynn Kennedy, *Born Southern: Childbirth, Motherhood and Social Networks in the Old South* (Baltimore: Johns Hopkins University Press, 2010), 160; and Thomas D. Morris, *Southern Slavery and the Law, 1619–1860* (Chapel Hill: University of North Carolina Press, 2004), 85.

40. Bush, *Slave Women in Caribbean Society*, 112. Natalie Zacek makes an important observation that these strict ideologies of white female chastity and virtue changed overtime in the British Caribbean. In the early years of settlement, white men far outnumbered white women in the Leeward Islands, but as more women arrived toward the eighteenth century marriage and family became more realistic for men. This is the moment when ideologies of the virtuous white woman solidified, as stated in Zacek, *Settler Society*, 170. For further reading on white women in the British West Indies, see Bush, *Slave Women in Caribbean Society*, 11–13; Jones, *White Women and Colonialism*; Cecily Jones, *Engendering Whiteness*; Susan Dwyer Amussen, *Caribbean Exchanges: Slavery and the Transformation of English Society, 1650–1700* (Chapel Hill: University of North Carolina Press, 2007); and Mair, *A Historical Study of Women in Jamaica*.

41. Zacek, *Settler Society*, 171.

42. For an example of terrorizing techniques employed by colonial authorities in Jamaica that went beyond the living, see Brown, *The Reaper's Garden*, 129–56 and Paton, *No Bond But the Law*. Sally E. Hadden illuminates the state as a perpetrator of violence alongside slave owners in *Slave Patrols: Law and Violence in Virginia and the Carolinas* (Cambridge, Mass.: Harvard University Press, 2001).

43. For the text from which I draw on the concept of unstable identities, see Judith Butler, *Gender Trouble: Feminism and the Subversion of Identity* (New York: Routledge, 1990) wherein she explains that gender is performed and therefore produced and these repeated performances result in the effect of a norm or static state of being: or a "true gender." Gender (and other social identities) is maintained, argues Butler, by "the tacit collective agreement to perform, produce, and sustain discrete and polar genders as cultural fictions is obscured by the credibility of those productions—and the punishments that attend not agreeing to believe in them," 178.

44. For a discussion about the solidification of racial categories through the policing

of sex, see Fischer, *Suspect Relations*. This chapter applies much of Fischer's argument to the context of eighteenth-century Barbados. My argument differs however, in my focus on an elite white woman due to the lack of a substantial population of lower-class white women in the colony and a large gap in the archives concerning lower court cases. Moreover, I am interested in how elite discourses and the illicit behavior of white women shaped the limits for enslaved women in this Caribbean Society.

45. For an early discussion of this method, see Kevin J. H. Dettmar, *The Illicit Joyce of Postmodernism: Reading Against the Grain* (Madison: University of Wisconsin Press, 1996). For a study that "reads along the grain" in order to access the affective conditions in colonial archives, see Ann Laura Stoler, *Along the Archival Grain: Epistemic Anxieties and Colonial Common Sense* (Princeton, N.J.: Princeton University Press, 2009).

46. According to the Oxford English Dictionary, "bias" connotes several different definitions. The one I am specifically using here is common in sewing/tailoring referring to cutting, "on the bias: diagonally, across the texture." In addition to stretching the archive to accentuate other figures who otherwise would not appear, "reading along the bias grain" can also mean explicitly confronting the "bias"—" a swaying influence, impulse, or weight"—of the archive in historical narration. See "bias," Online Oxford English Dictionary, accessed March 20, 2015.

47. I use subjection here in the Foucauldian sense, as Judith Butler explains, "Foucault refers to subjection in *Discipline and Punish*, and this word, as is well known, carries a double meaning: *assujettissement* means both subjection (in the sense of subordination) and becoming a subject." Quoted from Judith Butler, "Bodies and Power, Revisited," *Radical Philosophy: A Journal of Socialist and Feminist Philosophy* 114 (July/August 2002): 16.

48. G. W. Hegel, *Phenomenology of Spirit*, trans. A. V. Miller (Oxford: Clarendon, 1977). I take the phrase for this section head from Jennifer A. Glancy, "The Mistress-Slave Dialectic: Paradoxes of Slavery in Three Lxx Narratives," *Journal for the Study of the Old Testament* 21, 72 (December 1996): 71–87.

49. Orlando Patterson, *Slavery and Social Death: A Comparative Study* (Cambridge, Mass.: Harvard University Press, 1982), 79. The concept of honor receives a thorough interrogation in relation to the law in Ariela Gross, *Double Character: Slavery and Mastery in the Antebellum Southern Courtroom* (Princeton: Princeton University Press, 2000); esp. chap. 2 and in the context of colonial Virginia in Brown, *Good Wives, Nasty Wenches, and Anxious Patriarchs*, 174–86. See also Smallwood, *Saltwater Slavery*. Smallwood also discusses the process of Africans' commodification related to their reliance on their captors for food as a similar process of social death (esp. 43–45), my emphasis.

50. Patterson, *Slavery and Social Death*, 78–79 and Gross, *Double Character*, 50 and chap. 2. For important scholarship on "honor" from the colonial Latin American and Spanish Caribbean scholarship see, Renato Barahona, *Sex Crimes, Honour, and the Law in Early Modern Spain, Vizcaya, 1528–1735* (Toronto: University of Toronto Press, 2003); Sueann Caulfield, Sarah C. Chambers, and Lara Putnam, eds., *Honor, Status, and Law in Modern Latin America* (Durham, N.C.: Duke University Press, 2005); Lyman L. Johnson

and Sonya Lipsett-Rivera, eds., *The Faces of Honor: Sex, Shame, and Violence in Colonial Latin America* (Minneapolis: University of Minnesota Press, 1998); Martha Santos, *Cleansing Honor with Blood: Masculinity, Violence, and Power in the Backlands of Northeast Brazil, 1845–1889* (Stanford, Calif.: Stanford University Press, 2012); Pete Sigal, ed., *Infamous Desire: Male Homosexuality in Colonial Latin America* (Chicago: University of Chicago Press, 2003); Ann Twinam, "Honor, Sexuality, and Illegitimacy in Colonial Spanish America," in *Sexuality and Marriage in Colonial Latin America*, ed. Asunción Lavrin (Omaha: University of Nebraska Press, 1992), 118–55; and Ann Twinam, *Public Lives, Private Secret: Gender, Honor, Sexuality, and Illegitimacy in Colonial Spanish America* (Stanford, Calif.: Stanford University Press, 1999). Several historians discuss honor, sexuality, and gender in the early modern British Atlantic and the antebellum U.S., including John Addy, *Sin and Society in the Seventeenth Century* (London: Routledge, 1989); Ruth H. Bloch, *Gender and Morality in Anglo-American Culture, 1650–1800* (Berkeley: University of California Press, 2003); Brown, *Good Wives, Nasty Wenches, and Anxious Patriarchs*, esp. 179–86; Fischer, *Suspect Relations*; Kenneth S. Greenberg, *Honor and Slavery: Lies, Duels, Noses, Masks, Dressing as a Woman, Gits, Strangers, Humanitarianism, Death, Slave Rebellions, the Proslavery argument, Baseball, Hunting, Gambling in the Old South* (Princeton, N.J.: Princeton University Press, 1996); Arelia Gross, *Double Character*, esp. chap. 2; Eleanor Hubbard, *City Women: Money, Sex, and the Social Order in Early Modern London* (Oxford: Oxford University Press, 2013); Martin Ingram, *Church Courts, Sex and Marriage in England, 1570–1640* (Cambridge: Cambridge University Press, 1987); Philippa Levine, "Sexuality, Gender, and Empire," in *Gender and Empire*, ed. Philippa Levine (Oxford: Oxford University Press, 2004), 134–55; Clare A. Lyons, *Sex Among the Rabble: An Intimate History of Gender and Power in the Age of Revolution, Philadelphia, 1730–1830* (Chapel Hill: University of North Carolina Press, 2006); Lawrence Stone, *The Family Sex and Marriage in England, 1500–1800* (London: Weidenfeld and Nicolson, 1977); and Wilson, *The Island Race*.

51. Patterson, *Slavery and Social Death*, 79. See also Smallwood, *Saltwater Slavery*.

52. Patterson, *Slavery and Social Death*, 78–79. See also Gross, *Double Character*, 50 and chap. 2.

53. Patterson, *Slavery and Social Death*, 96.

54. Brown, *Good Wives, Nasty Wenches, and Anxious Patriarchs*, 176, 210.

55. Ibid., 100.

56. The word "mistress" is misleading in the literature. It supposes that the female in control of slaves was a married woman and under a husband's control. For scholarship on white women's role as "mistresses," and the concept of female honor in the British Caribbean see Welch, *Slave Society in the City*, 126–127. Other references discussing white women in the British Caribbean include Hilary Beckles, "White Women and Slavery in the Caribbean," *History Workshop* 36 (Autumn, 1993): 66–82; Burnard, "'A Matron in Rank, a Prostitute in Manners,'" 133–52; and Mair, *A Historical Study of Women in Jamaica*, 116, 176–77 and Jones, *Engendering Whiteness*, 167–83.

57. Welch, *Slave Society in the City*, 127, 133.

58. For other important discussions of white women and honor see, Elizabeth
Fox-Genovese, *Within the Plantation Household: Black and White Women of the Old
South* (Chapel Hill: University of North Carolina Press, 1988). In a double standard
throughout British West Indian societies, white community members tolerated, over-
looked, and even accepted the sexual license white men took with enslaved and free
women of color while condemning white women who engaged in interracial sex. At
the same time, honor for white men was attached to their property, legitimate birth,
and integrity in business practices. To a lesser extent, when a man's honor as a husband was challenged it was perceived as damaged by another man's molestation of his
wife more than the wife's behavior. In the *Crofts v. Harrison* case the key concern was
Crofts' unfair treatment by Judge Harrison and Agatha Moore was an appendage to
this case. Zacek argues that honor viewed in a trans-imperial frame outlines how
white societies in the Leeward Islands resisted and controlled metropolitan images of
Leeward colonists as deviant, sexually licentious, and prone to debauchery. To understand the myriad complexities of this argument, see Zacek, *Settler Society*, esp. chaps.
4 and 5. My discussion of honor in relation to Agatha Moore relates specifically to
exploring how white women experienced honor in relation to sexuality and the dis-
honoring of enslaved women.

59. Jones, *Engendering Whiteness*, 167, 172. See Stephanie Jones-Rogers' important
discussion of the economic power of married white women in the antebellum U.S. in
"'Nobody Couldn't Sell 'Em But Her'": Slaveowning Women, Mastery, and the Gendered Politics of the Antebellum Slave Market (Ph.D. dissertation, Rutgers University,
2012). For a partial list of scholarship on white women in plantation societies, see Sharon Block, *Rape and Sexual Power in Early America* (Chapel Hill: University of North
Carolina Press, 2006); Burnard, "'A Matron in Rank, a Prostitute in Manners'"; Cather-
ine Clinton, *The Plantation Mistress: Woman's World in the Old South* (New York: Pantheon, 1982); Fischer, *Suspect Relations*; Anne Frior Scott, *The Southern Lady: From
Pedestal to Politics, 1830–1930* (Chicago: University of Chicago Press, 1970); Fox-
Genovese, *Within the Plantation Household*; Glymph, *Out of the House of Bondage*; and
Brenda E. Stevenson, *Life in Black and White: Family and Community in the Slave South*
(Oxford: Oxford University Press, 1997). See also Brooke Newman, "Gender, Sexuality,
and the Formation of Racial Identities in the Eighteenth-Century Anglo Caribbean
World," *Gender and History* 22, 3 (November 2010): 585–602.

60. Welch, *Slave Society in the City*, 127 and Bush, *Slave Women in Caribbean Society*, 26.

61. To be clear I am discussing elite white women in Barbados. For scholarship on
non-elite women and men see, Jones, *Engendering Whiteness*, chap. 1; Welch, *Slave Society in the City*, 127; Hilary McD. Beckles, *White Servitude and Black Slavery in Barbados,
1627–1715* (Knoxville: University of Tennessee Press, 1989) and Karl Watson, *The Civilised Island: A Social History, 1750–1816*. Kathleen Brown makes an important point
that the laws in colonial Virginia did not protect servant and poor women who accused

men of rape; see *Good Wives, Nasty Wenches, and Anxious Patriarchs*, 192–94. For expertise on rape and colonial law, see Block, *Rape and Sexual Power* and Fischer, *Suspect Relations*. Fischer's study is vital understanding poor and servant women's sexual lives in colonial North Carolina.

62. Beckles, *Centering Woman*, 62; see also Fuentes, "Power and Historical Figuring," 564–84. The court records for the eighteenth century in Barbados are sparse at best and have not survived for the "slave courts."

63. See Handler, *Unappropriated People*, 15–21; Melanie Newton, *The Children of Africa in the Colonies*, 44–56; Pedro L. V. Welch and Richard Goodridge, *"Red" and Black over White: Free Coloured Women in Pre-Emancipation Barbados* (Bridgetown: Carib Research and Publications, 2000); and Welch, *Slave Society in the City*, 97.

64. See Chapter 3 of this book on brothel owner Rachael Pringle Polgreen, agency, and the commodification of sexuality.

65. Long, *The History of Jamaica*, 2: 335.

66. Ibid., 2: 336.

67. Patterson, *Slavery and Social Death*, 92.

68. Bush, *Slave Women in Caribbean Society*, 112.

69. Watson, "Obsession, Betrayal and Sex," 253.

70. Barbados Minutes of Council, 4 October 1743, CO31/21/D1: 65, NAL.

71. This refers to the northern part of the island of Barbados. See Watson, "Obsession, Betrayal and Sex," 255.

72. Barbados Minutes of Council, 4 October 1743, CO31/21/D1: 65, NAL.

73. Ibid.

74. Ibid.

75. Watson, "Obsession, Betrayal and Sex," 347.

76. Barbados Minutes of Council, 4 October 1743, CO31/21/D1: 76, NAL.

77. For discussion of the subjugation of white women in this time period, see Watson, "Obsession, Betrayal and Sex" and Burnard, "'A Matron in Rank, a Prostitute in Manners.'"

78. Watson, "Obsession, Betrayal and Sex," 262.

79. Ibid. It is unclear where Agatha Moore traveled during this case, perhaps to another island or to England. Archival evidence of Agatha Moore in Barbados ends with this case.

80. Barbados Minutes of Council, 4 October 1743, CO31/21/D1: 47, 63–64, NAL. White women appeared with more frequency in front of the Barbados Assembly. This governing body handled personal cases and petitions between white men and women and married couples. The Barbados Council served as a court of appeal for unsettled or contested cases.

81. Agatha Moore inherited property in Cheapside, Bridgetown from her grandmother Mary Thomsome while still an infant. Although this property would transfer to her husband upon marriage, it is possible, since this case did not end in divorce, that

Agatha Moore retained some economic resources after her "ruin." See Watson, "Obsession, Betrayal and Sex," 247.

82. Watson, "Obsession, Betrayal and Sex," 247.

83. Jones, *Engendering Whiteness*, 81. Jones' study on white women and property laws in Barbados remains the only full-length study of its kind. More scholarship exists for Jamaica including, Burnard, "Gay and Agreeable Ladies"; Burnard, "Evaluating Gender in Early Jamaica, 1674–1784"; Burnard, "'Rioting in Goatish Embraces'"; Mair, *A Historical Study of Women in Jamaica*; and Walker, "Pursuing Her Profits."

84. The term *feme covert* (spelled variously) referred to a married woman's condition in relation to her husband as a total dependent. On coverture, see Sir William Blackstone, *Commentaries of the Laws of England in Four Books* (Clark, N.J.: Lawbook Exchange, 1825), 442. For a range of scholarship on English women and property law, see Lloyd Bonefield, "Marriage Settlements and the 'Rise of the Great Estates': The Demographic Aspect," *Economic History Review* 2nd ser. 32 (1979): 483–93; Andrew Buck, Margaret Ferguson, and Nancy E. Wright, eds., *Women, Property, and the Letters of the Law in Early Modern England* (Toronto: University of Toronto Press, 2004); M. R. Chesterman, "Family Settlements on Trust: Landowners and the Rising Bourgeoise," in *Law, Economy, and Society, 1750–1914: Essays in the History of English Law*, ed. G. R. Rubin and David Sugarman (Abingdon: Professional Books, 1984); 124–67; Leonore Davidoff and Catherine Hall, *Family Fortunes: Men and Women of the English Middle Class, 1780–1850* (Chicago: University of Chicago Press, 1987); Amy Louise Erickson, *Women and Property in Early Modern England* (London: Routledge, 1993); Lee Holcombe, *Wives and Property: Reform of the Married Women's Property Law in Nineteenth-Century England* (Toronto: University of Toronto Press, 1983); Julia Rudolph, *Common Law and Enlightenment in England, 1689–1750* (Woodbridge: Boydell, 2013); Susan Staves, *Married Women's Separate Property in England, 1660–1833* (Cambridge, Mass.: Harvard University Press, 2013); and Tim Stretton and Krista J. Kesselring, eds., *Married Women and the Law: Coverture in England and the Common Law World* (Montreal: McGill-Queens University Press, 2013).

85. Linda De Pauw, "Women and the Law: The Colonial Period," *Human Rights* 6, 2 (1977): 107–13, quoted in Jones, *Engendering Whiteness*, 86.

86. Jones, *Engendering Whiteness*, 86.

87. Ibid., 107.

88. Ibid., 81. For Jamaican property laws and white women, see also Mair, *A Historical Study of Women in Jamaica*, 151.

89. Jones, *Engendering Whiteness*, 86–92.

90. For examples of white women managing their property in slaves and land, see Barbados Deeds 1775–1778, no. 182 and Recopied Wills, RB6/29–30, BDA. In many cases, white women circumvented colonial laws that transferred their property to their husbands by leaving their property "in trust" to a third party for the duration of their marriage. White women also formed these trusts to ensure their daughters and nieces would retain inheritance despite their marriages.

91. Barbados Minutes of Council, 4 October 1743, CO31/21/D1: 65, NAL.

92. Hartman, *Scenes of Subjection*, 81. For an earlier articulation of "discourse of seduction," see Terry Leahy, "Positively Experienced Boy/Man Sex: The Discourse of Seduction and the Social Construction of Masculinity," *Journal of Sociology* 28, 1 (March 1992): 71–88.

93. Hartman, *Scenes of Subjection,* 81.

94. Ibid.

95. For an important discussion of male sexuality, misogyny, and the complicated ideologies of white female victimhood and agency, see Thomas Foster, *Sex and the Eighteenth-Century Man: Massachusetts and the History of Sexuality in America* (Boston: Beacon, 2006), xix and 78.

96. Ibid.

97. Barbados Minutes of Council, 4 October 1743, CO31/21/D1: 65, NAL.

98. Watson, "Obsession, Betrayal and Sex," 256.

99. Michel Foucault, *The History of Sexuality*, trans. Robert Hurley, vol. 1, *An Introduction* (New York: Vintage, 1990), 97.

100. Ibid., 97.

101. Aliyyah I. Abdur-Rahman, "'The Strangest Freaks of Despotism': Queer Sexuality in Antebellum African American Slave Narratives," *African American Review* 40, 2 (2006): 226.

102. Beckles, *Centering Woman*, 22.

103. For scholarship on free people of color in Barbados refer to Beckles, *Natural Rebels*; Jerome Handler, *The Unappropriated People: Freedmen in the Slave Society of Barbados* (Baltimore: Johns Hopkins University Press, 1974); Newton, *The Children of Africa in the Colonies*; and Welch, *Slave Society in the City.*

104. See Beckles, "White Women and Slavery"; Glymph, *Out of the House of Bondage*; and Jones-Rogers, "Nobody Couldn't Sell 'Em But Her."

105. Morgan, *Laboring Women.*

106. Kirstin Olsen, *Daily Life in 18th-Century England* (Westport, Conn.: Greenwood, 1999), 43. See also, Fischer, *Suspect Relations*; Brown, *Good Wives, Nasty Wenches, and Anxious Patriarchs*; and Block, *Rape and Sexual Power in Early America.*

107. Jones, *Engendering Whiteness*, 29–30.

108. For example, see scholarship on Jamaica, which had a distinctly white male dominated population. See also Burnard, *Mastery, Tyranny and Desire*; Mair, *A Historical Study of Women in Jamaica*; and Marietta Morrissey, *Slave Women in the New World: Gender Stratification in the Caribbean* (Lawrence: University Press of Kansas, 1989).

109. Beckles, *Centering Woman*, 63.

110. Beckles, "White Women and Slavery," 63.

111. Ibid., 69.

112. See Beckles, "White Women and Slavery"; Bush, *Slave Women in Caribbean Society*; Glymph, *Out of the House of Bondage*; and Jones-Rogers, "'Nobody Couldn't Sell 'Em But Her.'"

113. See Newton, *Children of Africa in the Colonies*; Welch, *Slave Society in the City*; Handler, *Unappropriated People*; Welch and Goodridge, *"Red," and White over White*; and Christine Walker, "Pursuing Her Profits."

114. Newton, *The Children of Africa in the Colonies*, 48.

115. Ibid., 37.

116. Ibid., 53–54.

117. For a different perspective on this issue, see Walker, "Pursuing Her Profits," 482.

118. In order to assist my work in discovering the race of the women in these documents, I relied on the scholarship of Barbadian and other historians who have done extensive genealogical work with these same records, particularly identifying free(d) people of color. Their work includes Jerome S. Handler, Ronald Hughes, Melanie Newton, Pedro L.V. Welch and Ernest M. Whiltshire, *Freedmen of Barbados: Names and Notes for Genealogical and Family History Research* (Charlottesville: Virginia Foundation for the Humanities, 2007); Handler, *Unappropriated People*, and Newton, *Children of Africa in the Colonies*.

119. Although no laws existed preventing interracial marriage, Jerome Handler's research shows that "in Barbados, where the line between free(d) people and white was more rigidly drawn than in Jamaica, legal prohibitions against marriage were unnecessary; the force of social convention was sufficient . . . to prevent the social relationships which symbolically and in fact might have challenged these distinctions." Handler, *Unappropriated People*, 201. There is yet to be research that looks specifically at the property laws affecting the marriages between free(d) people of color. As of this writing, a sample of 175 wills for eighteenth-century Barbados revealed no single instance of a free woman of color manipulating couverture in her will. This might be due to several factors including low rates of marriage among the free(d) female population, restrictive laws against free(d) people of color as a group, the lack of interracial marriages and the small population of free(d) women who were able to leave wills. For a discussion the of wills and bequest patterns of white and free(d) people of color in Bridgetown see Welch, *Slave Society in the City*, 127–34 and chap. 8. In contrast, evidence in colonial North America suggests that free(d) women were subject to couverture laws in northern colonies like Massachusetts and Connecticut. For a discussion of coverture and Free(d) women of color see, Catherine Adams and Elizabeth H. Peck, *Love of Freedom: Black Women in Colonial and Revolutionary New England* (New York: Oxford University Press, 2010), 129.

120. Glymph, *Out of the House of Bondage*, 3–4.

121. Jones, *Engendering Whiteness*, chaps. 3 and 5.

122. Will of Elvira Cox, 7 September 1792, Recopied Will Book, RB6/20: 502–503, BDA. For genealogy on Elvira Cox and the Alleyne families see, *Genealogies of Barbados Families: From Caribbeana and the Journal of the Barbados Museum and Historical Society*, ed. James C. Brandow (Baltimore: Genealogical Publishing, 1983), 424.

123. Will of Elvira Cox, 7 September, 1792, Recopied Will Book, RB6/20: 502–503, BDA

124. Baptism Record, "Frances a negro slave the [property] of Flora Cox," 25 April, 1793, Joanne McRee, *Barbados Records: Baptisms* (Black Rock, Barbados: Barbados Department of Archives, 1984), 221.

125. Estate Inventory of Elvira Cox, 1794, Bridgetown, Barbados, BDA. Jones, *Engendering Whiteness*, 172; Morgan, *Laboring Women*, 97.

126. Will of Mary Sisnett, 3 February 1794, Recopied Will Book, RB6/29: 247, BDA.

127. Ibid.

128. For a substantial statistical accounting of Barbados' wills and deeds, see Morgan, *Laboring Women* and Welch, *Slave Society in the City* (for Barbados), and Trevor Burnard, "Collecting and Accounting: Representing Slaves as Commodities in Jamaica, 1674–1784," in *Collecting Across Cultures: Material Exchanges in the Early Modern World*, ed. Daniela Bleichmar et al. (Philadelphia: University of Pennsylvania Press, 2011).

129. Will of Mary Sisnett, 3 February 1794, Recopied Will Book, RB6/29: 247, BDA.

130. Hannah Haynes to Samuel Drayton, 27 February 1778, Barbados Deeds 1775–1778, no. 182, RB1/146: 454, BDA.

131. Ibid.

132. Will of Mary Kidney, 30 September 1760, Recopied Will Book, RB6/30: 203–4, BDA.

133. Morgan, *Laboring Women*, 84.

134. This argument is not new. Morgan deftly illustrates this in *Laboring Women*. I bring attention to the sexual construction of enslaved women that is both an extension of and constituent to reproduction.

135. Will of Elizabeth Grant, 9 August 1766, Recopied Will Book, RB6/31: 153–56, BDA. For genealogies of the Grant, Moore and Edey families—relatives of Elizabeth Grant—see *Genealogies of Barbados families*, ed. James C. Brandow, 254, 712.

136. Jones, *Engendering Whiteness*, 172 and Morgan, *Laboring Women*, 97.

137. See Morgan, *Laboring Women*.

138. Bush, *Slave Women in Caribbean Society*; Morgan, *Laboring Women*; Long, *The History of Jamaica*; Richard Ligon, *A True and Exact History of the Island of Barbados*, ed. Karen Ordahl Kupperman (Indianapolis: Hackett, 2011); and Beckles, *Centering Women*.

139. Long, *The History of Jamaica*, vol. 2, bk. 2, 280.

140. See J. B. Moreton, *West India Customs and Manners: Containing Strictures on the Soil, Cultivation, Produce, Trade, Officers, and Inhabitants: With the Method of Establishing, and Conducting a Sugar Plantation. To which is Added, the Practice of Training New Slaves* (London: Printed for J. Parsons; W. Richardson; H. Gardner; and J. Walter, 1793), esp. 107–23.

141. Moreton, *West India Customs and Manners*, 121.

142. Long, *The History of Jamaica*, vol. 2, bk. 3, 535.

143 .Morgan, *Laboring Women*, chap. 1 and Bush, *Slave Women in Caribbean Society*, chap. 1.

144. Beckles, *Centering Woman*, 62.

145. Barbara Bush, "The Eye of the Beholder," in *Engendering Caribbean History*, ed. Verene Shepherd (Kingston: Ian Randle, 2011), 203. See also Morgan, *Laboring Women* for a discussion of early modern travelers' writings and their impact on the treatment of enslaved and indigenous women.

146. See Morgan, *Laboring Woman* and Sasha Turner, "Home-Grown Slaves: Women, Reproduction, and the Abolition of the Slave Trade, Jamaica 1788–1807," *Journal of Women's History* 23, 3 (Fall 2011): 39–62.

147. Will of Mary Sisnett, 3 February 1794, RB6/29:247, BDA.

148. Barbados Minutes of Council, CO31/21/D1: 51, NAL.

149. The name Withers refers to Mr. Withers, Agatha Moore's father. Agatha Moore's maiden name was Withers and she and her husband lived in her father's house on High Street in Bridgetown at the time of this case. See Watson, "Obsession, Betrayal and Sex," 243.

150. Barbados Minutes of Council, CO31/21 D1: 68, NAL.

151. Ibid., 58.

152. Ibid., 69.

153. Ibid.

154. "The Barbados Slave Act of 1661," modified in 1676, 1682, and 1688, made it a capital offense for a slave to murder or attempt to murder a white person. For the text of these laws, see Baskett, *Acts of Assembly*.

155. Tartiman, *Scenes of Subjection*, 81.

156. Baskett, *Acts of Assembly*, 118–26.

157. See Brown, *Good Wives, Nasty Wenches, and Anxious Patriarchs*, esp. 75–80, wherein she discusses the case of Thomas Hall, a white indentured servant who was likely a hermaphrodite.

158. See, for example, Barbara Bush's discussion of the denigrating sexual images and sexual exploitation of enslaved women in the Caribbean in *Slave Women in Caribbean Society*, esp. 1, 15910–18.

159. Long, *The History of Jamaica*, vol. 2, bk. 2, 276–77.

160. Ibid., vol. 2, bk. 3, 541.

161. Consider annual slave sales or the dissolution of estates when insolvent. The enslaved were vulnerable to their owner's economic situation.

162. Watson, "Obsession, Betrayal and Sex," 254.

163. Ibid.

164. The concept of "relations of power" is borrowed from Foucault who argues that "we need a new economy (read theory) of power relations" that tracks how power relations are acted out—or more specifically, how power relations (which connote a *relationship* between entities) can be understood as struggles or a series of strategies employed to achieve submission of the other. See Michel Foucault, "The Subject and Power," *Critical Inquiry* 8, 4 (Summer 1982): 777–95.

165. See Block, *Rape and Sexual Power* and Fischer, *Suspect Relations*.

Chapter 4. Molly: Enslaved Women, Condemnation, and Gendered Terror

Epigraphs: Portion of Journal of Nicolas Cresswell, 16 September 1774, Bridgetown, Barbados, X10/10, BDA, my emphasis; James Stephen, *The Slavery of the British West India Colonies Delineated, as it Exists in both Law and Practice, and Compared with the Slavery of other Countries, Ancient and Modern* (London: J. Butterworth and Son, 1824–1830), 301, http://hdl.handle.net/2027/nyp.33433075911267, accessed 25 March 2013; Barbados Minutes of Council, 5 December 1767, Lucas MSS: 157–58, BPL.

1. "To Anr. Edwards Constable, for apprehending a Negro woman Slave named Molly, late belonging to Isaac Wray, Executed according to Law." Barbados Minutes of Council, 18 April 1769, Lucas MSS: 186, BPL. See also Governor Spry's directive for the execution of another slave Sam Clift where the governor states, "you are hereby empowered to press some Negro to assist in the Execution hereof." Barbados Minutes of Council, 20 June 1769, Lucas MSS: 228, BPL. See also Karl Watson, "Capital Sentences Against Slaves in Barbados in the Eighteenth Century: An Analysis," in *In the Shadow of the Plantation: Caribbean History and Legacy*, ed. Alvin O. Thompson (Kingston: Ian Randle, 2002), 204.

2. Barbados Minutes of Council, 19 February 1769, Lucas MSS: 172, BPL.

3. Baskett, *Acts of Assembly*, 123–24.

4. Goveia, *The West Indian Slave Laws*, 34.

5. Barbados Minutes of Council, 20 December 1768, Lucas MSS: 157, BPL.

6. Moore, *The Public Acts in Force*, 159. On two previous occasions, representatives of the Barbados Council and the governor spoke out against commemorations of condemned slaves. On one occasion, in 1757, an enslaved man was accused of murdering an infant and the Governor's secretary directed Bridgetown authorities to prevent the man's family from having "any plays, Dancing, or Cabells . . . in honour to or Memory of the said Murderer." Welch, *Slave Society in the City*, 148–49. My concentrated attention to Molly allows us to consider the gendered expectations of enslaved women in an urban setting and the arbitrary nature of slave laws.

7. There is a vast literature on slave laws and the following include scholarship from North America and the Caribbean and covers colonial and antebellum slave societies. For reference to these works see, Edward L. Ayers, *Vengeance and Justice: Crime and Punishment in the Nineteenth-Century American South* (New York: Oxford University Press, 1984); Alexandra K. Brown, "'A Black Mark on Our Legislation': Slavery, Punishment, and the Politics of Death in Nineteenth-Century Brazil," *Luso-Brazilian Review* 37, 2 (2000): 96–121; Margaret Burnham, "An impossible Marriage: Slave Law and Family Law," *Law and Inequality* 5 (1987): 187–225; Robert J. Cottrol, "Liberalism and Paternalism: Ideology, Economic Interest, and the Business of Law of Slavery," *American Journal of Legal History* 31 (1987): 359–73; Richard Cover, *Justice Accused: Antislavery and the Judicial Process* (New Haven, Conn.: Yale University Press, 1975); Jonathan Dalby, *Crime and Punishment in Jamaica: A Quantitative Analysis of the Assize Court Records, 1756–1856* (Mona: Social History Project, Department of History, University of

the West Indies, 2000); James Epstein, *Scandal of Colonia Rule: Power and Subversion in the British Atlantic during the Age of Revolution* (New York: Cambridge University Press, 2012); Andrew Fede, "Legitimized Violent Slave Abuse in the American South, 1619–1865: A Case Study of Law and Social Change in Six Southern States," *American Journal of Legal History* 29 (1985): 93–150; Andrew Fede, *People without Rights: An Interpretation of the Fundamentals of the Law of Slavery in the U.S. South* (New York: Garland, 1992); Barbara Jane Fields, "Race and Ideology in American History," in *Region, Race and Reconstruction: Essays in Honor of C. Vann Woodward*, ed . J. Morgan Kousser and James M. McPherson (New York: Oxford University Press, 1982): 143–77; Paul Finkelman, "The Crime of Color," *Tulane Law Review* 67 (1993): 2063–2112; Paul Finkelman, "Northern Labor Law and Southern Slave Law: The Application of the Fellow Servant Rule to Slaves," *National Black Law Journal* 11 (1989): 212–32; William W. Fischer, III, "Ideology and Imagery in the Law of Slavery," *Chicago-Kent Law Review* 68 (1993): 1051–86; Daniel J. Flanigan, "Criminal Procedure in Slave Trials in the Antebellum South," *Journal of Southern History* 40 (November 1974): 537–64; V. A. C. Gatrell, *The Hanging Tree: Execution and the English People, 1770–1868* (New York: Oxford University Press, 1994); Elizabeth Fox-Genovese and Eugene D. Genovese, *Fruits of Merchant Capital: Slavery and Bourgeois Property in the Rise and Expansion of Capitalism* (New York: Oxford University Press, 1983); Elizabeth Fox-Genovese and Eugene D. Genovese, "Slavery, Economic Development, and the Law: The Dilemma of the Southern Political Economists, 1800–1861," *Washington and Lee Law Review* 41 (Winter 1984): 1–29; Claudia Dale Goldin, *Urban Slavery in the American South, 1820–1860* (Chicago: University of Chicago Press, 1976); Sally E. Hadden, *Slave Patrols: Law and Violence in Virginia and the Carolinas* (Cambridge, Mass.: Harvard University Press, 2001); Douglas Hay and E. P. Thompson, *Albion's Fatal Tree: Crime and Society in Eighteenth-Century England* (New York: Pantheon, 1976); A. Leon Higginbotham, Jr., *In the Matter of Color: Race and the American Legal Process: The Colonial Period* (New York: Oxford University Press, 1978); A. Leon Higginbotham, Jr., and Barbara K. Kopytoff, "Property First, Humanity Second: The Recognition of the Slave's Human Nature in Virginia Civil Law," *Ohio State Law Journal* 50 (1989): 511–40; Michael S. Hindus, *Prison and Plantation: Crime, Justice, and Authority in Massachusetts and South Carolina, 1767–1878* (Chapel Hill: University of Chapel Hill Press, 1980); Arthur F. Howington, *What Sayeth the Law: The Treatment of Slavery and Free Blacks in the State and Local Courts of Tennessee* (New York: Garland, 1989); Thomas N. Ingersoll, "Slave Codes and Judicial Practice in New Orleans, 1718–1807," *Law and History Review* 13 (Spring 1995): 23–62; Walter Johnson, "Inconsistency, Contradiction, and Complete Confusion: The Everyday Life of the Law of Slavery," *Law and Social Inquiry* 22 (Spring 1997): 405–33; Walter Johnson, *Soul by Soul: Life Inside an Antebellum Slave Market* (Cambridge, Mass.: Harvard University Press, 1999); Marvin D. Jones, "Darkness Made Visible: Law, Metaphor and the Racial Self," *Georgetown Law Journal* 82 (1993): 437–511; Winthrop D. Jordan, *White over Black: American Attitudes Toward the Negro, 1550–1812* (New York: Norton, 1968); Terrance F. Kiley, " 'The Hollow Words': An Experiment in Legal Historical Method as Applied to the Institution of Slavery," *De*

Paul Law Review 25 (1976): 842–94; Mindie Lazarus-Black, "John Grant's Jamaica: Notes Towards a Reassessment of Courts in the Slave Era," *Journal of Caribbean History* 27, 2 (1993): 144–59; Mindie Lazarus-Black, *Legitimate Acts and Illegal Encounters: Law and Society in Antigua and Barbuda* (Washington, D.C.: Smithsonian Institution Press, 1994); Alex Lichtenstein, "'That Disposition to Theft, with Which They Have Been Branded': Moral Economy, Slave Management, and the Law," *Journal of Social History* 22, 3 (1988): 413–30; Peter Linebaugh, *The London Hanged: Crime and Civil Society in the Eighteenth Century* (Cambridge: Cambridge University Press, 1992); Louis P. Masur, *Rites of Execution: Capital Punishment and the Transformation of American Culture, 1776–1865* (New York: Oxford University Press, 1989); Michael Meranze, *Laboratories of Virtue: Punishment, Revolution, and the Transformation of Authority in Philadelphia, 1760–1835* (Chapel Hill: University of North Carolina Press, 1996); Diana Paton, "Punishment, Crime, and the Bodies of Slaves in Eighteenth-Century Jamaica," *Journal of Social History* 34, 4 (2001): 923–54; Thomas D. Morris, "'As If the Injury Was Effected by the Natural Elements of Air or Fire': Slave Wrongs and the Liability of Masters," *Law and Society Review* 16 (1981–82): 569–99; Thomas D. Morris, "Slaves and the Rules of Evidence in Criminal Trials," *Chicago-Kent Law Review* 68 (1993): 1209–40; Thomas D. Morris, *Southern Slavery and the Law, 1619–1860* (Chapel Hill: University of North Carolina Press, 1996); Anupama Rao, "Discipline and the Other Body: Correction, Corporeality, and Colonial Rule," *Interventions* 3, 2 (2001): 159–68; Judith K. Schafer, *Slavery, Civil Law and the Supreme Court in Antebellum Louisiana* (Baton Rouge: Louisiana State University Press, 1994); Philip J. Schwartz, *Twice Condemned: Slaves and the Criminal Laws of Virginia, 1705–1865* (Baton Rouge: Louisiana State University Press, 1988); David Vincent Trotman, *Crime in Trinidad: Conflict and Control in a Plantation Society, 1838–1900* (Knoxville: University of Tennessee Press, 1986); Alan Watson, *Slave Laws in the Americas* (Athens: University of Georgia Press, 1989); and Thomas J. Wren, "A Two-Fold Character: The Slave as Person and Property," *Southern Studies* 24 (Winter 1985): 417–31.

8. Vincent Brown, "Spiritual Terror and Sacred Authority in Jamaican Slave Society," *Slavery and Abolition* 24, 1 (2003): 31.

9. See Diana Paton, "Punishment, Crime, and the Bodies of Slaves in Eighteenth-Century Jamaica," *Journal of Social History* 34, 4 (2001): 935. Paton offers an important comparative perspective of slave trials in Jamaica in the same period. Her assessment of crimes and punishments provides an unprecedented view into the colonial Caribbean slave courts. However, unlike the remarkable slave trial summaries for eighteenth-century Jamaica, no slave court records or summaries of trials for Barbados have been located. It is likely they did not survive from that era.

10. Barbados Minutes of Council, 15 March 1736/7, Lucas MSS: 196–97, BPL. See Paton, "Punishment, Crime, and the Bodies of Slaves," 935, for an example of slave executions that were deemed questionable by the Jamaican legislature.

11. Moore, *The Public Acts in Force*, 117–18.

12. Baskett, *Acts of Assembly*, 123–24.

13. Paton, "Punishment, Crime, and the Bodies of Slaves," 934. Paton describes the various reasons slave owners sent their slaves to trial.

14. Brown, *The Reaper's Garden*, 77.

15. Hall, *Acts Passed in the Island of Barbados*, 119.

16. Ibid.

17. Goveia, *The West Indian Slave Laws*, 34.

18. Stephen, *The Slavery of the British West India Colonies*, 324–26.

19. Barbados Minutes of Council, 15 March 1736/7, Lucas MSS: 196–97, BPL.

20. Act of 1739, No. 180, Sect. 1, in Hall, *Acts Passed in the Island of Barbados*, 325.

21. Ibid., 321.

22. See Chapter 1 discussion of Bess and Grigg in this book. Such bodily punishment included public whippings and brandings; in one instance it was suggested that instead of death, "a legg of the negroe Davy, should be taken off." Barbados Minutes of Council, 18 February 1756, Lucas MSS: 85 (1 October 1755–20 December 1758, Ref 388.981 3326, Reel 11, Vol. 25), BPL.

23. Barbados Minutes of Council, 19 February 1769, Lucas MSS: 172, BPL.

24. Ibid.

25. Stephen, *The Slavery of the British West India Colonies*, 2: 321; "Act of 1739, No. 180. Sect. 1," in Hall, *Acts Passed in the Islands of Barbados*; my emphasis.

26. Stephen, *The Slavery of the West India Colonies*, 2: xviii.

27. Ibid.

28. "A Certificate of the Justices of the Peace who tried & found guilty two Negro Slaves named Sambo & Nick, burnt alive for the murder of John Horsham Apothecarrry for Payment to Benjamin Alleyne Cox Esqr. For the Sum of Five Pounds Seventeen Shillings and one half penny: (exclusive of the Secretarys fee for the order being disbursed by him for the Expences of the said Execution," Barbados Minutes of Council, 16 March 1784, CO28/60:141, NAL. See also Stephen, *The Slavery of the West India Colonies*, 2: x–xvii.

29. Stephen, *The Slavery in the British West India Colonies*, 2: xviii, xxvi; Watson, "Capital Sentences Against Slaves," 208–9. Watson's account, taken from an editorial in *Barbados Mercury*, differs significantly from that of Stephen and presumes the guilt of the enslaved.

30. Paton, "Punishment, Crime, and the Bodies of Slaves," 935; Brown, *The Reaper's Garden*, 77.

31. "Testimony of Captain Thomas Lloyd," in Lambert, *House of Commons Sessional Papers*, 82: 48.

32. See, for example, David Barry Gaspar, "'To Bring their Offending Slave to Justice': Compensation and Slave Resistance in Antigua 1669–1763," *Caribbean Quarterly* 30, 3/4 (September–December 1984): 45–59. Gaspar analyzes compensation records in Antigua where slave owners were compensated for fugitive slaves who had not returned. The absence of a body certainly provides evidence of slaves absconding. It also brings up questions of the murder of slaves by their owners who could claim their slaves ran away to claim compensation.

33. Paton discusses the rate and reasons of slave acquittal in Jamaica in "Punishment, Crime, and the Bodies of Slaves," 933–34.

34. Goveia, *The West Indian Slave Laws*, 20. See also Brown, *The Reaper's Garden*, 76–77.

35. Hartman, *Scenes of Subjection*, 80.

36. Higman, *Slave Populations of the British West Indies*, 314–348.

37. For discussions of social death, see Patterson, *Slavery and Social Death*; Hartman, *Lose Your Mother*; Smallwood, *Saltwater Slavery*; and Brown, "Social Death and Political Life," 1231–49.

38. Leland de la Durantaye, *Giorgio Agamben: A Critical Introduction* (Stanford, Calif.: Stanford University Press, 2009), 206.

39. Ibid., 206.

40. Portion of Journal of Nicolas Cresswell, 16 September 1774, X10/10, BDA.

41. Hartman, *Scenes of Subjection*, 83–84. For a major study on the dual condition of the enslaved as object and subject in antebellum U.S. slave law see Ariela J. Gross, *Double Character*.

42. Stephen, *The Slavery of the British West India Colonies*, 2: 321.

43. Ibid.

44. Hartman, *Scenes of Subjection*, 69. See also Smallwood, *Saltwater Slavery*, 33–64 for her discussion of the commodification process captive Africans endured from West Africa to the Americas

45. For a discussion of penal systems in early modern Europe see Michel Foucault, *Discipline and Punish: The Birth of the Prison*, trans. Alan Sheridan (New York: Random House, 1977).

46. See Linebaugh, *The London Hanged*; Gatrell, *The Hanging Tree*; Foucault, *Discipline and Punish*; and James Epstein, *Scandal of Colonia Rule*.

47. See Lambert, *House of Commons Sessional Papers*, vols. 71, 72.

48. Brown, "Spiritual Terror," 31.

49. Diana Paton, "Punishment Crime, and the Bodies of Slaves in Eighteenth-Century Jamaica," *Journal of Social History* 34, 4 (2001): 923.

50. For a meticulous analysis of the differences between West Indian slave laws and English common laws see Stephen, *The Slavery of the West India Colonies*, 2: 284–327.

51. Ibid.

52. David Barry Gaspar, "With a Rod of Iron: Barbados Slave Laws as a Model for Jamaica, South Carolina, and Antigua, 1661–1697," in *Crossing Boundaries: Comparative History of Black People in Diaspora*, ed. Darlene Clark Hine and Jacqueline McLeod (Bloomington: Indiana University Press, 1999), 347.

53. Hadden, *Slave Patrols*, 42–71.

54. Testimony of William Fitzmaurice, 9 March 1791, in Lambert, *House of Commons Sessional Papers*, 82: 230.

55. Brown, "Spiritual Terror and Sacred Authority," 25. For further analyses on

relationships between women of color and white men, see Welch, *Slave Society in the City*; Bush, *Slave Women in Caribbean Society*; and Burnard, *Mastery, Tyranny and Desire*.

56. "Wanted to Hire . . . a negro Woman," 22 February 1783, *Barbados Mercury*, CO28/60: 9, vol. XI, NAL.

57. Beckles, *Natural Rebels*, 60.

58. Hartman, *Scenes of Subjection*, 95.

59. For a study on the significance of reproduction to slave owners in Barbados see Morgan, *Laboring Women*.

60. Gasper, "With a Rod of Iron," 347. See also Goveia, *The West Indian Slave Laws of the Eighteenth Century*.

61. Hall, *Acts Passed in the Island of Barbados*, 114–15, 118, 130–31, 185–87.

62. Ibid., 355.

63. Ibid.

64. Baskett, *Acts of Assembly*, 120.

65. No such references appear in the Barbados Minutes of Council referring to executed enslaved women.

66. Bush, *Slave Women in Caribbean Slave Society*, 28.

67. For an excellent and thorough exploration of the effects of amelioration on enslaved women, see Sasha Turner, "Home-Grown Slaves: Women, Reproduction, and the Abolition of the Slave Trade, Jamaica 1788–1807," *Journal of Women's History* 23, 3 (Fall 2011): 39–62.

68. See Turner, "Home-Grown Slaves."

69. This is an approximation based on Karl Watson's chapter, "Capital Sentences Against Slaves."

70. For a rare study on black female executions in U.S. colonial and antebellum history, see David V. Baker, "Black Female Executions in Historical Context," *Criminal Justice Review* 33, 1 (March 2008): 64–88.

71. Barbados Minutes of Council, 6 August 1700, CO31/5: 527, NAL.

72. Ibid., 6 August 1700, CO31/5: 528, NAL.

73. Ibid.

74. Ibid., 20 February 1727, CO31/17: 12, NAL.

75. Ibid., "Eve," 21 January 1729, CO31/18: 5; "Peggy," 14 October 1729, CO31/18:5; "[Quamina]," 8 October 1740, CO31/21:25, NAL.

76. Ibid., 21 January 1728/9, CO31/18: 28, NAL.

77. Ibid., 18 November 1729, CO31/18: 28, NAL.

78. The Barbados Court of Exchequer was not a criminal court. Its purpose was to recover property from defaulters of debt. Any evidence of Bascom's murder of the enslaved woman was extraneous to the fact that he owed her owner for the loss. For an explanation of the functions of the various courts in colonial Barbados, see Erwin C. Surrency, "Report on Court Procedures in the Colonies, 1700," *American Journal of Legal History* 9, 1 (January 1965): 234–246.

79. Hartman, *Scenes of Subjection*, 51.

80. Quoted in Watson, "Capital Sentences Against Slaves," 217.

81. Brown, "Spiritual Terror," 29.

82. Ibid., 29.

83. Barbados Minutes of Council, 20 December 1768, Lucas MSS: 159, BPL.

84. Brown, "Spiritual Terror," 24–53.

85. Ibid., 33.

86. Barbados Minutes of Council, 20 June 1769, Lucas MSS: 228, BPL.

87. Foucault, *Discipline and Punish*, 111.

88. Reverend H. E. Holder, *A Short Essay on the Subject of Negro Slavery, With a Particular Reference to The Island of Barbadoes* (London: Couchman and Fry, 1785), 815S, Bb. 28, British Library (hereafter BL); my emphasis.

89. Ibid.

90. Ibid.

91. Ibid.

92. Foucault, *Discipline and Punish*, 111.

93. Barbados Minutes of Council, 20 June 1769, Lucas MSS: 228–29, BPL.

94. Ibid.

95. Ibid.

96. Ligon, *The True and Exact History of the Island of Barbadoes*, 72.

97. Pinckard, *Notes on the West Indies*, 272–73.

98. Ibid., 273.

99. Portion of Journal of Nicolas Cresswell, 16 September 1774, X10/10, BDA.

100. Alexander Barclay, *A Practical View of the Present State of Slavery in The West Indies; or An Examination of Mr. Stephen's, "Slavery of the British West India Colonies": Containing More Particularly An Account of the Actual Condition of the Negroes in Jamaica: With Observations on the Decrease of Slaves Since the Abolition of the Slave Trade, and on the Probable Effects of Legislative Emancipation: Also, Strictures on the Edinburgh Review, and on the Pamphlets of Mr. Cooper and Mr. Bickell* (London: Smith, Elder & Co., 1828), 131.

101. Barclay, *A Practical View of the Present State*, 131.

102. Ibid., 132.

103. Ibid., 133.

104. Brown, *The Reaper's Garden*, 212–16.

105. Ibid.

106. For an excellent and in-depth account of funerary practices and politics, see Brown, *The Reaper's Garden*. Also see Handler and Lange, *Plantation Slavery*; Handler, "An African Pipe from a Slave Cemetery in Barbados, West Indies," in *The Archaeology of the Clay Tobacco Pipe*, ed. P. Davey, America, British Archaeological Reports, International Series 175 (Oxford: BAR, 1983), 245–54; Handler, "An African-Type Slave Burial [from] Newton Plantation, Barbados," *African American Archaeology* 15, 1 (1995): 5; Handler, "A Prone Burial from a Plantation Cemetery in Barbados, West Indies:

Possible Evidence for an African-Type Witch or Other Negatively Viewed Person," *Historical Archaeology* 30 (1996): 76–86; and Handler, "An African-Type Healer/Diviner and His Grave Goods: A Burial from a Plantation Slave Cemetery in Barbados, West Indies," *International Journal of Historical Archaeology* 1 (1997): 91–130.

107. The term "socio-sexual" is taken from Beckles, *Centering Woman*, 22.

Chapter 5. Venus: Abolition Discourse, Gendered Violence, and the Archive

Epigraphs: Diana Paton, "Decency, Dependence, and the Lash: Gender and the British Debate over Slave Emancipation, 1830–34," *Slavery and Abolition* 17, 3 (December 1996): 163; "Testimony of Captain Cook," in Lambert, *House of Commons Sessional Papers*, 82: 201–2.

1. "Testimony of Captain Cook," 201–2.

2. "Testimony of Hercules Ross, Esq.," in Lambert, 82: 252.

3. *Abridgement of the Minutes of Evidence, Taken before a Committee of the Whole House, To Whom it was Referred to Consider of the Slave Trade, 1789* (London: Parliament House of Commons, 1789), 116.

4. Philip D. Curtain, *The Image of Africa: British Ideas and Action, 1780–1850* (Madison: University of Wisconsin Press, 1964), 1: 107.

5. *Abridgement of the Minutes of Evidence*, 116–29.

6. "Testimony of Henry Hew Dalrymple," in Lambert, 82: 305.

7. Several accounts in the *House of Common Sessional Papers* remark on the crane in Kingston harbor used for unloading and loading ships but also specifically for the suspension of slaves above the ground for the purpose of whipping. Mr. Fitzmaurice, an overseer and a Kingston store clerk, commented that punishments in town, occurred "in the most public place, and [slaves] were sent there on that account, and for the conveniency of the crane and the weights." See "Testimony of William Fitzmaurice," in Lambert, 82: 206. See also Chapter 1 of this book.

8. For a rare example of a poem discussing sexual violence, see *West India Customs and Manners: Containing Strictures on the Soil, Cultivation, Produce, Trade, Officers, and Inhabitants: with the Method of Establishing, and Conducting a Sugar Plantation. To which is Added, the Practice of Training New Slaves. By J. B. Moreton, Esq. A New Edition, Volume 8* (Oxford: J. Parsons, W. Richardson, and J. Walter, 1793), 154–55.

9. "Testimony of Hercules Ross, Esq.," in Lambert, 252.

10. For evidence of numerous deaths resulting from whippings, see Lambert, 82: 55, 64, 68, 152, 155.

11. Hartman, "Venus in Two Acts," 7.

12. I have chosen to let these questions stand alone to signify the glaring silence of these records on the feelings, thoughts, and circumstances of these enslaved women during and following these violent acts. Although as noted in note 10 there are several mentions of enslaved women dying from wounds of whippings, the loss of their perspective and the ultimate fate of these women is permanent. There are, however, several

historical studies on African healing practices and medicinal knowledge the enslaved might have used in an attempt to heal the wounds from such torture. African captives and the Caribbean-born enslaved populations both retained and recreated cosmological and healing practices throughout the period of slavery. Choosing not to contextualize such important practices in the above discussion is to point out that our desire to know that bodies were healed and to fill in the silences with more sources derived from colonial authorities lessens the impact of the violence the enslaved endured and from which some died. For work on African healing, religious and medicinal practices, see for example, James Sweet, *Recreating Africa: Culture, Kinship, and Religion in the African-Portuguese World, 1441–1770* (Chapel Hill: University of North Carolina Press, 2003) and Judith Carney and Richard Nicholas Rosomoff, *In the Shadow of Slavery: Africa's Botanical Legacy in the Atlantic World* (Berkeley: University of California Press, 2001).

13. Foucault, "Lives of Infamous Men," in *Power, Truth, Strategy*, ed. Meaghan Morris and Paul Patton (Sydney: Feral Publications, 1979), 81.

14. For the rest of the chapter I refer to the campaign to end the slave trade as "abolition" following Chris Brown, who makes the distinction between abolitionism and anti-slavery movements. See Christopher Leslie Brown, *Moral Capital: Foundations of British Abolitionism* (Chapel Hill: University of North Carolina Press, 2006), 17–18 n14.

15. Hartman, *Scenes of Subjection*, 20.

16. Paton, *No Bond But the Law*, 83. In context, Paton makes an important argument about historians' lack of attention to the prison boom in the late eighteenth-century Caribbean (Jamaica in particular) that coexisted with corporeal forms of slave punishment. See for example, Paton, "Decency, Dependence and the Lash," 163–84.

17. Paton, *No Bond But the Law*, 20.

18. Ibid., 5–6.

19. Hartman, "Venus in Two Acts," 7. See also Paton, *No Bond But the Law*, 83.

20. Hartman, *Scenes of Subjection*, 3–4.

21. Nicole Fleetwood, *Troubling Vision: Performance, Visuality, and Blackness* (Chicago: University of Chicago Press, 2011), 9.

22. For a full account of the impossibilities of recovering enslaved women from the archives of slavery see Hartman, "Venus in Two Acts."

23. Several notable texts of abolition and slavery use these records, but the particularities of the structure and specific content of these documents or the production of particularly gendered discourses remain unexamined. One exception is David Brion Davis's mention of the political concerns of witness veracity or neutrality surrounding the gathering of evidence on both sides of the debate. However Davis argues that each side of the abolition debate believed that the evidence gathered would discredit the other side. See Davis, *The Problem of Slavery in the Age of Revolution* (Ithaca, N.Y.: Cornell University Press, 1975), 421–22 and n 62. By centering enslaved women in an analysis of the Privy Council report, new ways of understanding this archive, this historical moment, and enslaved women's condition are illuminated. For the history of the pivotal

years 1787–1792 in the British abolition movement and the event that led up to the production of the Report, see Robin Blackburn, *The Overthrow of Colonial Slavery, 1776–
1848* (London: Verso, 1988), 141–42; Seymour Drescher, *Abolition: A History of Slavery
and Antislavery* (Cambridge: Cambridge University Press, 2009), 213–23; and Davis,
421–22.

24. Seymour Drescher, *Capitalism and Antislavery* (New York: Oxford University
Press, 1987), 87–88.

25. Paton, "Decency, Dependence and the Lash," 170.

26. Turner, "Home-Grown Slaves: Women, Reproduction, and the Abolition of the
Slave Trade, Jamaica 1788–1807," 45.

27. Ibid.

28. The issue about the motivations of British abolitionists has a long historiographical trail. See Brown, *Moral Capital*, 4–18 and Turner, "Home Grown Slaves," 42. For recent scholarship pointing to the complexities of abolitionists' intentions during the slave
trade debates, Brown's text explores the myriad political actors and events that culmi-
nated to form the abolition *movement* in 1787–1788, arguing that the American Revolution was the catalyst that brought variously committed groups to mobilize a movement.
For other examples of these debates, see Blackburn, *The Overthrow of Colonial Slavery*
and Drescher, *Abolition*. Blackburn emphasizes the antislavery and anticolonial en-
meshment of the era leading up to the ending of the slave trade and slavery in the British empire while devoting significant attention to the role of the enslaved in antislavery
activity and politics. Drescher downplays the involvement of the enslaved while arguing
that several humanitarian groups and politicians across the Atlantic effectively and necessarily forced slavery's demise. Scholarship on the slave trade, abolition, and antislavery movements proliferated over the last several decades. For a sample of these texts, see
Jonathan Aitken, *John Newton: From Disgrace to Amazing Grace* (London: Continuum,
2007); Roger T. Anstey, "Capitalism and Slavery: A Critique," *Economic History Review*
2nd ser. 21 (1968): 307–20; Roger Anstey, *The Atlantic Slave Trade and British Abolition,
1760–1810* (London: Humanities Press, 1975); James Bandinel, *Some Account of the Trade
in Slaves From Africa* (London: Frank Cass, 1968); Thomas Bender, ed., *The Antislavery
Debate: Capitalism and Abolitionism as a Problem in Historical Interpretation* (Berkeley:
University of California Press, 1992); Blackburn, *The Overthrow of Colonial Slavery*; Brycchan Carey, *British Abolitionism and the Rhetoric of Sensibility: Writing, Sentiment, and
Slavery, 1760–1807* (Basingstoke: Palgrave Macmillan, 2005); Brycchan Carey, *From
Peace to Freedom: Quaker Rhetoric and the Birth of American Antislavery, 1657–1761*
(New Haven, Conn.: Yale University Press, 2012); Reginald Coupland, *The British Anti-
slavery Movement* (London: Frank Cass, 1964); Melinda Elder, *The Slave Trade* (Krum-
lin: Ryburn, 1992); David Eltis, *Economic Growth and the Ending of the Transatlantic
Slave Trade* (Oxford: Oxford University Press, 1987); Moira Ferguson, *Subject to Others:
British Women Writers and Colonial Slavery, 1670–1834* (London: Routledge, 1992); Wil-
liam Hague, *William Wilberforce: The Life of the Great Anti-Slave Trade Campaigner*
(London: HarperPress, 2007); Robert Harms, *The Diligent: A Voyage Through the Worlds*

of the Slave Trade (New York: Basic, 2002); Adam Hochschild, *Bury the Chains: The First International Human Rights Movement* (Basingstoke: Macmillan, 2005); Maurice Jackson, *Let This Voice Be Heard: Anthony Benezet, Father of Atlantic Abolitionism* (Philadelphia: University of Pennsylvania Press, 2010); Peter Kitson et al., eds., *Slavery, Abolition and Emancipation: Writings in the British Romantic Period*, 8 vols. (London: Chatto and Windus, 1999); Frank J. Klingberg, *The Anti-Slavery Movement in England: A Study in English Humanitarianism* (Oxford: Oxford University Press, 1928); Averil Mackenzie-Grieve, *The Last Years of the English Slave Trade: Liverpool 1750–1807* (London: Putnam, 1941); John Oldfield, *Popular Politics and British Anti-Slavery: The Mobilisation of Public Opinion Against the Slave Trade, 1787–1807* (London: Frank Cass, 1998); John Pinfold, ed., *The Slave Trade Debate: Contemporary Writings for and Against* (Oxford: Bodleian, 2007); James A. Rawley and Stephen D. Behrendt, *The Transatlantic Slave Trade: A History*, rev. ed. (Lincoln: University of Nebraska Press, 2005); Marcus Rediker, *The Slave Ship: A Human History* (London: John Murray, 2008); C. Duncan Rice, *The Rise and Fall of Black Slavery* (London: Macmillan, 1975); Marika Sherwood, *After Abolition: Britain and Slave Trade Since 1807* (New York: Tauris, 2007); Folarin Shyllon, *James Ramsay: The Unknown Abolitionist* (Edinburgh: Canongate, 1977); Howard Temperley, "The Ideology of Antislavery," in *The Abolition of the Atlantic Slave Trade Origins and Effects in Europe, Africa, and the Americas*, ed. David Eltis and James Walvin (Madison: University of Wisconsin Press, 1981), 335–50; Hugh Thomas, *The Slave Trade: The Story of the Atlantic Slave Trade, 1440–1870* (New York: Simon and Schuster, 1997); David Turley, *The Culture of English Antislavery, 1780–1860* (London: Routledge, 1991); James Walvin, *England, Slaves, and Freedom, 1776–1838* (Jackson: University Press of Mississippi, 1986); James Walvin, ed., *Slavery and British Society: 1776–1846* (Baton Rouge: Louisiana State University Press, 1982); James Walvin, *Questioning Slavery* (London: Routledge, 1996); and Eric Williams, *Capitalism and Slavery* (London: André Deutsch, 1964).

29. Barbados planters made it difficult to pass ameliorative laws in the colony. Although other British Caribbean colonies passed such legislation in the late eighteenth-century, including the Leeward Islands, Grenada and Jamaica, Barbados remained a stronghold in preserving their system of slavery. Caroline Quarrier Spence, "Ameliorating Empire: Slavery and Protection in the British Colonies, 1783–1865 (PhD diss., Harvard University, 2014), 6, 18, 235–236.

30. Davis, *The Problem of Slavery*, 425–26; Seymour Drescher, "Public Opinion and Parliament in the Abolition of the British Slave Trade," in *The British Slave Trade: Abolition, Parliament and People*, ed. Stephen Farrell, Melanie Unwin, and James Walvin (Edinburgh: Edinburgh University Press, 2007), 44 and Blackburn, *The Overthrow of Colonial Slavery*, 142.

31. Drescher, "Public Opinion and Parliament," 47.

32. Brown, *Moral Capital*, 385.

33. Ibid., 49–50.

34. Drescher, *Abolition*, 214.

35. Blackburn, *The Overthrow of Colonial Slavery*, 137–38.

36. Drescher, "Public Opinion and Parliament," 50.

37. Ibid., 54–56.

38. See Lambert, 71–72 (1788–1789).

39. Laurent Dubois, *Avengers of the New World: The Story of the Haitian Revolution* (Cambridge: Harvard University Press, 2004), 21.

40. Davis, *The Problem of Slavery*, 422.

41. Ibid., 422–23.

42. Hartman, *Scenes of Subjection*, 19.

43. Brown, *Moral Capital*, 450; Drescher, *Abolition*, 215–16; Blackburn, *The Overthrow of Colonial Slavery*, 422.

44. Drescher, *Abolition*, 205–41; Blackburn, *The Overthrow of Colonial Slavery*, chaps. 3–5, 109–212.

45. Davis, *The Problem of Slavery*, 422. Davis explains that the abolitionists, "were embarrassed by the moral character and social status of many of their witnesses," and the proslavery contingent had difficulty finding neutral testimony (422).

46. Blackburn, *The Overthrow of Colonial Slavery*, 138.

47. For reference to their complete narratives, see Olaudah Equiano, *The Life of Olaudah Equiano, or Gustavus Vassa, the African written by Himself* (Boston: Isaac Knapp, 1837) and Quobna Ottobah Cugoano, *Thoughts and Sentiments on the Evil of Slavery and Other Writings*, ed. Vincent Carretta (New York: Penguin, 1999). For scholarship on black activism around abolition and antislavery, see Vincent Carretta, *Equiano, the African: Biography of a Self-Made Man* (Athens: University of Georgia Press, 2005); Vincent Carretta, ed., *Unchained Voices: An Anthology of Black Authors in the English-Speaking World of the Eighteenth Century* (Lexington: University Press of Kentucky, 1996); Vincent Carretta and Philip Gould, eds., *Genius in Bondage: Literature of the Early Black Atlantic* (Lexington: University Press of Kentucky, 2001); Kathleen Chater, *Untold Histories: Black people in England and Wales during the Period of the British Slave trade, c. 1660–1807* (Manchester: Manchester University Press, 2009); Angelo Costanzo, *Surprising Narrative: Olaudah Equiano and the Beginnings of Black Autobiography* (New York: Greenwood, 1987); Charles T. Davis and Henry Louis Gates, Jr., *The Slave's Narrative* (Oxford: Oxford University Press, 1985); Paul Edwards and David Dabydeen, eds., *Black Writers in Britain 1760–1890* (Edinburgh: Edinburgh University Press, 1991); Peter Fryer, *Staying Power: The History of Black People in Britain* (London: Pluto, 1984); Gretchen Gerzina, *Black England: Life Before Emancipation* (London: Allison & Busby, 1999); Peter Linebaugh and Marcus Rediker, *The Many-Headed Hydra: Sailors, Slaves, Commoners, and the Hidden History of the Revolutionary Atlantic* (London: Verso, 2000); Mary Prince, *The History of Mary Prince: A West Indian Slave Narrative* (Mineola, N.Y.: Dover, 2004); Keith A. Sandiford, *Measuring the Moment: Strategies of Protest in Eighteenth-Century Afro-English Writing* (London: Associated University Presses, 1988); Verene Shepherd, *I Want to Disturb My Neighbour: Lectures on Slavery, Emancipation, and Postcolonial Jamaica* (Kingston: Ian Randle, 2007); Folarin Shyllon, *Black People in Britain, 1555–1833* (London: Oxford University Press, for Institute of Race

Relations, 1977); James Walvin, *Making the Black Atlantic: Britain and the African Diaspora* (London: Cassell, 2000); and Eric Williams, *Capitalism and Slavery, with a New Introduction by Colin Palmer* (Chapel Hill: University of North Carolina Press, 1994).

48. "Testimony of John Orde, Esq.," in Lambert, 72, part 2, 170.

49. "Testimony of Robert Hibbert, Esq.," in Lambert, 72, part 2, 71.

50. "Testimony of Thomas Kerby," in Lambert, 72, part 2, 6.

51. "Testimony of Governor David Perry Esquire, Governor of Barbados," in Lambert, 72, part 2, 171.

52. Higman, *Slave Populations of the British Caribbean*, 303–78.

53. Morgan, *Laboring Women*, 12–39.

54. Ibid. See also Bush, *Slave Women in Caribbean Society*, esp. chap. 1.

55. See Verene Shepherd and Bridget Brereton eds., *Engendering History: Caribbean Women in Historical Perspective* (New York: Macmillan, 1995).

56. For detailed examples of conditions after the Consolidated Slave Act, see Turner, "Home-Grown Slaves."

57. "Testimony of Dr. Jackson, M.D.," in Lambert, 82: 54.

58. Ibid., 57.

59. Ibid., 54.

60. Ibid., 58.

61. Ibid., 56.

62. "Testimony of Major General Tottenham," in Lambert, 82: 125.

63. Ibid., 128.

64. Ibid., 127.

65. Ibid., 128.

66. Rhodda Reddick, "Women and Slavery in the Caribbean: A Feminist Perspective," *Latin American Perspectives* 12, 1 (Winter 1985): 63–80. See also Orlando Patterson, *The Sociology of Slavery: An Analysis of the Origins, Development and Structure of Negro Slave Society in Jamaica* (Rutherford, N.J.: Fairleigh Dickson University Press, 1967), esp. 104–12.

67. Reddick, "Women and Slavery," 67–68. Kenneth Morgan, "Slave Women and Reproduction in Jamaica, ca. 1776–1834," in *Women and Slavery: The Modern Atlantic*, ed. Gwyn Campbell, Suzanne Miers, and Joseph Calder Miller (Athens: Ohio University Press, 2007), 38. See also Beckles, *Natural Rebels*; Higman, *Slave Populations of the British Caribbean*; Bush, *Slave Women in Caribbean Society*; and Morgan, *Laboring Women*.

68. "Testimony of Captain Cook," in Lambert 201–2.

69. "Testimony of Hercules Ross, Esq.," 252.

70. Hartman, "Venus in Two Acts," 7.

71. Feldman, *Formations of Violence*, 7.

72. "Testimony of William Fitzmaurice," 205.

73. "Testimony of Hercules Ross, Esq.," 253.

74. "Testimony of Mr. Coor," in Lambert, 82: 72.

75. Ibid., 99.

76. "Testimony of Mr. John Terry," in Lambert, 82: 107.

77. Hartman, *Scenes of Subjection*, 51.

78. "Testimony of Hercules Ross, Esq.," 253.

79. See "wanton," Online Oxford English Dictionary.

80. "Testimony of Mr. Davison," in Lambert, 82: 182.

81. "Testimony of Mr. Coor," 72.

82. "Testimony of Hercules Ross, Esq.," 255.

83. Fred Moten, *In the Break: The Aesthetics of the Black Radical Tradition* (Minneapolis: University of Minnesota Press, 2003), 6.

84. Hartman, "Venus in Two Acts," 4.

85. See, for example, work on slavery in the colonial Spanish empire, such as Herman Bennett, *Colonial Blackness: A History of Afro-Mexico* (Bloomington: Indiana University Press, 2010); Jane Landers, *Black Society in Spanish Florida* (Urbana: University of Illinois Press, 1999); and Block, *Ordinary Lives*. One might argue however, that it is not the amount of source materials available, but the nature of such sources, that is always mitigated by European and ecclesiastical interpretations of enslaved and free black voices in the Spanish Caribbean context. Those sources too, were produced by religious, racial, and gendered ideologies that shaped how black bodies were interrogated and how black voices were translated. No archive is free from such bias, but the British archive is particularly economic and racialized in form and context.

86. For a range of scholarship covering these issues, see Michel Foucault, "The Subject and Power," *Critical Inquiry* 8 (Summer 1982); Gordon, *Ghostly Matters*; Ranajit Guha, *A Subaltern Studies Reader* (Minneapolis: University of Minnesota Press, 1997); David Scott, *Conscripts of Modernity: The Tragedy of Colonial Enlightenment* (Durham, N.C.: Duke University Press, 2004); Spivak, "Can the Subaltern Speak?"; and Trouillot, *Silencing the Past*.

87. Moten, *In the Break*, 12 and Hartman, "Venus in Two Acts," 3.

88. For a discussion of rhetorical genres in general, see Amy Devitt, *Writing Genres* (Carbondale: Southern Illinois University Press, 2004).

89. Ibid., 13.

90. Moten, *In the Break*, 6.

91. Ibid.

92. Ibid., 5–7.

Epilogue

Epigraph: Ta-Nehisi Coates, "Letter to My Son," *Atlantic* (4 July 2015).

1. M. NourbeSe Philip, *Zong!* (Middletown, Conn.: Wesleyan University Press, 2008), 196.

ACKNOWLEDGMENTS

So many people and institutions have made it possible for me to write this book. I am thrilled for the opportunity to acknowledge this support. I have been supported by funding and fellowships from the Fulbright IIE, University of California, Berkeley and the Ida B. Jackson Fellowship, the Ford Foundation, the Carolina Postdoc for faculty Diversity, the Charles Warren Center for the Study of American History at Harvard University, and the Schomburg Center for Research in Black Culture Scholars-in-Residence Fellowship with funding by the National Endowment for the Humanities, as well as research support from the Women's and Gender Studies and History Departments at Rutgers University. (Any views, findings, conclusions, or recommendations expressed in this book do not necessarily reflect those of the National Endowment for the Humanities.) Rutgers School of Arts and Sciences deans Douglas Greenberg and James Swenson facilitated the leave time I used to finish the book. Bob Lockhart has been a supportive, patient, and generous editor from our first conversation. I thank him for all the work he put into getting the book to publication. I extend profound thanks to the University of Pennsylvania Press, Early American Studies series editors, especially Kathleen Brown, and the anonymous reviewers who provided such substantive and vital feedback. I also want to thank Roy Tahtinen who provided the artistic inspiration for the amazing cover design and Sebastian Araya for the cartography.

From the very beginning of this intellectual journey, Sarah Poindexter pointed the way and encouraged me to pursue my dreams. Alice Walker, Zora Neale Hurston, and Bob Marley were the muses who initiated my journey. I have been incredibly lucky to work with amazing mentors at several institutions. At UC Santa Cruz I am indebted to David Anthony, Jacqueline Nassy Brown, Rosie Cabrerra, and Angela Davis. I am still thinking through what it meant to meet Ula Taylor and Saidiya Hartman for the first time in Cape Coast, Ghana. These two incredible women became my mentors and much, much more. They pushed me to reach higher than I might have otherwise. I am so thankful for their unconditional support and dear friendship—meeting them changed my life. I also met Patricia Penn Hilden and Timothy Reiss on my first trip to Barbados. I am ever so thankful for their unyielding encouragement through this work and the trials of this process. VèVè Amasasa Clark has been a warm, protective presence even in her physical absence and Stephen Small a wonderful advisor. Mercy Romero saw the spirits in the book. Erin Winkler has been a dear friend and source of strength. Kristen Block and Tuyen Tran gave me hundreds of pep talks and Jenny Shaw sat with me to finish an important draft. Patch Garcia was a vigorous cheerleader, Nicole Branch provided a home, Amber Randolph did so much work to keep me nourished and Anne Tahtinen kept the porch light on and a basket of treats in my room. They are the midwives of this book. My deepest gratitude goes to them for their sustaining friendship.

During my long stay in Barbados I met people who shared archives, advice and created homes away from home. Vice-Chancellor Sir Hilary McDonald Beckles, KA, wrote me a pivotal letter for the Fulbright fellowship providing me with the funding to conduct research in Barbados. His scholarship serves as a foundation for my own. Professor Pedro Welch, from University of the West Indies, Cave Hill took me on as an advisee and shared archives, wisdom, and insight into the world of Bridgetown. It was he who helped me shape a vague and broad project into a study of urban slavery. Professor Karl Watson gives the best tour of Bridgetown and he opened his research on enslaved executions that formed the basis for chapter four. He continues to be a great source of knowledge. Professor Martyn Bowden also shared records with me and his scholarship on Bridgetown's geography helped me to imagine the sensorial and geographic experience of this town in the eighteenth century. Natalie and L. Marguerita Smith, Jasper Blades, Gregg, Z' Dana and Z' Dari Scantlebury, Barbara Rock and Jackie and Penny Lewis have become my Bajan family. Patricia Stafford, Kristen Block, Jenny Shaw, Denise Challenger and Tara Inniss brought much needed company and inspiration in my last months on the island. Maureen and Rashidie Mullins provided a wonderful home and Linda Bull offered a gorgeous view of the vast Atlantic Ocean on the east coast of the island. My deep gratitude goes out to the staff at the Barbados Department of Archives, UWI library, Bridgetown Public Library and the Barbados Museum and Historical Society, particularly, Mr. David Williams, Ms. Ingrid Cumberbatch, and the assistant archivists including Brian Inniss, Stacia Adams, Charmaine Payne, Karen Proverbs and Rudolph (Timothy) Sealy. Mr. Kevin Farmer, Ms. Angela

Boyce, and the Barbados Museum and Historical Society and Patricia Stafford provided much needed assistance in the final stages of this work.

Throughout the last several years my work has benefitted from the support of fellowships during which I was welcomed into many different academic communities. The feedback I received was invaluable. At UNC-Chapel Hill, the Women's and Gender Studies Department welcomed me into their community. I extend my gratitude for this time and space to Michelle Berger, Karen Booth, E. Jane Burns, Barbara Harris, Joanne Herschfield, Tanya Shields, and Silvia Tomášková. Sibby Anderson Thompkins became a dear colleague. My colleagues in the Carolina Postdoc Program, especially Sergio Chavez and Emily Cheng became vital friends during my two-years in Chapel Hill. Elyse Crystall and Karen Booth invited me into their home when I first arrived and made my transition from the Bay Area so much easier. Kennetta Perry's unending support through the ups and downs of work and life has made it possible to reach the end of a long road. Katherine Charron always reminds me of how friendship is precious, that I have something important to say, and not to go down the rabbit hole. To the wonderful women of healing: Myisha and Teena Priest and Ula Taylor took care of me at the most challenging moments and Mimi Alvarez who walked me to the finish line. These words do not do justice to the deep appreciation I owe them but their care and kindness is something that stays with me always. Amber Alsobrooks, Laura Deloye and Allison Meyers—we met at the end of a journey and the beginning of another, I'm so appreciative of our enduring connection. Adriane Lenz-Smith and Tina Campt made my intellectual community rich, valuable, and vital. Jennifer Morgan is an extraordinary scholar and mentor. I am humbled by her welcoming me into the field and as a colleague. Vincent Brown and Walter Johnson provided a beautiful space to continue my work at Harvard's Charles Warren Center before joining the Rutgers faculty. I would like to thank Arthur Patton-Hock and Larissa Kennedy for their administrative labors on our behalf. Many thanks to my colleagues at the CWC: Suzanna Reiss, Edward Ruegemer, Kristen Block, Joshua Guild, Paul Kramer, Cynthia Young, Gunther Peck, and Patrick Wolfe (whose presence in this world I will miss so much—rest in peace, dear friend). Conversations with Emily Alyssa Owens enhanced my work as well. In Boston/Cambridge, Rani Neutill, Keith Jones and Jen Brody, Timothy McCarthy, and Meredith Sterling made the time in the cold much warmer.

I spent two wonderful years at the Schomburg Center for Research in Black Culture, thanks to the generosity of Khalil Muhammed, Farah Jasmine

Griffith, and Diana Lachatanere. Farah's support extended beyond the Schomburg and for that I am so grateful. My colleagues on this fellowship provided rigor, laughter, and comradery in the course of shaping the book, especially, Zakiya Adair, Yarimar Bonilla, Rafe Dalleo, Belinda Edmonson, Anthony Foy, David Goldberg, Regine Jackson, Ryan Kernan, Kevin Meehan, Nancy Mirabal, Andrew Rosa, and Salamishah Tillet. I was also fortunate to spend time as a Ford Fellow at Barnard College thanks to the wonderful mentorship of Kim Hall and Tina Campt. I thank Yvette Christiansë and Jennifer Morgan for engaging my work at a seminar hosted by the Institute for Research on Women and the Africana Studies Departments at Barnard and Jennifer Brier for sharing her time at the "Little Berks" during my revisions process. I want to thank Brian Connolly, Emily Landau, Jennifer Spear, and Sharon Block, for providing important feedback on this work.

My colleagues at Rutgers have helped knead and shape this book with critical care. It has been a dream come true to work with Deborah Gray White, the scholar who opened the field to studies on enslaved women. Her wise counsel, good humor, and support have ushered this book into existence. I thank her for understanding. The Chairs of WGS and History at Rutgers (past and present) have provided important support for the last several years including Mary Hawkesworth, Leslie Fishbein, Abena Busia, Paul Clemons, Jim Masschaele, Mark Wasserman, and Barbara Cooper. Mary Hawkesworth has been an enthusiastic reader and mentor and Seth Koven gave so much time and care to this book and generous support to me especially in the crucial last stages. Nancy Hewitt and Julie Livingston provided critical feedback on drafts of the book and I thank them both for their kindness, mentorship, and incredible generosity. Many other colleagues across campus offered their help, wrote letters, and urged me on including: Radhika Balakrishnan, Barbara Balliet, Mia Bay, Rudy Bell, Alastair Bellany, Ethel Brooks, Carolyn Brown, Kim Butler, Sylvia Chan-Malik, Cheryl Clarke, Paul Clemons, Belinda Davis, Carlos Decena, James Delbourgo, Rachel Devlin, Zaire Dinzey-Flores, Ann Fabian, Melissa Fienberg, Nicole Fleetwood, Nikol Alexander Floyd, Joanne Givand, Judy Gerson, Anne Gregory, Monique Gregory, Paul Hannebrink, Jochen Hellbeck, Annie Hogan, Bayo Holsey, Allan Isaac, Jennifer Jones, Temma Kaplan, Suzy Kiefer, Kathy Lopez, Nelson Maldonado-Torres, Carter Mathes, Jennifer Middlestat, Donna Murch, Jamie Pietruska, Jasbir Puar, Walter Rucker, Aldo Lauria Santiago, Lousia Schien, Johanna Schoen, Kyla Schuller, Peter Silver, Michelle Stephens, Mary Trigg, Camila Townsend, and Yana van der Meulen Rodgers.

Many thanks to colleagues outside of Rutgers for writing groups, support groups, andyour collegial presence in my life during this project especially, LaKisha Simmons, Sharon Heijin Lee, Rosanne Adderley, Herman Bennett, Luisa Heredia, Tamara Walker, Jason Young, Daina Berry, Erica Dunbar, Kathleen Wilson, Carina Ray, LaShawn Harris, Leslie Harris, Jen Manion, Danielle McGuire, Natasha Lightfoot, Sarah Cervenak, Felix Germaine, Jennifer Morgan, and Melanie Newton. Tracy Grinnell's keen editorial eye helped me to get the book in wonderful shape. Jesse Bayker and Naomi Bland were extraordinary research assistants over the last few years and Dara Walker, Stina Soderling, Ben Resnick-Day, Vishal Kamath, and Lytton McDonnell provided critical technical help.

I owe infinite gratitude for the love, years of patience, the moments of holding me upright, long conversations, and steadfast encouragement from my dear friends and community. Special and heartfelt thanks to David Peed, Tracye Stormer, Erin Winkler, Carrie Maynard, Tracy Grinnell, Eréndira Rueda, Jesse Moya, Daniel Konecky, Keenan Hakim Booker, Suzanna Reiss, Ms. Mary Wooten, Ms. Madeline Randolph, Maggie Cutts, Sebastian Araya, Kennetta Perry, Nicole Fleetwood, Pagan Morris, Hana Mori Böttger, Para Ambardar, Jasmine Oberste, Andrew Powell, Allison Briscoe-Smith, Nicole Branch, Bobbi Wunsch, Jonathan Cohen, Jennifer Pasinosky, John Littrell, Charles Peterson, Meredith Gadsby, Christina Perez, Rhiannon Welch, Nathan Horell, Amber, Marcus and Grace Randolph, Mercy Romero, Katherine Charron, Danielle Di Silverio, Judy Barrett, Abosede George, Karin Hurley, Jill Chenault, Javane Strong, Heather Koppleson, Pacino Bing, Rafiki Carter, Josh Renick, Ife Sherman, Kisha Simmons, Staci Konecky, Yvahn Martin, Azure Thompson, Anne Eller, Eduardo Contreras, David Blasher, Jerome Haferd, Charlie Tripp, and Lucy Ames.

Thank you to my family, Jose, Mari, and Andrew Fuentes, Maria Elena (Nena), Alma, Edmund, Steve, and Hector Fuentes, Annie and Roy Tahtinen, Sarah Petrini and Lisa Bridges, Mary, Dolly, and Cathy Connell, Gina Neri, Patch Garcia, Jake and Edie Ducich. And, to the new generation born in the final months of this book: Leo Vincent Tahtinen, Calvin and Caitlin Fuentes, and Avery Petrini Bridges, I hope you find a love of books on your journey through the world.